The AI Product Manager's Handbook

Develop a product that takes advantage of machine learning to solve AI problems

Irene Bratsis

BIRMINGHAM—MUMBAI

The AI Product Manager's Handbook

Copyright © 2023 Packt Publishing

Publishing Product Manager: Dinesh Chaudhary

Senior Editor: Tazeen Shaikh

Technical Editor: Rahul Limbachiya

Copy Editor: Safis Editing

Project Coordinator: Farheen Fathima

Proofreader: Safis Editing

Indexer: Pratik Shirodkar

Production Designer: Alishon Mendonca

Marketing Coordinators: Shifa Ansari and Vinishka Kalra

First published: February 2023

Production reference: 2230223

Published by Packt Publishing Ltd.

Livery Place

35 Livery Street

Birmingham

B3 2PB, UK.

ISBN 978-1-80461-293-4

www.packtpub.com

For those courageous enough to believe they deserve their heart's desires... evermore.

– Irene Bratsis

Contributors

About the author

Irene Bratsis is a director of digital product and data at the **International WELL Building Institute (IWBI)**. She has a bachelor's in economics, and after completing various MOOCs in data science and big data analytics, she completed a data science program with Thinkful. Before joining IWBI, Irene worked as an operations analyst at Tesla, a data scientist at Gesture, a data product manager at Beekin, and head of product at Tenacity. Irene volunteers as NYC chapter co-lead for Women in Data, has coordinated various AI accelerators, moderated countless events with a speaker series with Women in AI called WaiTalk, and runs a monthly book club focused on data and AI books.

About the reviewer

Akshat Gurnani is a highly qualified individual with a background in the field of computer science and machine learning. He has a master's degree in computer science and a deep understanding of various machine learning techniques and algorithms. He has experience working on various projects related to natural language processing, computer vision, and deep learning. He has also published several research papers in top-tier journals and conferences and has a proven track record in the field. He has a passion for keeping up to date with the latest developments in their fields and has a strong desire to continue learning and contributing to the field of artificial intelligence.

Table of Contents

Preface   **xv**

Part 1 – Lay of the Land – Terms, Infrastructure, Types of AI, and Products Done Well

1

Understanding the Infrastructure and Tools for Building AI Products   **3**

Definitions – what is and is not AI   4

ML versus DL – understanding the difference   6

ML   6

DL   7

Learning types in ML   8

Supervised learning   8

Unsupervised learning   9

Semi-supervised learning   10

Reinforcement learning   11

The order – what is the optimal flow and where does every part of the process live?   11

Step 1 – Data availability and centralization   11

Step 2 – Continuous maintenance   12

Database   13

Data warehouse   13

Data lake (and lakehouse)   14

Data pipelines   14

Managing projects – IaaS   15

Deployment strategies – what do we do with these outputs?   16

Shadow deployment strategy   17

A/B testing model deployment strategy   17

Canary deployment strategy   17

Succeeding in AI – how well-managed AI companies do infrastructure right   18

The promise of AI – where is AI taking us?   19

Summary   20

Additional resources   20

References   21

2

Model Development and Maintenance for AI Products 23

Understanding the stages of NPD	23	Training – when is a model ready for market?	28
Step 1 – Discovery	24		
Step 2 – Define	24	Deployment – what happens after the workstation?	32
Step 3 – Design	25		
Step 4 – Implementation	25	Testing and troubleshooting	34
Step 5 – Marketing	25	Refreshing – the ethics of how often we update our models	36
Step 6 – Training	26		
Step 7 – Launch	26	Summary	38
Model types – from linear regression to neural networks	27	Additional resources	39
		References	40

3

Machine Learning and Deep Learning Deep Dive 41

The old – exploring ML	42	Emerging technologies – ancillary and related tech	52
The new – exploring DL	43		
Invisible influences	44	Explainability – optimizing for ethics, caveats, and responsibility	53
A brief history of DL	45		
Types of neural networks	46	Accuracy – optimizing for success	54
		Summary	55
		References	55

4

Commercializing AI Products 59

The professionals – examples of B2B products done right	60	The rebels – examples of red ocean products	64
The artists – examples of B2C products done right	61	The GOAT – examples of differentiated disruptive and dominant strategy products	65
The pioneers – examples of blue ocean products	63	The dominant strategy	66

The disruptive strategy   67   Summary   68

The differentiated strategy   67   References   69

5

AI Transformation and Its Impact on Product Management   71

Money and value – how AI could   Sickness and health – the benefits of
revolutionize our economic systems   72   AI and nanotech across healthcare   79

Goods and services – growth in   Basic needs – AI for Good   80
commercial MVPs   74   Summary   81

Government and autonomy – how AI   Additional resources   82
will shape our borders and freedom   77   References   82

Part 2 – Building an AI-Native Product

6

Understanding the AI-Native Product   87

Stages of AI product development   88   UX designers/researchers   94

Phase 1 – Ideation   88   Customer success   95

Phase 2 – Data management   89   Marketing/sales/go-to-market team   95

Phase 3 – Research and development   90   Investing in your tech stack   95

Phase 4 – Deployment   91   Productizing AI-powered

AI/ML product dream team   91   outputs – how AI product
                                                 management is different   96
AI PM   92
                                                 AI customization   98
AI/ML/data strategists   92
                                                 Selling AI – product management as
Data engineer   92   a higher octave of sales   99

Data analyst   93   Summary   100

Data scientist   93   References   101

ML engineer   93

Frontend/backend/full stack engineers 94

7

Productizing the ML Service   103

Understanding the differences between AI and traditional software products   103
How are they similar?   104
How are they different?   105

B2B versus B2C – productizing business models   110
Domain knowledge – understanding the needs of your market   110

Experimentation – discover the needs of your collective   112

Consistency and AIOps/MLOps – reliance and trust   113

Performance evaluation – testing, retraining, and hyperparameter tuning   114

Feedback loop – relationship building   115

Summary   116

References   116

8

Customization for Verticals, Customers, and Peer Groups   117

Domains – orienting AI toward specific areas   118
Understanding your market   119
Understanding how your product design will serve your market   120
Building your AI product strategy   121

Verticals – examination into four areas (FinTech, healthcare, consumer goods, and cybersecurity)   123
FinTech   123
Healthcare   125
Cybersecurity   126

Anomaly detection and user and entity behavior analytics   126

Value metrics – evaluating performance across verticals and peer groups   127
Objectives and key results   128
Key performance indicators   128

Thought leadership – learning from peer groups   130

Summary   130

References   131

9

Macro and Micro AI for Your Product   133

Macro AI – Foundations
and umbrellas   134
ML   135
Robotics   139
Expert systems   140
Fuzzy logic/fuzzy matching   140
Micro AI – Feature level   141
ML (traditional/DL/
computer vision/NLP)   141
Robotics   143
Expert systems   143

Fuzzy logic/fuzzy matching   144
Successes – Examples that inspire   144
Lensa   145
PeriGen   145
Challenges – Common pitfalls   146
Ethics   146
Performance   147
Safety   148
Summary   149
References   149

10

Benchmarking Performance, Growth Hacking, and Cost   151

Value metrics – a guide to north star
metrics, KPIs and OKRs   152
North star metrics   153
KPIs and other metrics   156
OKRs and product strategy   157
Hacking – product-led growth   159
The tech stack – early signals   160
Customer Data Platforms (CDPs)   161
Customer Engagement Platforms (CEPs) 162
Product analytics tools   162

A/B testing tools   163
Data warehouses   164
Business Intelligence (BI) tools   164
Growth-hacking tools   165
Managing costs and pricing – AI is
expensive   166
Summary   166
References   167

Part 3 – Integrating AI into Existing Non-AI Products

11

The Rising Tide of AI 171

Evolve or die – when change is the only constant 172

The fourth industrial revolution – hospitals used to use candles 174

Working with a consultant 175
Working with a third party 176
The first hire 177

The first AI team 177
No-code tools 178

Fear is not the answer – there is more to gain than lose (or spend) 178
Anticipating potential risks 179

Summary 181

12

Trends and Insights across Industry 183

Highest growth areas – Forrester, Gartner, and McKinsey research 184
Embedded AI – applied and integrated use cases 184
Ethical AI – responsibility and privacy 186
Creative AI – generative and immersive applications 187
Autonomous AI development – TuringBots 187

Trends in AI adoption – let the data speak for itself 188
General trends 188

Embedded AI – applied and integrated use cases 189
Ethical AI – responsibility and privacy 190
Creative AI – generative and immersive applications 191
Autonomous AI development – TuringBots 191

Low-hanging fruit – quickest wins for AI enablement 192
Summary 193
References 194

13

Evolving Products into AI Products 197

Venn diagram – what's possible and what's probable 198

List 1 – value 199
List 2 – scope 200

List 3 – reach   201

Data is king – the bloodstream of the company   202

Preparation and research   202

Quality partnership   203

Benchmarking   204

The data team   204

Defining success   205

Competition – love your enemies   205

Product strategy – building a blueprint that works for everyone   207

Product strategy   208

Red flags and green flags – what to look for and watch out for   212

Red flags   212

Green flags   213

Summary   214

Additional resources   214

Index   217

Other Books You May Enjoy   226

Preface

It's hard to come across anyone that doesn't have strong opinions and reactions about AI these days. I've witnessed my own feelings and conclusions about it ebb and flow as the years have gone on. When I was a student, I felt a tremendous amount of excitement and optimism about where AI, and the fourth industrial revolution that accompanies it, would take us. That was quickly tempered when I started my book club, and I started a monthly practice of reading books about how bias and dependence on AI were compromising our lives in seen and unseen ways. Then, I started moderating events, where I brought together people from virtually every corner of AI and machine learning, who spoke not just on how they're leveraging this technology in their own work but on their own beliefs about how AI will impact us in the future.

This brings us to one of the greatest debates we find ourselves returning to with every major advancement in technology. Do we dare adopt powerful technology even when we're aware of the risks? As far as I see it, we don't have a choice, and the debate is only an illusion we indulge ourselves in. AI is here to stay, and nihilistic fears about it won't save us from any harm it may cause. Pandora's box is open, and as we peer into what remains of it, we find that hope springs eternal.

AI is holding up a mirror to our biases and inequalities, and so far, it's not a flattering reflection. It's my hope that, with time, we will learn how to adopt AI responsibly in order to minimize its harm and optimize its greatest contributions to our modern civilization. I wanted to write a book about AI product management because it's the makers of products that bring nebulous ideas into the "real" world. Getting into the details about how to ideate, build, manage and maintain AI products with integrity, to the best of my ability, is the greatest contribution I can make to this field at this present moment. It's been an honor to write this book.

Who this book is for

This book is for people that aspire to be AI product managers, AI technologists, and entrepreneurs, or for people that are casually interested in the considerations of bringing AI products to life. It should serve you if you're already working in product management and you have a curiosity about building AI products. It should also serve you if you already work in AI development in some capacity and you're looking to bring those concepts into the discipline of product management and adopt a more business-oriented role. While some chapters in the book are more technically focused, all of the technical content in the book can be considered beginner level and accessible to all.

What this book covers

Chapter 1, Understanding the Infrastructure and Tools for Building AI Products, offers an overview of the main concepts and areas of infrastructure for managing AI products.

Chapter 2, Model Development and Maintenance for AI Products, delves into the nuances of model development and maintenance.

Chapter 3, Machine Learning and Deep Learning Deep Dive, is a broader discussion of the difference between traditional deep learning and deep learning algorithms and their use cases.

Chapter 4, Commercializing AI Products, discusses the major areas of AI products we see in the market, as well as examples of the ethics and success factors that contribute to commercialization.

Chapter 5, AI Transformation and Its Impact on Product Management, explores the ways AI can be incorporated into the major market sectors in the future.

Chapter 6, Understanding the AI-Native Product, gives an overview of the strategies, processes, and team building needed to empower the success of an AI-native product.

Chapter 7, Productizing the ML Service, is an exploration of the trials and tribulations that may come up when building an AI product from scratch.

Chapter 8, Customization for Verticals, Customers, and Peer Groups, is a discussion on how AI products change and evolve over various types of verticals, customer types, and peer groups.

Chapter 9, Macro and Micro AI for Your Product, gives an overview of the various ways you can leverage AI in ways big and small, as well as some of the most successful examples and common mistakes.

Chapter 10, Benchmarking Performance, Growth Hacking, and Cost, explains the benchmarking needed to gauge product success at the product level rather than the model performance level.

Chapter 11, The Rising Tide of AI, is a revisit to the concept of the fourth industrial revolution and a blueprint for products that don't currently leverage AI.

Chapter 12, Trends and Insights across Industry, dives into the various ways we're seeing AI trending across industries, based on prominent and respected research organizations.

Chapter 13, Evolving Products into AI Products, is a practical guide on how to deliver AI features and upgrade the existing logic of products to successfully update products for AI commercial success.

Conventions used

The text conventions used throughout this book are as follows:

> **Tips or important notes**
> Appear like this.

Get in touch

Feedback from our readers is always welcome.

General feedback: If you have questions about any aspect of this book, email us at customercare@packtpub.com and mention the book title in the subject of your message.

Errata: Although we have taken every care to ensure the accuracy of our content, mistakes do happen. If you have found a mistake in this book, we would be grateful if you would report this to us. Please visit www.packtpub.com/support/errata and fill in the form.

Piracy: If you come across any illegal copies of our works in any form on the internet, we would be grateful if you would provide us with the location address or website name. Please contact us at copyright@packt.com with a link to the material.

If you are interested in becoming an author: If there is a topic that you have expertise in and you are interested in either writing or contributing to a book, please visit authors.packtpub.com.

Share Your Thoughts

Once you've read *The AI Product Manager's Handbook*, we'd love to hear your thoughts! Scan the QR code below to go straight to the Amazon review page for this book and share your feedback.

https://packt.link/r/1-804-61293-6

Your review is important to us and the tech community and will help us make sure we're delivering excellent quality content.

Download a free PDF copy of this book

Thanks for purchasing this book!

Do you like to read on the go but are unable to carry your print books everywhere?

Is your eBook purchase not compatible with the device of your choice?

Don't worry, now with every Packt book you get a DRM-free PDF version of that book at no cost.

Read anywhere, any place, on any device. Search, copy, and paste code from your favorite technical books directly into your application.

The perks don't stop there, you can get exclusive access to discounts, newsletters, and great free content in your inbox daily

Follow these simple steps to get the benefits:

1. Scan the QR code or visit the link below

https://packt.link/free-ebook/9781804612934

2. Submit your proof of purchase
3. That's it! We'll send your free PDF and other benefits to your email directly

Part 1 –
Lay of the Land – Terms, Infrastructure, Types of AI, and Products Done Well

An AI product manager needs to have a comprehensive understanding of AI, along with all the varied components that lead to its success, if they're going to be successful in commercializing their products.

This first part consists of five cumulative chapters that will cover what the term AI encompasses and how to support infrastructure to make it successful within your organization. It will also cover how to support your AI program from a maintenance perspective, how to navigate the vast areas of **machine learning** (ML) and **deep learning** (DL) and choose the best path for your product, and how to understand current and future developments in AI products.

By the end of this part, you will understand AI terms and components, what an AI implementation means from an investment perspective, how to maintain AI products sustainably, and how to choose between the types of AI that would best fit your product and market. You will also learn how to understand success factors for ideating and building a **minimal viable product** (MVP), and how to make a product that truly serves its market.

This part comprises the following chapters:

- *Chapter 1, Understanding the Infrastructure and Tools for Building AI Products*
- *Chapter 2, Model Development and Maintenance for AI Products*
- *Chapter 3, Machine Learning and Deep Learning Deep Dive*
- *Chapter 4, Commercializing AI Products*
- *Chapter 5, AI Transformation and Its Impact on Product Management*

1

Understanding the Infrastructure and Tools for Building AI Products

Laying a solid foundation is an essential part of understanding anything, and the frontier of **artificial intelligence (AI)** products seems a lot like our universe: ever-expanding. That rate of expansion is increasing with every passing year as we go deeper into a new way to conceptualize products, organizations, and the industries we're all a part of. Virtually every aspect of our lives will be impacted in some way by AI and we hope those reading will come out of this experience more confident about what AI adoption will look like for the products they support or hope to build someday.

Part 1 of this book will serve as an overview of the lay of the land. We will cover terms, infrastructure, types of AI algorithms, and products done well, and by the end of this section, you will understand the various considerations when attempting to build an AI strategy, whether you're looking to create a native-AI product or add AI features to an existing product.

Managing AI products is a highly iterative process, and the work of a product manager is to help your organization discover what the best combination of infrastructure, training, and deployment workflow is to maximize success in your target market. The performance and success of AI products lie in understanding the infrastructure needed for managing AI pipelines, the outputs of which will then be integrated into a product. In this chapter, we will cover everything from databases to workbenches to deployment strategies to tools you can use to manage your AI projects, as well as how to gauge your product's efficacy.

This chapter will serve as a high-level overview of the subsequent chapters in *Part 1* but it will foremost allow for a definition of terms, which are quite hard to come by in today's marketing-heavy AI competitive landscape. These days, it feels like every product is an AI product, and marketing departments are trigger-happy with sprinkling that term around, rendering it almost useless as a descriptor. We suspect this won't be changing anytime soon, but the more fluency consumers and customers alike have with the capabilities and specifics of AI, machine learning (ML), and data science, the more we should see clarity about how products are built and optimized. Understanding the context of AI is important for anyone considering building or supporting an AI product.

In this chapter, we will cover the following topics:

- Definitions – what is and is not AI

- ML versus DL – understanding the difference

- Learning types in ML

- The order – what is the optimal flow and where does every part of the process live?

- DB 101 – databases, warehouses, data lakes, and lakehouses

- Managing projects – IaaS

- Deployment strategies – what do we do with these outputs?

- Succeeding in AI – how well-managed AI companies do infrastructure right

- The promise of AI – where is AI taking us?

Definitions – what is and is not AI

In 1950, a mathematician and world war II war hero Alan Turing asked a simple question in his paper *Computing Machinery and Intelligence – Can machines think?*. Today, we're still grappling with that same question. Depending on who you ask, AI can be many things. Many maps exist out there on the internet, from expert systems used in healthcare and finance to facial recognition to natural language processing to regression models. As we continue with this chapter, we will cover many of the facets of AI that apply to products emerging in the market.

For the purposes of applied AI in products across industries, in this book, we will focus primarily on ML and deep learning (DL) models used in various capacities because these are often used in production anywhere AI is referenced in any marketing capacity. We will use AI/ML as a blanket term covering a span of ML applications and we will cover the major areas most people would consider ML, such as DL, computer vision, natural language processing, and facial recognition. These are the methods of applied AI that most people will come across in the industry, and familiarity with these applications will serve any product manager looking to break into AI. If anything, we'd like to help anyone who's looking to expand into the field from another product management background to choose which area of AI appeals to them most.

We'd also like to cover what is and what isn't ML. The best way for us to express it as simply as we can is: if a machine is learning from some past behavior and if its success rate is improving as a result of this learning, it is ML! *Learning is the active element.* No models are perfect but we do learn a lot from employing models. Every model will have some element of hyperparameter tuning, and the use of each model will yield certain results in performance. Data scientists and ML engineers working with these models will be able to benchmark performance and see how performance is improving. If there are fixed, hardcoded rules that don't change, it's not ML.

AI is a subset of computer science, and all programmers are effectively doing just that: giving computers a set of instructions to fire away on. If your current program doesn't learn from the past in any way, if it simply executes on directives it was hardcoded with, we can't call this ML. You may have heard the terms *rules-based engine* or *expert system* thrown around in other programs. They are considered forms of AI, but they're not ML because although they are a form of AI, the rules are effectively replicating the work of a person, and the system itself is not learning or changing on its own.

We find ourselves in a tricky time in AI adoption where it can be very difficult to find information online about what makes a product *AI*. Marketing is eager to add the AI label to their products but there still isn't a baseline of explainability with what that means out in the market. This further confuses the term AI for consumers and technologists alike. If you're confused by the terms, particularly when they're applied to products you see promoted online, you're very much not alone.

Another area of confusion is the general term that is AI. For most people, the concept of AI brings to mind the *Terminator* franchise from the 1980s and other futurist depictions of inescapable technological destruction. While there certainly can be a lot of harm to come from AI, this depiction represents what's referred to as *strong AI* or **artificial general intelligence (AGI)**. We still have ways to go for something such as AGI but we've got plenty of what's referred to as **artificial narrow intelligence** or **narrow AI (ANI)**.

ANI is also commonly expressed as *weak AI* and is what's generally meant when you see AI plastered all over products you find online. ANI is exactly what it sounds like: a narrow application of AI. Maybe it's good at talking to you, at predicting some future value, or at organizing things; maybe it's an expert at that, but its expertise won't bleed into other areas. If it could, it would stop being ANI. These major areas of AI are referred to as strong and weak in comparison to human intelligence. Even the most convincing conversational AIs out there, and they are quite convincing, are demonstrating an illusionary intelligence. Effectively, all AI that exists at the moment is weak or ANI. Our *Terminator* days are still firmly in our future, perhaps never to be realized.

For every person out there that's come across Reddit threads about AI being sentient or somehow having ill will toward us, we want to make the following statement very clear. AGI does not exist and there is no such thing as sentient AI. This does not mean AI doesn't actively and routinely cause humans harm, even in its current form. The major caveat here is that unethical, haphazard applications of AI already actively cause us both minor inconveniences and major upsets. Building AI ethically and responsibly is still a work in progress. While AI systems may not be sentiently plotting the downfall of humanity, when they're left untested, improperly managed, and inadequately vetted for bias, the applications of ANI that are deployed already have the capacity to do real damage in our lives.

For now, can machines think like us? No, they don't think like us. Will they someday? We hope not. It's my personal opinion that the insufferable aspects of the human condition end with us. But we do very much believe that we will experience some of our greatest ails, as well as our wildest curiosities, to be impacted considerably by the benevolence of AI and ML.

ML versus DL – understanding the difference

As a product manager, you're going to need to build a lot of trust with your technical counterparts so that, together, you can build an amazing product that works as well as it can technically. If you're reading this book, you've likely come across the phrase ML and DL. We will use the following sections titled *ML* and *DL* to go over some of the basics but keep in mind that we will be elaborating on these concepts further down in *Chapter 3*.

ML

In its basic form, **ML** is made up of two essential components: *the models used* and *the training data it's learning from*. These data are historical data points that effectively teach machines a baseline foundation from which to learn, and every time you retrain the models, the models are theoretically improving. How the models are chosen, built, tuned, and maintained for optimized performance is the work of data scientists and ML engineers. Using this knowledge of performance toward the optimization of the product experience itself is the work of product managers. If you're working in the field of AI product management, you're working incredibly closely with your data science and ML teams.

We'd like to also make a distinction about the folks you'll be working with as an AI product manager. Depending on your organization, you're either working with data scientists and developers to deploy ML or you're working with ML engineers who can both train and upkeep the models as well as deploy them into production. We highly suggest maintaining strong relationships with any and all of these impacted teams, along with DevOps.

All ML models can be grouped into the following four major learning categories:

- Supervised learning
- Unsupervised learning
- Semi-supervised learning
- Reinforcement learning

These are the four major areas of ML and each area is going to have its particular models and algorithms that are used in each specialization. The learning type has to do with whether or not you're labeling the data and the method you're using to reward the models you've used for good performance. These learning types are relevant whether your product is using a DL model or not, so they're inclusive of all ML models. We will be covering the learning types in more depth in the following section titled *Learning types in ML*.

DL

DL is a subset of ML, but the terms are often used colloquially as almost separate expressions. The reason for this is DL is based on neural network algorithms and ML can be thought of as… the rest of the algorithms. In the preceding section covering ML, we looked at the process of taking data, using it to train our models, and using that trained model to predict new future data points. Every time you use the model, you see how *off* it was from the correct answer by getting some understanding of the rate of error so you can iterate back and forth until you have a model that works well enough. Every time, you are creating a model based on data that has certain patterns or *features*.

This process is the same in DL, but one of the key differences of DL is that patterns or features in your data are largely picked up by the DL algorithm through what's referred to as **feature learning** or **feature engineering** through a hierarchical layered system. We will go into the various algorithms that are used in the following section because there are a few nuances between each, but as you continue developing your understanding of the types of ML out there, you'll also start to group the various models that make up these major areas of AI (ML and DL). For marketing purposes, you will for the most part see terms such as *ML, DL/neural networks*, or just the general umbrella term of *AI* referenced where DL algorithms are used.

It's important to know the difference between what these terms mean in practice and at the model level and how they're communicated by non-technical stakeholders. As product managers, we are toeing the line between the two worlds: what engineering is building and what marketing is communicating. Anytime you've heard the term **black box model**, it's referring to a neural network model, which is DL. The reason for this is DL engineers often can't determine how their models are arriving at certain conclusions that are creating an opaque view of what the model is doing. This opacity is double-sided, both for the engineers and technologists themselves, as well as for the customers and users downstream who are experiencing the effects of these models without knowing how they make certain determinations. The DL neural networks are mimicking the structure of the way humans are able to think using a variety of layers of neural networks.

For product managers, DL poses a concern for explainability because there's very little we can understand about how and why a model is arriving at conclusions, and, depending on the context of your product, the importance of explainability could vary. Another inherent challenge is these models essentially learn autonomously because they aren't waiting for their engineer to choose the features that are most relevant in the data for them; the neural networks themselves do the feature selection. It learns with very little input from an engineer. Think of the models as the *what* and the following section of learning types as the *how*. A quick reminder that as we move on to cover the learning styles (whether a model is used in a supervised, unsupervised, semi-supervised, or reinforcement learning capacity), these learning styles apply to both DL and traditional ML models.

Let's look at the different learning types in ML.

Learning types in ML

In this section, we will cover the differences between supervised, unsupervised, semi-supervised, and reinforcement learning and how all these learning types can be applied. Again, the learning type has to do with whether or not you're labeling the data and the method you're using to reward the models you've used for good performance. The ultimate objective is to understand what kind of learning model gets you the kind of performance and explainability you're going to need when considering whether or not to use it in your product.

Supervised learning

If humans are labeling the data and the machine is looking to also correctly label current or future data points, it's supervised learning. Because we humans know the answer the machines are trying to arrive at, we can see how off they are from finding the correct answer, and we continue this process of training the models and retraining them until we find a level of accuracy that we're happy with.

Applications of supervised learning models include classification models that are looking to categorize data in the way spam filters do or regression models that are looking for relationships between variables in order to predict future events and find trends. Keep in mind that all models will only work to a certain point, which is why they require constant training and updating and AI teams are often using ensemble modeling or will try various models and choose the best-performing one. It won't be perfect either way, but with enough hand-holding, it will take you closer and closer to the truth.

The following is a list of common supervised learning models/algorithms you'll likely use in production for various products:

- **Naive Bayes classifier**: This algorithm *naively* considers every feature in your dataset as its own independent variable. So, it's essentially trying to find associations probabilistically without having any assumptions about the data. It's one of the simpler algorithms out there and its simplicity actually is what makes it so successful with classification. It's commonly used for binary values such as trying to decipher whether or not something is spam.

- **Support vector machine (SVM)**: This algorithm is also largely used for classification problems and will essentially try to split your dataset into two classes so that you can use it to group your data and try to predict where future data points will land along these major splits. If you're not seeing compelling groups between the data, SVMs allow you to add more dimensions to be able to see groupings easier.

- **Linear regression models**: These have been around since the 1950s and they're the simplest models we have for regression problems such as predicting future data points. They essentially use one or more variables in your dataset to predict your dependent variable. The *linear* part of this model is trying to find the best line to fit your data, and this line is what dictates how it predicts. Here, we once again see a relatively simple model also being heavily used because of how versatile and dependable it is.

- **Logistic regression**: This model works a lot like linear regression in that you have independent and dependent variables, but it's not predicting a numerical value; it's predicting a future binary categorical state such as whether or not someone might default on a loan in the future, for instance.

- **Decision trees**: This algorithm works well with both predicting something categorical as well as something numerical, so it's used for both kinds of ML problems, such as predicting a future state or a future price. This is less common so decision trees are used often for both kinds of problems, which has contributed to its popularity. Its comparison to a tree comes from the nodes and branches that effectively function like a flow chart. The model learns from the flow of past data to predict future values.

- **Random forest**: This algorithm builds from the previous decision trees and is also used for both categorical and numerical problems. The way it works is it splits the data into different *random"*samples, creates decision trees for each sample, and then takes an average or majority vote for its predictions (depending on whether you're using it for categorical or numerical predictions). It's hard to understand how a random forest comes to conclusions, so if interpretability isn't super high on the list of concerns, you can use it.

- **K-nearest neighbors** (**KNNs**): This algorithm exclusively works on categorical as well as numerical predictions, so it's looking for a future state and it offers results in groups. The number of data points in the group is set by the engineer/data scientist, and the way the model works is by grouping the data and determining characteristics the data shares with its neighbors and giving its best guess based on those neighbors for future values.

Now that we've covered supervised learning, let's discuss unsupervised learning next.

Unsupervised learning

If the data is unlabeled and we're using machines to label the data and find patterns we don't yet know of, it's unsupervised. Effectively, we humans either know the right answer or we don't, and that's how we decipher which camp the ML algorithms belong to. As you might imagine, we take the results of unsupervised learning models with some hesitancy because it may be finding an organization that isn't actually helpful or accurate. Unsupervised learning models also require large amounts of data to train on because the results can be wildly inaccurate if it's trying to find patterns out of a small data sample. As it ingests more and more data, its performance will improve and become more refined over time, but once again, there is no *correct* answer.

Applications of unsupervised learning models include clustering and dimensionality reduction. Clustering models segment or group data into certain areas. These can be used for things such as looking for patterns in medical trials or drug discovery, for instance, because you're looking for connections and groups of data where there might not already be obvious answers. Dimensionality reduction essentially removes the features in your dataset that contribute less to the performance you're looking for and will simplify your data so that your most important features will best improve your performance to separate real signals from the noise.

The following is a list of common unsupervised learning models/algorithms you'll likely use in production for various products:

- **K-means clustering**: This algorithm will group data points together to better see patterns (or clusters), but it's looking for some optimal number of clusters as well. This is unsupervised learning, so the model is looking to find patterns that it can learn from because it's not given any information (or supervision) to go off from the engineer that's using it. Also, the number of clusters assigned is a hyperparameter and you will need to choose what number of clusters is optimal.

- **Principal component analysis** (**PCA**): Often, the largest problem with using unsupervised ML on very large datasets is there's actually too much uncorrelated data to find meaningful patterns. This is why PCA is used so often because it's a great way to reduce dimension without actually losing or discarding information. This is especially useful for massive datasets such as finding patterns in genome sequencing or drug discovery trials.

Next, let's jump into semi-supervised learning.

Semi-supervised learning

In a perfect world, we'd have massive well-labeled datasets with which to create optimal models that don't overfit. **Overfitting** is when you create and tune a model to the dataset you have but it fits a bit too well, which means it's optimized for that particular dataset and doesn't work well with more diverse data. This is a common problem in data science. We live in an imperfect world and we can find ourselves in situations where we don't have enough labeled data or enough data at all. This is where semi-supervised learning comes in handy. We give some labeled datasets and also include a dataset that is unlabeled to essentially give the model nudges in the right direction as it tries to come up with its own semblance of finding patterns.

It doesn't quite have the same level of absolute truth associated with supervised learning, but it does offer the models some helpful clues with which to organize its results so that it can find an easier path to the right answer.

For instance, let's say you're looking for a model that works well with detecting patterns in photos or speech. You might label a few of them and then see how the performance improves over time with the examples you don't label. You can use multiple models in semi-supervised learning. The process would be a lot like supervised learning, which learns with labeled datasets so that it knows exactly how off it is from being correct. The main difference between supervised learning and semi-supervised learning is that you're predicting a portion of the new unlabeled data and then, essentially, checking its accuracy against the labeled data. You're adding unlabeled new data points into the training set so that it's *training* on the data it's gotten correct.

Finally, to wrap up this section, let's take a brief look at reinforcement learning.

Reinforcement learning

This area of ML effectively learns with trial and error, so it's learning from past behavior and adapting its approach to finding the best performance by itself. There's a sequence to reinforcement learning and it's really a system based on weights and rewards to reinforce correct results. Eventually, the model tries to optimize for these rewards and gets better with time. We see reinforcement learning used a lot with robotics, for instance, where robots are trained to understand how to operate and adjust to the parameters of the real world with all its unpredictability.

Now that we've discussed and understood the different ML types, let's move on and understand the optimal flow of the ML process.

The order – what is the optimal flow and where does every part of the process live?

Companies interested in creating value with AI/ML have a lot to gain compared to their more hesitant competitors. According to McKinsey Global Institute, *"Companies that fully absorb AI in their value-producing workflows by 2025 will dominate the 2030 world economy with +120% cash flow growth."* The undertaking of embracing AI and productionizing it – whether in your product or for internal purposes – is complex, technical debt-heavy, and expensive. Once your models and use cases are chosen, making that happen in production becomes a difficult program to manage and this is a process many companies will struggle with as we see companies in industries other than tech starting to take on the challenge of embracing AI. Operationalizing the process, updating the models, keeping the data fresh and clean, and organizing experiments, as well as validating, testing, and the storage associated with it, are the complicated parts.

In an effort to make this entire process more digestible, we're going to present this as a step-by-step process because there are varying layers of complexity but the basic components will be the same. Once you have gotten through the easy bit and you've settled on the models and algorithms you feel are optimal for your use case, you can begin to refine your process for managing your AI system.

Step 1 – Data availability and centralization

Essentially, you'll need a central place to store the data that your AI/ML models and algorithms will be learning from. Depending on the databases you invest in or legacy systems you're using, you might have a need for an ETL pipeline and data engineering to make the layers of data and metadata available for your productionized AI/ML models to ingest and offer insights from. Think of this as creating the pipeline needed to feed your AI/ML system.

AI feeds on data, and if your system of delivering data is clunky or slow, you'll run into issues in production later. Choosing your preferred way of storing data is tricky in and of itself. You don't know how your tech stack will evolve as you scale, so choosing a cost-effective and reliable solution is a mission in and of itself. For example, as we started to add more and more customers at a cybersecurity company we were previously working for, we noticed the load time for certain customer-facing dashboards was lagging behind. Part of the issue was the number of customers, and their metadata was too large to support the pipelines we already had in place.

Step 2 – Continuous maintenance

At this point, you have your models and algorithms and you've chosen a system for delivering data to them. Now, you're going to be in the flow of constantly maintaining this system. In DevOps, this is referred to as **continuous integration (CI)**/**continuous delivery (CD)**. In the later chapters, we will cover the concept of **AI Operations (AIOps)** but for now, the following is a list of the stages tailored for the continuous maintenance of AI pipelines. The following are the four major components of the continuous maintenance process:

- **CI**: Testing/validating code and components, along with data, data schemas, and models

- **CD**: Code changes or updates to your model are passed on continuously so that once you've made changes, they are slated to appear in the testing environment before going to production without pauses

- **CT**: We've mentioned the idea of continuous learning being important for ML, and **continuous training** productionizes this process so that as your data feeds are refreshed, your models are consistently training and learning from that new data

- **CM**: We can't have ML/AI models continuously running without also **continuously monitoring** them to make sure something isn't going horribly wrong

You can't responsibly manage an AI program if you aren't iterating your process constantly. Your models and hyperparameters will become stale. Your data will become stale and when an iterative process like this stagnates, it will stop being effective. Performance is something you'll constantly be staying up to date on because the lack of performance will be self-evident, whether it is client-facing or not. With that said, things can also go wrong. For example, lags in performance or in the frequency of the model updating can lead to people losing their jobs, not getting a competitive rate on a mortgage, or getting an unfair prison sentence. Major consequences can arise from downstream effects due to improper model maintenance. We recommend exploring the *Additional resources* section at the end of this chapter for more examples and information on how stagnant AI systems can wreak havoc on environments and people.

B 101 – databases, warehouses, data lakes, and lakehouses

AI/ML products run on data. Where and how you store your data is a big consideration that impacts your AI/ML performance, and in this section, we will be going through some of the most popular storage vehicles for your data. Figuring out the optimal way to store and access and train your data is a specialization in and of itself, but if you're in the business of AI product management, eventually, you're going to need to understand the basic building blocks of what makes your AI product work. In a few words, data does.

Because AI requires big data, this is going to be a significant strategic decision for your product and business. If you don't have a well-oiled machine, pun intended, you're going to run into snags that will impair the performance of your models and, by extension, your product itself. Having a good grasp of the most cost-effective and performance-driven solution for your particular product, and finding the balance within these various facets, is going to help your success as a product manager. Yes, you will depend on your technical executives for a lot of these decisions, but you'll be at the table helping make these decisions, so some familiarity is needed here.

Let's look at some of the different options to store data for AI/ML products.

Database

Depending on your organization's goals and budget, you'll be centralizing your data somehow between a data lake, a database, and a data warehouse, and you might even be considering a new option: the data lakehouse. If you're just getting your feet wet, you're likely just storing your data in a relational database so that you can access it and query it easily. Databases are a great way to do this if you have a relatively simple setup. With a relational database, there's a particular schema you're operating under if you wanted to combine this data with data that's in another database; you would run into problems aligning these schemas later.

If your primary use of the database is querying to access data and use only a certain subset of your company's data for general trends, a relational database might be enough. If you're looking to combine various datasets from disparate areas of your business and you're looking to accomplish more advanced analytics, dashboards, or AI/ML functions, you'll need to read on.

Data warehouse

If you're looking to combine data into a location where you can centralize it somewhere and you've got lots of structured data coming in, you're more likely going to use a data warehouse. This is really the first step toward maturity because it will allow you to leverage insights and trends across your various business units quickly. If you're looking to leverage AI/ML in various ways, rather than one specific specialized way, this will serve you well.

Let's say, for example, that you want to add AI features to your existing product as well as within your HR function. You'd be leveraging your customer data to offer trends or predictions to your customers based on the performance of others in their peer group, as well as using AI/ML to make predictions or optimizations for your internal employees. Both these use cases would be well served with a data warehouse.

Data warehouses do, however, require some upfront investment to create a plan and design your data structures. They also require a costly investment as well because they make data available for analysis on demand, so you're paying a premium for keeping that data readily available. Depending on how advanced your internal users are, you could opt for cheaper options, but this option would be optimal for organizations where most of your business users are looking for easily digestible ways to analyze data. Either way, a data warehouse will allow you to create dashboards for your internal users and stakeholder teams.

Data lake (and lakehouse)

If you're sitting on lots of raw, unstructured data, and you want to have a more cost-effective place to store it, you'd be looking at a data lake. Here, you can store unstructured, semi-structured, as well as structured data that can be easily accessed by your more tech-savvy internal users. For instance, data scientists and ML engineers would be able to work with this data because they would be creating their own data models to transform and analyze the data on the fly, but this isn't the case at most companies.

Keeping your data in a data lake would be cheap if you've got lots of data your business users don't need immediately, but you won't ever really be able to replace a warehouse or a database with one. It's more of a "nice to have." If you're sitting on a massive data lake of historical data you want to use in the future for analytics, you'll need to consider another way to store it to get those insights.

You might also come across the term **lakehouse**. There are many databases, data warehouses, and data lakes out there. However, the only lakehouse we're aware of has been popularized by a company called Databricks, which offers something like a data lake but with some of the capabilities you get with data warehouses, namely, the ability to showcase data, make it available and ingestible for non-technical internal users, and create dashboards with it. The biggest advantage here is that you're storing it and paying for the data to be stored upfront with the ability to access and manipulate it downstream.

Data pipelines

Regardless of the tech you use to maintain and store your data, you're still going to need to put up pipelines to make sure your data is moving, that your dashboards are refreshing as readily as your business requires, and that data is flowing the way it needs to. There are also multiple ways of processing and passing data. You might be doing it in batches (batch processing) for large amounts of data being moved at various intervals, or in real-time pipelines for getting data in real time as soon as it's generated. If you're looking to leverage predictive analytics, enable reporting, or have a system in place to move, process, and store data, a data pipeline will likely be enough. However, depending on what your data is doing and how much transformation is required, you'll likely be using both data pipelines and perhaps, more specifically, ETL pipelines.

ETL stands for **extract, transform, and load**, so your data engineers are going to be creating specific pipelines for more advanced systems such as centralizing all your data into one place, adding data or data enrichment, connecting your data with **CRM (customer relationship management)** tools, or even transforming the data and adding structure to it between systems. The reason for this is that it's a necessary step when using a data warehouse or database. If you're exclusively using a data lake, you'll have all the metadata you need to be able to analyze it and get your insights as you like. In most cases, if you're working with an AI/ML product, you're going to be working with a data engineer who will power the data flow needed to make your product a success because you're likely using a relational database as well as a data warehouse. The analytics required to enable AI/ML features will most likely need to be powered by a data engineer who will focus on the ETL pipeline.

Managing and maintaining this system will also be the work of your data engineer, and we encourage every product manager to have a close relationship with the data engineer(s) that supports their products. One key difference between the two is that ETL pipelines are generally updated in batches and not in real time. If you're using an ETL pipeline, for instance, to update historical daily information about how your customers are using your product to offer client-facing insights in your platform, it might be optimal to keep this batch updating twice daily. If you need insights to come in real time for a dashboard that's being used by your internal business users and they rely on that data to make daily decisions, however, you likely will need to resort to a data pipeline that's updated continuously.

Now, that we understand the different available options to store data and how to choose the right option for the business, let's discuss how to manage our projects.

Managing projects – IaaS

If you're looking to create an AI/ML system in your organization, you'll have to think about it as its own ecosystem that you'll need to constantly maintain. This is why you see MLOps and AIOps working in conjunction with DevOps teams. Increasingly so, we will start to see managed services and **infrastructure-as-a-service (IaaS)** offerings coming out more and more. There has been a shift in the industry toward companies such as Determined AI and Google's AI platform pipeline tools to meet the needs of the market. At the heart of this need is the desire to ease some of the burdens from companies left scratching their heads as they begin to take on the mammoth task of getting started with an AI system.

Just as DevOps teams became popular with at-scale software development, the result of decades of mistakes, we will see something similar with MLOps and AIOps. Developing a solution and putting it into operation are two different key areas that need to work together. This is doubly true for AI/ML systems. The trend now is on IaaS. This is an important concept to understand because companies just approaching AI often don't have an understanding of the cost, storage, compute power, and investment required to do AI properly, particularly for DL AI projects that require massive amounts of data to train on.

At this point, most companies haven't been running AI/ML programs for decades and don't have dedicated teams. Tech companies such as MAANG (Meta, Amazon, Apple, Netflix, Google) are leading the cultural norms with managing AI/ML, but most companies that will need to embrace AI are not in tech and are largely unprepared for the technical debt AI adoption will pose for their engineering teams to manage.

Shortcuts taken to get AI initiatives off the ground will require code refactoring or changing how your data is stored and managed, which is why strategizing and planning for AI adoption is so crucial. This is why so many of these IaaS services are popping up to help keep engineering teams nimble should they require changes in the future as well. The infrastructure needed to keep AI teams up and running is going to change as time goes on, and the advantage of using an IaaS provider is that you can run all your projects and only pay for the time your AI developers are actually using data to train models.

Deployment strategies – what do we do with these outputs?

Once you're happy with the models you've chosen (including their performance and error rate), you've got a good level of infrastructure to support your product and chosen AI model's use case; you're ready to go to the last step of the process and deploy this code into production. Keeping up with a deployment strategy that works for your product and organization will be part of the continuous maintenance we've outlined in the previous section. You'll need to think about things such as how often you'll need to retrain your models and refresh your training data to prevent model decay and data drift. You'll also need a system for continuously monitoring your model's performance so this process will be really specific to your product and business, particularly because these periods of retraining will require some downtime for your system.

Deployment is going to be a dynamic process because your models are trying to effectively make predictions of real-world data for the most part, so depending on what's going on in the world of your data, you might have to give deployment more or less of your attention. For instance, when we were working for an ML property-tech company, we were updating, retraining, and redeploying our models almost daily because we worked with real estate data that was experiencing a huge skew due to rapid changes in migration data and housing price data due to the pandemic. If those models were left unchecked and there weren't engineers and business leaders on both sides of this product, on the client's end and internally, we might not have caught some of the egregious liberties the models were making on behalf of under-representative data.

There are also a number of well-known deployment strategies you should be aware of. We will discuss them in the following subsections.

Shadow deployment strategy

In this deployment strategy (often referred to as **shadow mode**), you're deploying a new model with new features along with a model that already exists so that the new model that's deployed is only experienced as a *shadow* of the model that's currently in production. This also means that the new model is handling all the requests it's getting just as the existing model does but it's not showing the results of that model. This strategy allows you to see whether the shadow model is performing better on the same real-world data it's getting without interrupting the model that's actually live in production. Once it's confirmed that the new model is performing better and that it has no issues running, it will then become the predominant model fully deployed in production and the original model will be retired.

A/B testing model deployment strategy

With this strategy, we're actually seeing two slightly different models with different features to get a sense of how it's working in the live environment concurrently. The two models are set up at the same time and the performance is optimized to reward conversion. This is effectively like an experiment where you're looking at the results of one model over another and you're starting with some hypothesis or expectation of how one is performing better than another, and then you're testing that hypothesis to see whether you were right. The differences in your models do, however, have to be slight because if there's too much variety between the features of the two, you actually won't understand what's creating the most success for you.

Canary deployment strategy

Here, we see a more gradual approach to deployment where you actually create subsets of users that will then experience your new model deployment. Here, we're seeing the number of users that are subjected to your new model gradually increasing over time. This means that you can have a buffer time between groups of users to understand how they're reacting and interacting with this new model. Essentially, you're using varying groups of your own users as testers before you release to a new batch so you can catch bugs more gradually as well. It's a slow but rewarding process if you have the patience and courage.

There are more strategies to choose from but keep in mind that the selection of these strategies will depend on the nature of your product, and what's most important to your customers and users is your budget, your metrics and performance monitoring, your technical capacity and knowledge, and the timeline you have. Beyond your deployment, you're going to have to help your business understand how often they should be doing code refactoring and branching as well.

Now that we've discussed the different deployment strategies, let's see what it takes to succeed in AI.

Succeeding in AI – how well-managed AI companies do infrastructure right

It's indicative of the complexity of ML systems that many large technology companies that depend heavily on ML have dedicated teams and platforms that focus on building, training, deploying, and maintaining ML models. The following are a few examples of options you can take when building an ML/AI program:

- **Databricks has MLflow**: MLflow is an open source platform developed by Databricks to help manage the complete ML life cycle for enterprises. It allows you to run experiences and work with any library, framework, or language. The main benefits are experiment tracking (so you can see how your models are doing between experiments), model management (to manage all versions of your model between teammates), and model deployment (to have a quick view of deployment in view in the tool).

- **Google has TensorFlow Extended (TFX)**: This is Google's newest product built on TensorFlow and it's an end-to-end platform for deploying production-level ML pipelines. It allows you to collaborate within and between teams and offers robust capabilities for scalable, high-performance environments.

- **Uber has Michelangelo**: Uber is a great example of a company creating their own ML management tool in-house for collaboration and deployment. Earlier, they were using disparate languages, models, and algorithms and had teams that were siloed. After they implemented Michelangelo, they were able to bring in varying skill sets and capabilities under one system. They needed one place for a reliable, recreatable, and standardized pipeline to create, manage, predict, and deploy their data at scale.

- **Meta has FBLearner Flow**: Meta also created its own system for managing its numerous AI projects. Since ML is such a foundational part of their product, Meta needed a platform that would allow the following:

  - Every ML algorithm that was implemented once to have the ability to be reusable by someone else at a later date

  - Every engineer to have the ability to write a training pipeline that can be reused

  - Make model training easy and automated

  - Everybody to have the ability to search past projects and experiments easily

  Effectively, Facebook created an easy-to-use knowledge base and workflow to centralize all their ML ops.

- **Amazon has SageMaker**: This is Amazon's product that allows you to build, train, and deploy your ML models and programs with their own collection of fully managed infrastructure tools and workflows. The idea of this product is to meet their customers where they are and offer low-code or no-code UIs, whether you employ ML engineers or business analysts. The ability to use their infrastructure is also great if you're already using Amazon services for your cloud infrastructure so that you can take it a step further to automate and standardize your ML/AI program and operations at scale.

- **Airbnb has Bighead**: Airbnb created its own ML infrastructure in an effort to create standardization and centralization between their AI/ML organizations. They used a collection of tools such as Zipline, Redspot, and DeepThought to orchestrate their ML platform in an effort to do the same as Facebook and Uber: to mitigate errors and discrepancies and minimize repeatable work.

As we can see, there are multiple platforms that can be used to create, train, and deploy ML models. Finally, let's see what the future of AI looks like.

The promise of AI – where is AI taking us?

So, where is this era of AI implementation headed and what does it mean for all industries? At this point, we're looking at an industry of geopolitical influence, a technologically obvious decision that comes with a lot of responsibility, cost, and opportunity. As long as companies and product managers are aware of the risks, costs, and level of investment needed to properly care for an AI program, use it as a source of curiosity, and apply AI/ML to projects that create success early on and build from that knowledge, those that invest in AI will find themselves experiencing AI's promise. This promise is rooted in quantifying prediction and optimization. For example, Highmark Inc. saved more than $260M in 2019 by using ML for fraud detection, GE helped its customers save over $1.6B with their predictive maintenance, and 35% of Amazon's sales come from their recommendation engine.

When a third of your revenues are coming from an AI algorithm, there's virtually no argument. Whatever investment you make in AI/ML, make sure you're leveraging it to its maximum capacity by properly planning and strategizing, finding capable talent that's aware of the space and potential dangers, and choosing the right scalable infrastructure to limit your refactoring.

As long as your AI/ML projects are directly married to outcomes that impact cost savings or revenue, you'll likely experience success within your own career if you're overseeing these projects. The recommendation of starting small, applying it to a clear business goal, tracking that goal, and showing off its effectiveness is a smart strategy because this chapter details the many areas of maintaining an AI program, as well as potential areas where it might experience hurdles. Justifying the time, investment in headcount, and infrastructure expenses will be challenging if you're not able to communicate the strength and capabilities of AI to even your most hesitant executive.

This will also be important for your technical resources (data scientists, data engineers, and ML engineers) as well as for your business stakeholders. It's one thing to know more about the ML algorithms you'll be using or to get a few recommendations about how to best store your data, but you really won't have the intimacy and fluency needed to truly be an agent of change within your organization if you don't iterate with your own projects and grow your knowledge and intuition about what works best from there. We learn through iteration and we build confidence the more we complete a task successfully. This will be the case for you as a product manager as well.

In the previous example, GE offered cost savings to its customers, Highmark prevented future bottlenecks by predicting fraud, and Amazon grew its revenues through ML. When we think about the promise of AI and where it's taking us, these examples drive the idea that this is the home of the latest industrial revolution. It's not just something that will offer benefits to companies but to everyone all at once. The distribution of the benefits may not be completely equal because, ultimately, it's the companies that are investing in this tech and they will look to experience the highest return on this investment first, but the point stands that consumers, as well as businesses, will experience benefits from AI.

Summary

We've covered a lot in this chapter, but keep in mind that a lot of the concepts present here will be returned to in subsequent chapters for further discussion. It's almost impossible to overstate the infrastructure AI/ML will need to be successful because so much of the performance is dependent on how we deliver data and how we manage deployments. We covered the basic definitions of ML and DL, as well as the learning types that both can employ. We also covered some of the basics of setting up and maintaining an AI pipeline and included a few examples of how other companies manage this kind of operation.

Building products that leverage AI/ML is an ambitious endeavor, and this first chapter was meant to provide enough of a foundation for the process of setting up an AI program overall, so that we can build on the various aspects of that process in the following chapters without having to introduce too many new concepts so late in the book. If you're feeling overwhelmed, it only means you're grasping the scale necessary for building with AI. That's a great sign! In *Chapter 2*, we will get into the specifics of using and maintaining the ML models we briefly introduced earlier in this chapter.

Additional resources

For additional information, you can refer to the following resources:

- *Weapons of Math Destruction* by Cathy O'Neil: https://www.amazon.com/Weapons-Math-Destruction-Increases-Inequality/dp/0553418815

- *Invisible Women: Exposing Data Bias in a World Designed for Men* by Caroline Criado Perez: https://www.amazon.com/Invisible-Women-Data-World-Designed/dp/1419735217/ref=sr_1_1?keywords=invisible+women&qid=1673296808&sr=8-1

- *The Ethical Algorithm: The Science of Socially Aware Algorithm Design* by Michael Kearns, Aaron Roth: https://www.amazon.com/Ethical-Algorithm-Science-Socially-Design/dp/0190948205/

- *Artificial Unintelligence: How Computers Misunderstand the World* by Meredith Broussard: https://www.amazon.com/Artificial-Unintelligence-Computers-Misunderstand-World/dp/026253701X/

- *Algorithms of Oppression: How Search Engines Reinforce Racism* by Safiya Umoja Noble: https://www.amazon.com/Algorithms-Oppression-Search-Engines-Reinforce/dp/1479837245/

- *Race After Technology: Abolitionist Tools for the New Jim Code* by Ruha Benjamin: https://www.amazon.com/Race-After-Technology-Abolitionist-Tools/dp/1509526404/

- *The Age of Surveillance Capitalism: The Fight for a Human Future at the New Frontier of Power* by Shoshana Zuboff: https://www.amazon.com/Age-Surveillance-Capitalism-Future-Frontier/dp/1541758005/

- *Automating Inequality: How High-Tech Tools Profile, Police, and Punish the Poor* by Virginia Eubanks: https://www.amazon.com/Automating-Inequality-High-Tech-Profile-Police/dp/1250074312/

- *Data Feminism* by Catherine D'Ignazio: https://www.amazon.com/Feminism-Strong-Ideas-Catherine-DIgnazio/dp/0262044005/

References

- https://www.canva.com/careers/topic/machine-learning/

- *Model Deployment Strategies*: https://neptune.ai/blog/model-deployment-strategies

- *AI Helps DuoLingo Personalize Language Learning*: https://www.wired.com/brandlab/2018/12/ai-helps-duolingo-personalize-language-learning/#:~:text=The%20learning%20behind%20the%20lingo,data%20and%20make%20intelligent%20predictions

- https://www.crunchbase.com/organization/ggwp-65c2

- https://www.cbinsights.com/company/anon-ai

- *AI-50 America's Most Promising Artificial Intelligence Companies*: https://www.forbes.com/sites/alanohnsman/2021/04/26/ai-50-americas-most-promising-artificial-intelligence-companies/?sh=3b5e27ef77cf

- https://www.lacework.com/labs/

- `https://www.crunchbase.com/organization/lacework/company_financials`

- *SHEIN's AI Program Matches Local Demand at Scale*: `https://www.psfk.com/2022/06/sheins-consumer-to-manufacturer-ai-program-matches-local-demand-at-scale.html#:~:text=Shein's%20AI%20engine%20can%20quickly,brand%20much%20cheaper%20operating%20costs`

- *Product Led Growth, Wes Bush*

- *Mind the Gap – It's Not AI/ML Unless It's in Production: Data Strategy Series Part 4*: `https://www.credera.com/insights/mind-gap-not-ai-ml-unless-production-data-strategy-series-part-4`

- *Airbnb's End-to-End ML Platform*: `https://medium.com/acing-ai/airbnbs-end-to-end-ml-platform-8f9cb8ba71d8`

- *Amazon SageMaker*: `https://aws.amazon.com/sagemaker/`

- *Introducing FBLearner Flow: Facebook's AI backbone*: `https://engineering.fb.com/2016/05/09/core-data/introducing-fblearner-flow-facebooks-ai-backbone/`

- *Meet Michelangelo: Uber's Machine Learning Platform*: `https://www.uber.com/blog/michelangelo-machine-learning-platform/`

- *TFX is an end-to-end platform for deploying production ML pipelines*: `https://www.tensorflow.org/tfx`

- *Managed MLflow Managing the complete machine learning lifecycle*: `https://www.databricks.com/product/managed-mlflow`

- *Discover Lakehouse*: `https://www.databricks.com/discoverlakehouse?utm_medium=paid+search&utm_source=google&utm_campaign=13039235745&utm_adgroup=125064728314&utm_content=product+page&utm_offer=discoverlakehouse&utm_ad=576656880219&utm_term=what%20is%20a%20lakehouse&gclid=CjwKCAjwx7GYBhB7EiwA0d8oe_HabROASQAaw7XYRq-VinQLswPqDyh8iPCT4032m8UN7H0B0uNyVBoCZ-QQAvD_BwE`

- *Computing Machinery and Intelligence*: `https://phil415.pbworks.com/f/TuringComputing.pdf`

- *Key requirements for an MLOps foundation*: `https://cloud.google.com/blog/products/ai-machine-learning/key-requirements-for-an-mlops-foundation`

- *How does TikTok use machine learning?*: `https://dev.to/mage_ai/how-does-tiktok-use-machine-learning-5b7i`

2

Model Development and Maintenance for AI Products

In this chapter, we will be exploring the nuances of model development, from linear regression to deep learning neural network models. We'll cover the variety of models that are available to use, as well as what's entailed for the maintenance of those models, from how they're developed and trained to how they're deployed and ultimately tested. This will be a basic overview to understand the end-to-end process of model maintenance that product managers can expect from the engineering and dev ops teams that support their products.

There's a lot involved with bringing any new product to market, and if you've been a product manager for a while, you're likely familiar with the **new product development** (**NPD**) process – or set of steps. As a precursor to the rest of the chapter, particularly for those that are unfamiliar with the NPD process, we're going to be summarizing each of the steps in the first section of this chapter. Overall, this chapter will cover the following topics:

- Understanding the stages of NPD

- Model types – from linear regression to neural networks

- Training – when is a model ready for market?

- Deployment – what happens after the workstation?

- Testing and troubleshooting

- Refreshing – the ethics of how often we update our models

Understanding the stages of NPD

In this section, we will be covering the various stages of the NPD cycle as it relates to the emergence of an AI/ML product. Through each stage, we'll cover the major foundational areas, from the ideation to the launch of an acceptable first version of a product. The steps are laid out incrementally from the discovery stage, in which you brainstorm about the need you're looking to address in the market and why that need needs to be bolstered by AI. In the define stage, you bring in your product requirements for your product. In the design stage, you bring in the active visual and experiential elements of your end product. In the implementation stage, you build it out. In the marketing stage, you craft a message for your broader audience. In the training stage, you put your product to the test and make sure it's being used as intended. Finally, in the launch stage, you release your product to a broader audience for feedback. Let's get into these stages in more detail in the following sections.

Step 1 – Discovery

In this phase, you're ideating. You look to isolate the particular problem you're trying to solve, and in the context of a **machine learning (ML)** product, a crucial part of this first phase is understanding why you're trying to solve that particular problem with ML in the first place. To borrow a phrase from Simon Sinek's popular book *Find Your Why* (https://simonsinek.com/books/find-your-why/), this is where you "find your why." This is the phase in which you contemplate the fundamentals of the problem at hand and look to isolate what is most urgent about the problem so that you can later address an unmet need or under-served customers.

This requires gathering qualitative and quantitative customer feedback about the particular issue they're facing that you're looking to address. The biggest focus here is creativity – to brainstorm potential solutions that you can then analyze and further explore (or discard) later.

Step 2 – Define

The second phase is all about defining your **minimal viable product (MVP)**. You've taken all the feedback about the problem and potential solutions in the first step, but now you're actually building a plan from those ideas. You have to start somewhere, right? So, this step is all about screening your ideas from the discovery stage to select the one that has the highest potential to solve your customers' biggest problem. This is where all those creative brainstorming sessions are put to the test and analyzed to best understand which of the ideas from phase one have legs. What you're looking for here is the minimum number of features you'd need to create a version of your product that will address the main problem areas – or assumptions of – for the customers you're looking to serve.

As far as your model goes, this is also where you define some metrics for model performance that will mark the minimum performance your model will need to reach in order to be a good, viable option for your customer. Remember, this is just for your MVP. The idea is that you first begin with your MVP and then you iterate through sprints or product development processes to incrementally make your product perform better or build in features your customers might prefer or need over time. Model performance will work the same way. As you partner with your customers, you will refine the product, the models, and the performance of those models together over time.

Step 3 – Design

In the first and second steps of this process, you identify the problem you want to solve, come up with ideas, and then define the minimum amount of work you'll need to take on the problem at hand. Now, in this third design step, you actually build out that MVP and start to piece together what it might look like. This is the step that's most heavy on finding the solution. In this step, you're coming up with mockups for how folks might interact with your product, what the UI might look like, and how the product experience might unfold. For AI products, this is also where you start to identify which of the models mentioned in the following section will best serve your product.

This step is all about creating a roadmap of the UI/UX elements. It's where you will want to involve some of your customers in the solution and, for an AI product, where you'll set some performance benchmarks and goals for your model to hit. Building performance into the design process and managing these expectations with eventual users of your product is a great way to crystalize the concept and test it early on.

Step 4 – Implementation

The implementation phase is where all the ideating and planning from the first three steps are put to the ultimate test. This is the phase in which you're actually working to materialize everything you just worked hard on strategizing. For all intents and purposes, this is essentially your first sprint, and as a product manager, you're effectively working as a project manager in this phase to make sure that what you end up with meets the needs you set out to address.

This is the doing part in which you actually bring in your engineers, ML engineers, developers, UI/UX folks, and project managers to create the MVP and achieve the performance your customers and the leadership are expecting. What you should be left with is a version of your MVP that does what you said it would do, as you said it would. You know you've succeeded with this step when your MVP meets the planning criteria.

Step 5 – Marketing

Marketing is happening in the background of all these steps because even part of *step 1* relates heavily to marketing. Understanding the language of your customer, their needs, and their pain points is a huge prerequisite for getting your messaging right. Marketing is the delivery and communication of your message to your wider market base, and the reason why it's *step 5* is that you want to have a working MVP before you craft the official message that will go out for your current and prospective customers to see.

With AI products, marketing undergoes specific scrutiny because the AI market is heavily competitive and companies are in a communication quagmire. If you communicate too much about your product and which models make it worthy of the AI stamp, you're giving away too much of the secret sauce. If you communicate too little about the actual tech that's giving it AI/ML capabilities, you're likely to face criticism that you're overselling your solutions' AI capabilities. We can say with a lot of confidence that most companies err on the side of under-communicating when it comes to AI products. This is the step in which you will need to agree with all your stakeholders on how you best want to communicate AI capabilities to the outside world.

Step 6 – Training

The process of training users and documenting your product happens in this sixth phase so that you can create the justifications for the choices you've made for your MVP and your product overall. Part of training your users on your product is also managing expectations for how they are to interpret the performance of your product. This part will be especially important with AI/ML products because they often optimize, rank, classify, recommend, or predict future values, and it will be especially important to help your customers understand when they can trust or question certain results.

This process is intuitive for the most part because when it comes to AI/ML, we don't know how far off we are from the predictions or optimizations until a future point in time. Part of the training that must happen, then, is to manage expectations with your customers about what margins of error are healthy for them to expect. This step is all about informing others about your product and how to best interact with it.

Step 7 – Launch

In this final step, we launch the product into the market officially. So far, you've spoken to your internal stakeholders and teams, received customer feedback, and maybe one or two customers have partnered with you to help create your offering and bring it to market. Maybe you've had a soft launch or gotten other beta testers/users to help you as well, but ultimately, the final step is your official hard launch. A big part of this final step is actually scaling back to your original definitions for performance and customer success. Is this final version of your product hitting the metrics you originally set with your customers? Is the performance of the product what everyone expected? Are you actively seeking to define future achievable goals?

Now that we've covered the process that's commonly followed in NPD, we can move on to the models that are commonly employed in that development cycle. In the following section, we will review the most popular ML model types that are commonly used in production, as well as some of the characteristics those models share.

Model types – from linear regression to neural networks

In the previous chapter, we looked at a few model types that you'll likely encounter, use, and implement in various types of products for different purposes. To jog your memory, here's a list of the ML models/ algorithms you'll likely use in production for various products:

- **Naive Bayes classifier**: This algorithm *"naively"* considers every feature in your dataset as its own independent variable, so it's essentially trying to find associations probabilistically without holding any assumptions about the data. It's one of the simpler algorithms out there and its simplicity is actually what makes it so successful with classification. It's commonly used for binary values, such as trying to decipher whether something is spam or not.

- **Support Vector Machine (SVM)**: This algorithm is also largely used for classification problems and will essentially try to split your dataset into two classes so that you can use it to group your data and try to predict where future data points will land along these major splits. If you don't see compelling groups within the data, SVMs allow you to add more dimensions to be able to see groupings more easily.

- **Linear regression**: These models have been around since the 50s and they're the simplest models we have for regression problems, such as predicting future data points. They essentially use one or more variables in your dataset to predict your dependent variable. The "linear" part of this model tries to find the best line to fit your data, and this line is what dictates how it makes predictions. Here, we once again see a relatively simple model heavily used because of how versatile and dependable it is.

- **Logistic regression**: This model works a lot like linear regression in that you have independent and dependent variables, but it doesn't predict a numerical value – it predicts a future binary categorical state, such as whether or not someone might default on a loan in the future, for instance.

- **Decision trees**: This algorithm works well for both categorical and numerical predictions, so it's used for both kinds of ML problems, such as predicting a future state or a future price. Decision trees are used often for both kinds of problems, which has contributed to its popularity. Its comparison to a tree comes from the nodes and branches, which effectively function like a flow chart. The model learns from the flow of past data to predict future values.

- **Random forest**: This algorithm builds from the previous decision trees and is also used for both categorical and numerical problems. The way it works is it splits the data into different "random" samples, creates decision trees for each sample, and then takes an average or majority vote for its predictions (depending on whether you're using it for categorical or numerical predictions). It's hard to understand how random forest comes to conclusions, so if interpretability isn't super high on the list of concerns, you can use it.

- **K-Nearest Neighbors (KNNs)**: This algorithm exclusively works on categorical and numerical predictions, so it looks for a future state and offers results in groups. The number of data points in the group is set by the engineer/data scientist and the way the model works is by grouping the data and determining characteristics that data shares with its neighbors and making the best guess for future values based on those neighbors.

- **K-means clustering**: This algorithm will group data points to see patterns (or clusters) better, but it looks for an optimal number of clusters as well. This is unsupervised learning, so the model looks to find patterns that it can learn from because it's not given any information (or supervision) to go off of from the engineer that's using it. Also, the number of clusters assigned is a hyperparameter, and you will need to choose what number of clusters is optimal.

- **Principal component analysis (PCA)**: Often, the largest problem with using unsupervised ML on very large datasets is there's actually too much uncorrelated data to find meaningful patterns. This is why PCA is used so often, because it's a great way to reduce dimensions without actually losing or discarding information. This is especially useful for massive datasets, such as finding patterns in genome sequencing or drug discovery trials.

- **Neural networks**: Deep learning models are lumped under the term neural networks for the most part because they all mimic the way the human brain processes information through layers of nodes and their edges. There are several neural network types with their own particulars, but for now, it suffices to say that neural networks are what make up the models used in what we call **deep learning**.

If you see that a product is labeled as an AI/ML product, it likely uses some form or combination of these aforementioned models. We will be going over these models in later chapters of this book but for now, this is a good introduction to the model types you'll most often come across where ML and AI are referenced. Now that we've introduced the models, let's go into how those models are trained and made ready for use in production.

Training – when is a model ready for market?

In this section, we will explore the standard process for gathering data to train a model and tune hyperparameters optimally to achieve a certain level of performance and optimization. In the implementation phase (*step 4* of the NPD process), we're looking for a level of performance that would be considered optimal based on the define phase (*step 2* of the NPD process) before we move to the next phase of marketing and crafting our message for what success looks like when using our product. A lot has to happen in the implementation phase before we can do that.

Data accessibility is the most important factor when it comes to AI/ML products. At first, you might have to start with third-party data, which you'll have to purchase, or public data that's freely available or easily scraped. This is why you'll likely want or need to partner with a few potential customers. Partnering with customers you can trust to stick with you and help you build a product that can be successful with real-world data is crucial to ending up with a product that's ready for market. The last thing you want is to create a product based on pristine third-party datasets or free ones that then becomes overfitted to real-world data and performs poorly with data coming from your real customers that it's never seen before.

Having a wide variety of data is important here, so in addition to making sure it's real-world data, you also need to make sure that your data is representative of many types of users. Unless your product caters to very specific user demographics, you're going to want to have a model trained on data that's as varied as possible for good model performance as well as good usability ethics. There will be more on that in the final section.

Iterative hyperparameter tuning will also be hugely important as you continuously retrain your models for performance. The performance metrics and benchmarks in the define phase (*step 2* of the NPD) will inform how your ML engineers will go about tuning their hyperparameters. Most of the time, we don't yet know what the optimal model architecture for a certain use case is. We want to explore how a model functions with various datasets and start somewhere so that we can see which hyperparameters give us superior performance.

Note

We always use the term hyperparameters when defining model optimizations because "parameters" refer to the boundaries within the training data that the model is using to make predictions. When it comes to adjustments to the model and how it functions, the term will always be **hyperparameter**.

Examples of what hyperparameters do include the degree of features that should be used in a linear model, the maximum depth that should be allowed for a decision tree model, how many trees should be included in a random forest model, or how many neurons or layers should be included for a neural network layer. In all these cases, we're looking at the external settings of the model itself and all these settings are worthy of scrutiny based on the model performance they produce. Having competent AI/ML engineers that are comfortable with navigating these shifts in performance will be important in creating a product that's set up for success.

We want to go into some applied examples of models and their comparisons to give product managers out there who are unfamiliar with AI/ML performance benchmarks a sense of how you can go about evaluating whether one model is better than another. The following are a few examples of performance metrics that your ML engineers will look at as they evaluate whether or not they're using optimal models. You'll notice some of the names are familiar from our previous list of model types.

These comparisons were done on a personal project, which was a model we had created to predict the price of Ether, a form of cryptocurrency. If you'd like to see the entire project outlined, you can do so here: `https://medium.com/analytics-vidhya/predicting-ether-prices-model-selection-for-machine-learning-8a50321f51a3`.

The first model we wanted to use was an **Ordinary Least Squares (OLS)** regression model because this is the most straightforward of the linear regression models that we wanted to select to give us a good baseline before we approached other model types.

The results of the OLS regression model are as follows:

```
The number of observations in training set is 723
The number of observations in test set is 181
R-squared of the model in the training set is: 0.8985831338240027
------Test set statistics------
R-squared of the model in the test set is: 0.8896944272555466
Mean absolute error of the prediction is: 42.39871596133024
Mean squared error of the prediction is: 7572.23276225187
Root mean squared error of the prediction is: 87.0185771100164
Mean absolute percentage error of the prediction is: 90.68081323695678
```

Figure 2.1 – OLS regression model results

There are a number of metrics that are automatically generated when you train a model. Here is an example of what the full set looks like, but for the purpose of comparison, we will be focusing on the **R-squared of the model in the test set** line in *Figure 2.1* to get the rate of error that's comparable between models. The **R-squared** metric is also referred to as the "coefficient of determination" and the reason why we use this particular metric so often in regression models is that it best assesses how far the data lies from the fitted regression line that the regression model creates. With the preceding OLS regression model, we see an R-squared of **0.889** for the test set using an 80/20 split of the training data. We used 80% of the data for training and the remaining 20% of the data for testing.

The next model we tested was a random forest to compare results with a tree-based model. One of our hyperparameters for this random forest example was setting our cross-validation to 10 so that it would run through the training 10 times and produce an average of those 10 as a final score. That average was an R-squared of 0.963, higher than our OLS model!

The results of the random forest model are as follows:

```
cross_val_score(randomforest, X_test, Y_test, cv=10)
```

```
array([0.9491968 , 0.94922887, 0.97426398, 0.96202586, 0.97348678,
       0.99491192, 0.9764517 , 0.96363981, 0.96975411, 0.98030483])
```

```
import statistics

data = [0.96906062, 0.94844658, 0.94470685, 0.97056179, 0.97284841,
        0.98021631, 0.98151656, 0.95956996, 0.95165316, 0.94865387]

x = statistics.mean(data)
print(x)
```

0.962723411

Figure 2.2 – Random forest model results

Finally, the last comparison was with our KNN model, which produced a score of 0.994. The hyperparameter we chose in this model was 6, which means we are looking for a group of 6 neighbors for each grouping. This KNN model gives us our best performance because we're ideally looking for the closest we can get to a perfect score of 1. However, we must keep this in mind with a caveat: although you are looking to get as close as you can to 1, the closer you get to 1, the more suspicious you should be of your model.

The results of the KNN model are as follows:

```
from sklearn import neighbors
from sklearn import neighbors
from numba import jit
import numpy
import matplotlib.pyplot as pyplot
import seaborn
from sklearn.datasets import make_regression
from sklearn.model_selection import train_test_split
from sklearn.neighbors import KNeighborsRegressor

# Build our model.
knn = neighbors.KNeighborsRegressor(n_neighbors=6)
knn.fit(X_train, Y_train)
knn.score(X_test, Y_test)
```

0.994602173372774

Figure 2.3 – KNN model results

Getting this high a score likely means that our model is not working well at all, or that it's working especially well on the training data but won't perform as well on new datasets. This phenomenon is called **overfitting** and it's a big topic of conversation in data science and ML circles. The reason for it is that, fundamentally, all models are flawed and are not to be trusted until you've done your due diligence in selecting the best model. This game of choosing the right model, training it, and releasing it into the wild must be done under intense supervision. This is especially true if you're charging for a product or service and attempting to win the confidence of customers that will be vouching on behalf of you and your products someday. If you're an AI/ML product manager, you should look for good performance that gets better and better incrementally with time, and you should be highly suspicious of excellent model performance from the get-go.

Once you have comprehensive, representative data that you're training your models on, and you've trained those models enough times and adjusted those models accordingly to get the performance you're seeking (and promising to customers), you're ready to move forward!

Now that we've gone over some of the major aspects of model maintenance, we can move on to what deployment looks like. Keep in mind that the entire process of ideating your product, choosing the right model to employ in your product, and gauging the performance of that model based on your training efforts is a collaborative effort. That collaboration doesn't end when you've trained your models; it intensifies. This is because you're now tasked with how exactly to integrate those models into the infrastructure of your product for your customers. Let's get into that in the following section.

Deployment – what happens after the workstation?

In *Chapter 1*, we discussed deployment strategies that can be used as you manage your AI/ML products in production. In this section, we'd like you to understand the avenues available from a DevOps perspective, where you will ultimately use and deploy the models in production outside of the training workstation or training environment itself. Perhaps you're using something such as GitLab to manage the branches of your code repository for various applications of AI/ML in your product and experimenting there. However, once you are ready to make changes or update your models after retraining, you'll push the new models into production regularly. This means you need a pipeline that can support this kind of experimentation, retraining, and deployment regularly. This section will primarily focus on the considerations after we place a finished ML model into production (a live environment) where it will be accessed by end users.

How you manage these future deployments will vary widely depending on whether your AI/ML product offering is **business-to-business (B2B)** or **business-to-consumer (B2C)**. If you're managing a B2C product, you'll likely make changes in phases and you'll likely use the deployment strategies outlined in *Chapter 1*, to manage how your updated product is received and when certain groups of users will see the new updated models. This is just the nature of a B2C product: it's one product going out to thousands, if not millions, of individual consumers, and your one product will mean many different things to individual users. If your product is a B2B product, then you manage expectations often at the customer level. One customer might have a different experience of your AI/ML product than another. The models you use could also very well change from one customer to another because the data you're using to train your models will be different from one customer to another.

Another thing to keep in mind is how you're going to handle discussions about your models and the collective training data you have among all your customers. With some products, you might not face much discussion about whether you use all your data to train your models. Some companies, however, are very particular about how their data is accessed and used. They might be okay with giving you historical data to train your model with as long as that data isn't being used to help the performance of other customers in their peer group, for example.

On the other hand, some customers might expect you to train your models on all the data you have to give your models the best shot at having as comprehensive a dataset as they possibly can. Remember that, as the strength of the models currently stands, the general rule is that the more data you have, the more examples you're able to give your models. This means that the more examples you have, theoretically, the stronger performance you should have across the board. Managing expectations with your customers and their threshold for data sharing is an important part of the deployment cycle because it's going to inform how often you update and how you deploy responsibly.

You'll likely have different teams that manage different areas of the deployment process. Perhaps your data scientists create and develop the models and train them, another team validates that work and the training data as well, and a third team of engineers deploys the models into the production environment. You might also have a team of ML engineers that specialize in different areas of this entire process.

Once you are ready to deploy your models, you will need to have a team analyze the deployment environment for the following reasons:

- To choose the best way to access the model (most often through an API or some UI/platform that's currently being used by your end user)

- To get a sense of how often it will be called

- To determine how many GPUs/CPUs and how much memory it will need to run

- To figure out how it will be continuously fed data

We'll leave the solutioning up to your onsite experts, but this is an important point for the AI/ML product manager to keep in mind: the time/money/effort/resources that will be required to keep your AI/ML algorithms running for your product will be a huge consideration when you choose the models and strategize how you'll deploy them in production.

The final part of deployment is training the end users on how to use the model and its results. Interpretability is important for any AI/ML project to succeed, but in the context of a product that's used and relied upon by end users, whether they are B2B or B2C customers, you will need to account for how to communicate through potentially confusing moments. Training your customers through in-app prompts or your customer success teams will allow your end users to learn how to activate your AI/ML features, access the data they need from these features, and interpret the output it gives them in a way that continuously reinforces your product's value – this is all part of managing your deployment.

Testing and troubleshooting

In *Chapter 1*, we discussed the idea of continuous maintenance, which included continuous integration, continuous delivery, continuous training, and continuous monitoring. This section will build on that and expand on how to test and troubleshoot issues related to ML products on an ongoing basis so that your product is set up for success. Once you've made your first deployment, we jump right into the continuous training and continuous maintenance portion of the continuous maintenance process we discussed in *Chapter 1*.

Remember, managing the performance of your models post-deployment is crucial and it will be a highly iterative, never-ending process of model maintenance. As is the case with traditional software development, you will continue to test, troubleshoot, and fix bugs for your AI/ML products as well. The only difference is that you will also screen for lags in performance and bugs related to your model.

Continuously monitoring your model makes sure that it's always working properly and that the outputs it generates are effective. The last thing you want is for your product to be spewing out wildly inaccurate recommendations or predictions. Imagine that your model operated incorrectly and it took your customer weeks or months to notice that this had serious negative consequences downstream. They would question your integrity as a company because they trusted you to maintain and keep up the platform that they rely on for their own workflows. As a result, they might cancel their contract with you, pull their data out of your database, or give you negative reviews and negative referrals to other prospective customers.

Even when all the aspects of your model work properly, you will still need to track the continuous performance of your model and its outputs. The metrics for success we looked at in the training section previously are the same metrics you'll create a log of that you routinely monitor to make sure model performance isn't lagging. In addition to statistical performance metrics such as the F-score or R-squared, you'll also want to keep track of your accuracy, recall, and precision rates. This entire process of monitoring your model's performance should be automated so that you're alerted when certain metrics go over a certain threshold, in the form of a flag of some sort so that you're not always having to manually check.

We don't just monitor the models themselves but we also continuously maintain the supporting code and documentation as well. This is notoriously a last priority for most companies that ultimately rely on the historical knowledge of the few developers that have been there the longest. Get it all documented and make it a practice of doing so regularly. You might find that there isn't enough training material or that the resources that currently exist just aren't adequate to explain what the product does. You might also find that the data feed that your model uses for training has issues with updates or wasn't properly connected in the first place. Perhaps it's an issue on your end users' side and they might not be accessing the AI/ML features of your product properly. Any number of these issues can happen routinely, which is why having teams devoted to the successful execution of your AI/ML product is crucial to its success.

Every model is going to have some form of degradation or drift over time. For example, if new data comes in that the model is training on that's not been cleaned in the same way that the training data was, your model's performance is going to suffer from a lack of uniformity in the data. Data hygiene is generally an important consideration when evaluating performance because it can wreak havoc and these kinds of changes might be hard to pinpoint.

Over months and years, if you see changes to how data is being reported and formatted, or if there are new fields or categories of data being added that weren't present when the models were first being trained, you're going to see the variance in your results. Data also can morph over time if your market changes or if the demographics of your users change. If major events impact the entirety of your dataset, this will adversely impact your model results because the baseline you built as your foundation will have been rendered unreliable because the majority of the training data might not apply to the new or current situation.

Outside of the training data, there is one last important area of drift, and that's what's often referred to as concept drift – or changes in your customer's expectations of what a correct prediction might be. For example, in some contexts, such as optimizing for a spam filter, you might find that certain new tactics mean that model outputs need to be reimagined to keep up with new trends in how spam emails evade the filter settings that originally worked well. Change is the only constant and the outside world is large and full of unpredictability. Any changes coming from outside factors could contribute to various types of concept drift, requiring us to go back to the drawing board and tweak our models and redeploy them to address a changing world.

Continuous monitoring and testing are a big reason why many companies will use an enterprise data science platform to keep track of their deployments. We highly recommend this if you have the budget for it because if you're working with many customers, as well as internal and external applications of your AI/ML models, you'll likely have many "reuse" use cases for your models. You'll benefit from the project tracking these platforms offer if you're managing at scale.

In this section, we covered some of the most important considerations when testing and troubleshooting the use of your models in production, and the importance of regular monitoring for maintaining a level of oversight, not only to keep on top of the technical performance and robustness of your models but also to remain ethical. In the following section, we will focus more on the ethical considerations when building products with AI/ML components to build responsibly and harness some industry best practices.

Refreshing – the ethics of how often we update our models

When we think about the amazing power we have as humans, the complex brain operations we employ for things such as weighing up different choices or deciding whether or not we can trust someone, we may find it hard or impossible to believe that we could ever use machines to do even a fraction of what our minds can do. Most of us make choices, selections, and judgments without fully understanding the mechanism that powers those experiences. However, when it comes to ML, with the exception of neural networks, we can understand the underlying mechanisms that power certain determinations and classifications. We love the idea that ML can mirror our own ability to come to conclusions and that we can employ our critical thinking skills to make sure that process is as free from bias as possible.

The power of AI/ML allows us to automate repetitive, boring, uninspiring actions. We'd rather have content moderators, for instance, be replaced with algorithms so that humans don't have to suffer through flagging disturbing content on the internet on a daily basis. However, ML models, for all their wonderful abilities, aren't able to reason the way we can. Automated structures that are biased or that degrade over time have the power to cause a lot of harm when they're deployed in a way that directly impacts humans and when that deployment isn't closely and regularly monitored for performance. The harm that can cause at scale, across all live deployments of AI/ML, is what keeps ethicists and futurists up at night.

Part of the danger with AI/ML is in the automation process itself. The types of drift we went over in the prior section impact how models derive meaning from the training data they learn from. Even when performance and maintenance appear normal, that doesn't mean that the models aren't taking liberties, resulting in real-world harm for the end user or for human beings that could be impacted downstream from the end user, whether or not they actually interact with the models themselves. A common example of this is the pervasive and unnecessary use of facial recognition software.

In February 2022, President Biden signed two pieces of legislation into law that expanded on AI accountability in the US: Artificial Intelligence for the Military Act of 2021 and the AICT Act of 2021. Will Griffin from *Fortune* magazine writes "*While this legislation falls far short of the calls for regulation consistent with the European Union model and desired by many in the A.I. ethics community, it plants the seeds of a thoughtful and inevitable A.I. ethics regulatory regime.*" It's important to remember that AI ethics and regulations vary depending on where you live. In the US, we still lag behind European standards both in terms of legislation that's put in place to rein in AI misconduct and in terms of how we enforce existing laws.

AI is still considered a wild west legislatively speaking, and we will likely see strides being made toward further defining the scope for how AI can interact with us as we see more and more use cases for AI products expand during this decade. Recently, the US made strides toward publishing a blueprint for an AI Bill of Rights that covers the following areas:

- Safe and effective systems
- Algorithmic discrimination protections

- Data privacy notices and explanation

- Human alternatives, consideration, and fallback

For now, we will use the European standards for framing how AI/ML product managers should think about their products because, even without deliberate laws that enforce AI ethics, entrepreneurs and technologists still face risks, such as losing customers, receiving bad press, or being taken to court, as a result of their algorithmic choices.

The European Commission outlines the following four key areas as ethical principles:

- **Respect for human autonomy**: "*AI systems should not unjustifiably subordinate, coerce, deceive, manipulate, condition or herd humans. Instead, they should be designed to augment, complement and empower human cognitive, social and cultural skills. The allocation of functions between humans and AI systems should follow human-centric design principles and leave meaningful opportunity for human choice.*"

- **Prevention of harm**: "*AI systems should neither cause nor exacerbate harm or otherwise adversely affect human beings. This entails the protection of human dignity as well as mental and physical integrity.*"

- **Fairness**: "*While we acknowledge that there are many different interpretations of fairness, we believe that fairness has both a substantive and a procedural dimension. The substantive dimension implies a commitment to: ensuring equal and just distribution of both benefits and costs, and ensuring that individuals and groups are free from unfair bias, discrimination and stigmatisation.*"

- **Explicability**: "*This means that processes need to be transparent, the capabilities and purpose of AI systems openly communicated, and decisions – to the extent possible – explainable to those directly and indirectly affected. Without such information, a decision cannot be duly contested. An explanation as to why a model has generated a particular output or decision (and what combination of input factors contributed to that) is not always possible. These cases are referred to as 'black box' algorithms and require special attention.*"

Citation

Bruschi, D., Diomede, N. *A framework for assessing AI ethics with applications to cybersecurity. AI Ethics* (2022). `https://doi.org/10.1007/s43681-022-00162-8`

Many companies might be tempted to create an AI ethics role within their companies and make it that person's problem or scapegoat if and when they fail to meet certain standards, but this is a lazy and unethical way of managing the ethics around your AI programs if that's all you choose to do. A better way would be to train and empower all of the resources that are involved in building your AI/ML products to be aware of the surrounding ethics and potential harm that could be caused to the customers or third parties interacting with your product.

While we must recognize the importance of understanding that recurring model updates are vital to maintaining good ethics with regard to ML and AI, as we've discussed previously in this chapter, it's also important to look into how your product can affect groups of people downstream who don't even use your product.

We don't exist in a vacuum. As we saw in the previous sections of this chapter, many factors at play already work against algorithms used in AI/ML products, which you have to keep track of even to stay on top of the natural chaos created by the constant input and output of data. This natural tendency that models have toward various types of drift is what demands a focus on ethics. According to a recent episode from TechTarget's *Today I Learned* podcast, FICO, the credit reporting and analytics vendor, conducted a survey of AI users and it showed that 67% of respondents do not monitor their models for accuracy or drift, which is pretty mind-blowing. These were AI users who were directly responsible for building and maintaining AI systems, which shows that the problems that come with unethical AI/data practices are a norm.

Ethical AI practices should be applied throughout every step we've outlined in this in-depth chapter on model maintenance. If we build AI/ML products that we are sure don't cause harm, both directly as part of our products' integrity and indirectly as part of our products' model maintenance, we can confidently market and promote our products without fear of retribution or punishment from the market that we want to serve. Every entrepreneur and technologist will have their own relationship with ethical business practices but, eventually, if you are a champion, promoter, or leader of a product that has come to market that harms others, you will be asked to explain what measures were put in place to inform your customers of the potential risks.

Summary

In this chapter, we covered the NPD cycle and a review of the common AI/ML model types. We also covered an overview of how to train, deploy, and troubleshoot the models that are chosen, giving us a reasonable foundation on what to expect when working with models in production. We also touched on some of the most important ethical practices, coming from some of the most rigorous standards that exist, when building products with AI/ML components.

If you're interested in expanding further on building ethical AI, we've provided some handy links in the following section for additional study. Keep in mind that we're at a critical juncture with regard to AI/ML ethics. We're building this ship as we're sailing it, and as AI/ML products continue to enter the zeitgeist, we will see additional measures put in place to reign in the potential harm caused by improper AI deployments through the diligent work of lawmakers and activists. We're not there yet, but with each new development, we get closer and closer to building a world that doesn't just embrace the promise of AI but limits the issues that AI poses as well.

So far, we've had a chance to introduce some of the main concepts we'll discuss throughout the book in *Chapter 1*. We've also gotten further into the requirements of maintaining ML models and familiarizing ourselves with the process of building products with AI/ML components in this chapter. These first two chapters are meant to serve as an introductory foundation so that we can get deeper into the concepts we've brought up so far in subsequent chapters. In *Chapter 3*, we'll focus on splitting deep learning from the broader umbrella term of ML, and discuss some of the differences between traditional ML algorithms and deep learning neural networks.

Additional resources

Reading about and familiarizing ourselves with AI ethics is important for everyone because AI is becoming increasingly impossible to avoid in our day-to-day lives. Additionally, if you actively work in the field of AI/ML as a data scientist, developer, engineer, product manager, or leader, it's doubly important that you're aware of the potential risks AI poses and how to build AI responsibly.

For further reading on ethical AI principles, we recommend the following reputable publications:

- *Blueprint for An AI Bill of Rights*: `https://www.whitehouse.gov/ostp/ai-bill-of-rights/`

- DoD Joint Artificial Intelligence Center Ethical Principles for AI: `https://www.defense.gov/News/Releases/Release/Article/2091996/dod-adopts-ethical-principles-for-artificial-intelligence/`

- National AI Initiative Office on *Advancing Trustworthy AI*: `https://www.ai.gov/strategic-pillars/advancing-trustworthy-ai/`

- Algorithmic Justice League: `https://www.ajl.org/library/research`

- AItruth.org 12 Tenets of Trust: `https://www.aitruth.org/aitrustpledge`

- Intel.gov's *Principles of AI ethics for the intelligence community*: `https://www.intelligence.gov/principles-of-artificial-intelligence-ethics-for-the-intelligence-community`

- European Commission's *Ethics Guidelines for Trustworthy AI*: `https://ec.europa.eu/futurium/en/ai-alliance-consultation.1.html`

- Ethics Guidelines for Trustworthy AI: `https://www.aepd.es/sites/default/files/2019-12/ai-ethics-guidelines.pdf`

- UNESCO Recommendations on AI Ethics: `https://en.unesco.org/artificial-intelligence/ethics`

- *"Today I Learned"* podcast on ethical AI, with insights from Scott Zoldi, the chief analytics officer at FICO: `https://www.techtarget.com/searchcio/podcast/How-machine-learning-model-management-plays-into-AI-ethics`

References

- *Find Your Why*, Simon Sinek: https://simonsinek.com/books/find-your-why/

- High-Level Expert Group on Artificial Intelligence Set Up By The European Commision: https://www.aepd.es/sites/default/files/2019-12/ai-ethics-guidelines.pdf

- Framing TRUST in Artificial Intelligence (AI) Ethics Communication: Analysis of AI Ethics Guiding Principles through the Lens of Framing Theory: https://www.proquest.com/docview/2721197134

- America must win the race for A.I. ethics: https://fortune.com/2022/02/15/america-must-win-the-race-for-a-i-ethics-tech-artificial-intelligence-politics-biden-dod-will-griffin/

- S.1776 - Artificial Intelligence for the Military Act of 2021: https://www.congress.gov/bill/117th-congress/senate-bill/1776/text?q=%7B%22search%22%3A%5B%22s1776%22%5D%7D&r=1&s=1

- S.1705 - AICT Act of 2021: https://www.congress.gov/bill/117th-congress/senate-bill/1705/text?r=82&s=1

3

Machine Learning and Deep Learning Deep Dive

In the age of AI implementation, the current period of AI we find ourselves in, we must understand the pros and cons of both **machine learning** (**ML**) and **deep learning** (**DL**) in order to best navigate when to use either technology. Some other terms you might have come across with respect to AI/ML tools are **applied AI** or **deep tech**. As we've mentioned a few times over the course of this book, the underlying tech that will, for the most part, power AI products will be ML or DL. That's because expert- or rule-based systems are slowly being powered by ML or not evolving at all. So, let's dive a bit further into these technologies and understand how they differ.

In this chapter, we will explore the relationship between ML and DL and the way in which they bring their own sets of expectations, explanations, and elucidations to builders and users alike. Whether you work with products that incorporate ML models that have been around since the 50s or use cutting-edge models that have sprung into use recently, you'll want to understand the implications either way. Incorporating ML or DL into your product will have different repercussions. Most of the time when you see an AI label on a product, it's built using ML or DL, so we want to make sure you come out of this chapter with a firm understanding of how these areas differ and what this difference will tangibly mean for your future products.

In *Chapter 1*, we discussed how we've grappled with the idea of using machines since the 50s, but we wanted to expand on the history of ML and DL **artificial neural networks** (**ANNs**) to give you a sense of how long these models have been around. In this chapter, we will cover the following topics to get more familiar with the nuances related to ML and DL:

- The old – exploring ML

- The new – exploring DL

- Emerging technologies – ancillary and related tech

- Explainability – optimizing for ethics, caveats, and responsibility

- Accuracy – optimizing for success

The old – exploring ML

ML models attempt to create some representation of reality in order to help us make some sort of data-driven decision. Essentially, we use mathematics to represent some phenomenon that's happening in the real world. ML essentially takes mathematics and statistics to predict or classify some future state. The paths diverge in one of two ways. The first group lies with the emergence of models that continue to progress through statistical models and the second group lies with the emergence of models that try to mimic our own natural neural intelligence. Colloquially, these are referred to as traditional ML and DL models.

You can think of all the models we covered in the *Model types – from linear regression to neural networks* section of *Chapter 2* as ML models, but we didn't cover ANNs in great depth. We'll discuss those further in the *Types of neural networks* section later on in this chapter. In this section, we will take a look at the traditional statistical ML models in order to understand both the historical relevance and prevalence of ML models. To recap the flow of ML, it's essentially a process of retrieving data, preparing that data through data processing, wrangling and feature engineering, running that data through a model and evaluating that model for performance, and tuning it as needed.

Some of the most reliable and prevalent models used in ML have been around for ages. **Linear regression** models have been around since the late 1800s and were popularized through the work of Karl Pearson and Sir Francis Galton, two British mathematicians. Their contributions gave way to one of the most popular ML algorithms used today, although unfortunately, both were prominent eugenicists. Karl Pearson is also credited with inventing **principle component analysis (PCA)**, an unsupervised learning method that reduces dimensions in a dataset, in 1901.

A popular ML method, **naive Bayes classifiers**, came onto the scene in the 1960s but they're based on the work of an English statistician named Thomas Bayes' and his theorem of conditional probabilities, which is from the 1700s. The logistic function was introduced by Belgian mathematician Pierre Francois Velhulst in the mid-1800s, and **logistic regression** models were popularized by a British statistician named David Cox in 1958.

Support vector machines (SVMs) were introduced in 1963 by Soviet mathematicians Vladimir Vapnik and Alexey Chervonenis from the Institute of Control Sciences at the Russian Academy of Sciences. The first decision tree analytical algorithm was also invented in 1963 by American statisticians James N. Morgan and John A. Sonquist from the University of Michigan and it was used in their **automatic interaction detection (AID)** program, but even that was derived from a *Porphyrian tree*, a classification tree-based diagram that was created by the eponymous Greek philosopher in the 3rd century BCE. Random forests, made up of an ensemble of multiple decision trees, were invented by an American statistician, Leo Breiman, from the University of California in 2001.

One of the simplest supervised learning models for classification and regression, the **KNN algorithm**, emerged from a technical analysis report that was done by statisticians Evelyn Fix and Joseph Lawson Hodges Jr. on behalf of the US Armed Forces in collaboration with Berkeley University in 1951. K-means clustering, a method of unsupervised ML clustering, was first proposed by a mathematician at UCLA named James MacQueen in 1967.

As you can see, many of the algorithms that are used most commonly in ML models today have their roots quite far in our modern history. Their simplicity and elegance add to their relevance today. Most of the models we've covered in this section were covered in *Chapter 2*, with the exception of DL ANNs. In the following section, we will focus on DL.

The new – exploring DL

Part of our intention with separating ML and DL conceptually in this book is really to create associations in the reader's mind. For most technical folks in the field, there are specific models and algorithms that come up when you see "ML" versus "DL" as a descriptor on a product. Quick reminder here that DL is a subset of ML. If you ever get confused by the two terms, just remember that DL is a form of ML that's grown and evolved to form its own ecosystem. Our aim is to demystify that ecosystem as much as possible so that you can confidently understand the dynamics at play with DL products as a product manager.

The foundational idea of DL is centered around our own biological neural networks and DL uses what's often the umbrella term of ANNs to solve complex problems. As we will see in the next section, much of the ecosystem that's been formed in DL has been inspired by our own brains, where the "original" neural networks are found. This inspiration comes not just from the function of the human brain, particularly the idea of learning through examples, but also from its structure as well.

Because this isn't an overly technical book meant for DL engineers, we will refrain from going into the terms and mathematics associated with DL. A basic understanding of an ANN would be helpful, however. As we go through this section, keep in mind that a neural network is composed of artificial neurons or nodes and that these nodes are stacked next to one another in layers. Typically, there are three types of layers:

- The input layer
- The hidden layer(s)
- The output layer

While we will go over the various types of ANNs, there are some basics to how these DL algorithms work. Think in terms of layers and nodes. Essentially, data is passed through each node of each layer and the basic idea is that there are weights and biases that are passed from each node and layer. The ANNs work through the data they're training on in order to best arrive at patterns that will help them solve the problem at hand. An ANN that has at least three layers, which means an input, output, and a minimum of one hidden layer, is "deep" enough to be classed as a DL algorithm. That settles the layers.

What about the nodes? If you recall, one of the simplest models we covered in prior chapters is the linear regression model. You can think of each node as its own mini-linear regression model because this is the calculation that's happening within each node of an ANN. Each node has its data, a weight for that data, and a bias or parameter that it's measuring against to arrive at an output. The summation of all these nodes making these calculations at scale gives you a sense of how an ANN works. If you can imagine a large scale of hundreds of layers, each with many nodes within each layer, you can start to imagine why it can be hard to understand why an ANN arrives at certain conclusions.

DL is often referred to as a black-box technology and this starts to get to the heart of why that is. Depending on our math skills, we humans can explain why a certain error rate or loss function is present in a simple linear regression model. We can conceptualize the ways a model, which is being fitted to a curve, can be wrong. We can also appreciate the challenge when presented with real-world data, which doesn't lay out a perfect curve, for a model. But if we increase that scale and try to conceptualize potentially billions of nodes each representing a linear regression model, our brains will start to hurt.

Though DL is often discussed as a bleeding-edge technological advancement, as we saw in the prior section, this journey also started long ago.

Invisible influences

It's important to understand the underlying relationships that have influenced ML and DL as well as the history associated with both. This is a foundational part of the storytelling but it's also helpful to better understand how this technology relates to the world around us. For many, understanding AI/ML concepts can be mystifying and unless you come from a tech or computer science background, the topics themselves can seem intimidating. Many will, at best, only acquire a rudimentary understanding of what this tech is and how it's come about.

We want to empower anyone interested in exploring this underlying tech that will shape so many products and internal systems in the future by making a deeper understanding more accessible. Already, there's favoritism going on. Most of the folks that intimately understand ML and DL already come from a computer science background whether it's through formal education or through boot camps and other technical training programs. That means that for the most part, the folks that have pursued study and entrepreneurship in this field have traditionally been predominantly white and predominantly male.

Apart from the demographics, the level of investment in these technologies, from an academic perspective, has gone up. Let's get into some of the numbers. Stanford University's AI index states that AI investment at the graduate level among the world's top universities has increased by 41.7%. That number jumps to 102.9 at the undergraduate level. An extra 48% of recipients of AI PhDs have left academia in the past decade in pursuit of the private sector's big bucks in the last 10 years. 10 years ago, only 14.2% of computer science PhDs were AI related. Now, that number is above 23%. The United States, in particular, is holding onto the talent it educates and attracts. Foreign students that come to the US to pursue an AI PhD stay at a rate of 81.8%.

The picture this paints is one of a world that's in great need of talent and skill in AI/ML. This high demand for the AI/ML skill set, particularly a demographically diverse AI skill set, is making it hard for those that have the hard skills in this field to stay in academia and the private sector handsomely rewards those that have these skills. In the start-up circuits, many VCs and investors are able to confidently solidify their investments when they know a company has somebody with an AI PhD, on staff, whether or not their product needs this heavy expertise. Placing a premium on human resources with these sought-after skills is likely not going to go away anytime soon.

We dream of a world where people from many competencies and backgrounds come into the field of AI because diversity is urgently needed and the opportunity that's ahead of us is too great for the gatekeeping that's been going on to prevail. It's not just important that the builders of AI understand the underlying tech and what makes its application of it so powerful. It's equally important for the business stakeholders that harness the capabilities of this tech to also understand the options and capabilities that lie before them. At the end of the day, nothing is so complicated that it can't be easily explained.

A brief history of DL

In 1943, Warren S. McCulloch and Walter Pitts published a paper, *A logical calculus of the ideas immanent in nervous activity*, which made a link between mathematics and neurology by creating a computer model based on the neural networks inherent in our own brains based on a combination of algorithms to create a "threshold" to mimic how we pass information from our own biological network of neurons. Then, in 1958, Frank Rosenblatt published a paper that would be widely considered the ancestor of neural nets, called *The Perceptron: A perceiving and recognizing automaton*. This was, for all intents and purposes, the first, simplest, and oldest ANN.

In the 1960s, developments toward backpropagation, or the idea that a model learns from layers of past mistakes as it trains its way through a dataset, made significant strides toward what would eventually make up the neural network. The most significant part of the development that was happening at this time was coupling the idea of inspiring mathematical models with the way the brain works based on networks of neurons and backpropagation because this created the foundation of ANNs, which learned through past iterations.

It's important to note here that many ANNs work in a "feedforward" motion in that they go through the input, hidden layers, and output layers sequentially and in one direction only, from input to output. The idea of backpropagation essentially allows for the ANNs to learn bi-directionally so that they're able to minimize the error in each node, resulting in a better performance.

It wasn't until 1986 when David Rumelhart, Geoffrey Hinton, and Ronald Williams published a famous paper, *Learning representations by back-propagating errors*, that people fully began to appreciate the role backpropagation plays in the success of DL. The idea that you could backpropagate through time, allowing neural networks to assign the appropriate weights as well as train a neural network with hidden layers, was revolutionary at the time.

After each development, there was much excitement for ML and the power of neural networks but between the mid-60s and the 80s, there was one significant issue: a lack of data as well as funding. If you've heard the term "AI winter," this is what it's referring to. Developments were made on the modeling side but we didn't have significant ways to apply the models that were being developed without the ability and willingness of research groups to get their hands on enough data to feed those models.

Then, in 1997, Sepp Hochreiter and Jürgen Schmidhuber published their groundbreaking work titled *Long Short-Term Memory*, which effectively allowed DL to "solve complex, artificial long-time lag tasks that had never been solved by previous recurrent network algorithms." The reason why this development was so important was it allowed the idea of sequences to remain relevant for DL problems. Because neural networks involve hidden layers, it's difficult for the notion of time to remain relevant, which makes a number of problems hard to solve. For instance, a traditional recurrent neural network might not be able to autocomplete a sentence in the way that a **Long short-term memory (LSTM)** can because it doesn't understand the time sequence involved in the completion of a sentence.

Today, most DL models require a ton of supervised datasets, meaning the neural networks that power DL need lots of examples to understand whether something is, for example, a dog or a horse. If you think about it a bit though, this doesn't actually relate that closely to how our brains work. A small child that's just emerging and learning about the world might need to be reminded once or twice about the difference between a dog and a horse, but you likely aren't reminding them of that difference thousands or millions of times.

In that sense, DL is evolving towards requiring fewer and fewer examples to learn. If you recall, in previous chapters, we went over supervised and unsupervised learning techniques, this becomes significant in the case of DL. Sure, these days we're able to gather massive amounts of data for DL models to learn from but the models themselves are evolving to improve without needing much data toward the ultimate goal of unsupervised DL that can be trained with small amounts of data.

So far, we've covered some of the histories and influences shaping the field of ML and DL more specifically. While we haven't gone into many of the technical concepts too heavily, this gives us a good foundation with which to understand how ML and DL have developed over time and why they've risen to prominence. In the following section, we will get more hands-on and get into the specific algorithms and neural networks that are used most heavily in DL.

Types of neural networks

We'd like to now turn your attention toward some of the most popular kinds of neural networks used in DL today. Some of these will sound familiar based on the previous section, but it will help to familiarize yourself with some of these concepts especially if you plan on working as a product manager for a DL product. Even if you aren't currently working in this capacity, you'll want to take a look through these in case your career does veer toward DL products in the future.

The following is a list of some of the most used ANNs in DL:

- **Multilayer perceptrons (MLPs)**
- **Radial basis function networks (RBFNs)**
- **Convolutional neural networks (CNNs)**
- **Recurrent neural networks (RNNs)**

- **Long short-term memory networks (LSTMs)**

- **Generative adversarial networks (GANs)**

- **Self-organizing maps (SOMs)**

- **Deep belief networks (DBNs)**

In the following section, we will touch on these various neural networks to give you an idea of what they are best suited for. As we did in the previous chapter with ML algorithms, we will describe some of the most popular use cases of each type of ANN so that we can understand, at least in a general sense, what some of the core competencies of each ANN are so that you can start to keep those ideas in mind should you pursue the creation of your own DL products in the future. If your aim is to specialize exclusively in supporting or building DL products of your own, this will be a great summary overview of each ANN.

MLPs

After David Rumelhart, Geoffrey Hinton, and Ronald Williams's paper *Learning representations by back-propagating errors* came out in 1986, MLPs were popularized because in that paper they used backpropagation to train an MLP. Unlike RNNs, MLPs are another form of feedforward neural network that uses backpropagation to optimize the weights. For this reason, you can think of MLPs as some of the most basic forms of ANNs because they were among the first to appear and today they're still used often to deal with the high compute power that's needed by some of the newer ANNs out there. Their accessibility and reliability are still useful today, which is why we wanted to start this list with MLPs to give us a good foundation for conceptualizing the rest of the DL algorithms.

The way they learn is the algorithm will send data forward through the input and middle layers to the output layer. Then, based on the results in the output layer, it will then calculate the error to assess how off it was at predicting values. This is where backpropagation comes in because it will get a sense of how wrong it was in order to then backpropagate the rate of error. It will then optimize itself to minimize that error by adjusting the weights in the network and will effectively update itself.

The idea is you would pass these steps through the model multiple times until you were satisfied with the performance. Remember the distinction between supervised and unsupervised learning in *Chapter 1*? Because MLPs use backpropagation to minimize their error rate by adjusting weights, MLPs are a supervised DL algorithm because they know based on our label data exactly how off they were from being right. These algorithms are also heavily used in ensembles with other ANNs as a final polishing stage.

RBFNs

RBFNs came on the scene in 1988 with D.S. Broomhead and David Lowe's paper *Multivariable Functional Interpolation and Adaptive Networks*. RBFNs differ from most other ANNs we will cover in this chapter in that they only have three layers. While most ANNs, including the MLPs we discussed in the preceding section, will have an input and output layer with several hidden layers in between, RBFNs only have one hidden layer. Another key difference is rather than having the input layer be a computational layer, the input layer only passes data to the hidden layer in RBFNs, so this ANN is incredibly fast. These DL algorithms are feedforward models, so they are computationally only really passing through two layers: the hidden layer and the output layer.

It would be helpful to think of these networks as similar to the KNN algorithm we discussed in the previous chapter, which aims to predict data points based on the data points around the value they're trying to predict. The reason for this is RBFNs look to approximate values based on the distance, radius, or Euclidean distance between points and they will cluster or group data in circles or spheres to better make sense of a complex multivariable dataset similar to how a K-means clustering algorithm from *Chapter 1* would. This is a highly versatile algorithm that can be used with both classification and regression problems in both supervised and unsupervised ways.

SOMs

SOMs were introduced in the 1980s by Tuevo Hohonen and are another example of unsupervised competitive learning ANNs in which the algorithm takes a multivariable dataset and reduces it into a two-dimensional "map." Each node will compete with the others to decide whether it's the one that should be activated, so it's essentially just a massive competition, which is how it self-organizes. Structurally though, SOMs are very different from most ANNs. There's really just one layer or node outside of the input layer, which is called the Kohonen layer. The nodes themselves are also not connected the way they are in more traditional ANNs.

The training of a SOM mirrors our own brain's ability to self-organize and map inputs. When we sense certain inputs, our brain organizes those inputs into certain areas that are apt for what we're seeing, hearing, feeling, smelling, or tasting. The SOM will similarly cluster data points into certain groupings. The way that happens is through a learning/training process where the algorithm sends out the data through the input layer and weights, randomly selecting input data points to test against the nodes until a node is chosen based on the distance between it and the data point, which then updates the weight of the node. This process is repeated until the training set is complete and the optimal nodes have been selected.

SOMs will also be in the same class of clustering algorithms such as K-means, or the RBFNs we touched on in the preceding section, in that they are useful for finding relationships and groupings in datasets that are unlabeled or undiscovered.

CNNs

CNNs, sometimes referred to as ConvNets, have multiple layers that are used largely for supervised learning use cases in which they detect objects, process images, and detect anomalies in medical and satellite images. The way this ANN works is through a feedforward, so it starts from the input layer and makes its way through the hidden layers to the ultimate output layer to categorize images. This type of ANN is characterized as categorical, so its ultimate goal is looking to put images into buckets of categories. Then, once they are categorized, it looks to group images by the similarities they share so that it can ultimately perform the object recognition that's used to detect faces, animals, plants, or signs on the street. CNNs can be used for things such as facial recognition, object identification, and self-driving cars or what's commonly referred to as computer vision applications of AI.

The four important layers in CNNs are as follows:

- The convolution layer
- The **rectified linear unit (ReLU)** layer
- The pooling layer
- The fully connected layer

The convolution layer turns an image into a matrix of pixel values that are 0s and 1s and then further reduces that matrix into a smaller matrix that's a derivative from the first. The ReLU layer effectively pares down the dimensions of the image that you pass to the CNN. Even color images are passed through a grayscale when they're originally assigned 0s and 1s. So, in the ReLU stage, the CNN actually gets rid of black pixels from the image so that it can reduce the image further and make it computationally easier for the model to process it. There's another layer that reduces the dimensions of the image in another way: the pooling layer.

While the ReLU layer pares down the gradient in the image itself, the pooling layer pares down the features of the image, so if we pass the CNN an image of a cat, the pooling layer is where we will see various features such as the ears, eyes, nose, and whiskers identified. You can think of the convolution, ReLU, and pooling layers as operations that take segments of each image you feed your model and concurrently fire the outputs of those prior steps as inputs into the fully connected layer, which is what actually passes through the neural network itself to classify the image. In essence, the convolution, ReLU, and pooling layers prepare the image to pass through the neural network to arrive at a conclusion.

RNNs

There are several operations that feedforward neural networks weren't able to do very well, including working with sequential data that is rooted in time, operations that needed to contextualize multiple inputs (not just the current input), and operations that require memorization from previous inputs. For these reasons, the main draw of RNNs is the internal memory they possess that allows them to perform and remember the kind of robust operations required of conversational AIs such as Apple's Siri. RNNs do well with sequential data and place a premium on the context in order to excel at working with time-series data, DNA and genomics data, speech recognition, and speech-to-text functions. In contrast to the preceding CNN example, which works with a feedforward function, RNNs work in loops.

Rather than the motion going from the input layer, through the hidden layers, and ultimately to the output layer, the RNN cycles through a loop back and forth and this is how it retains its short-term memory. This means the data passes through the input layer, then loops through the hidden layers, before it ultimately passes to the output layer. It's important to note that RNNs only have short-term memory, which is why there was a need for an LSTM network. More on that in the next section.

In essence, the RNN actually has two inputs. The first is the initial data that makes its way through the neural network and the second is actually the information and context it's acquired along the way. This is the framework with which it also effectively alters its own weights to current and previous inputs, so it's course-correcting as it goes through its loops. This process of retroactively adjusting weights to minimize its error rate is known as backpropagation, which you'll recall from the previous section (*A brief history of DL*) as this was a major advancement that has helped DL become so successful.

It's helpful to imagine that an RNN is actually a collection of neural networks that are continuously retrained and optimized for accuracy through backpropagation, which is why it's also considered a supervised learning algorithm. Because it's such a robust and powerful DL algorithm, we can see RNNs used for anything from captioning and understanding images to predicting time-series problems to natural language processing and machine translation.

LSTMs

LSTMs are basically RNNs with more memory power. Often, the way they manifest is through networks of the LSTM because what they do is actually connect layers of RNNs, which is what allows them to retain inputs over lags or longer periods of time. Much like a computer, LSTMs can write, read, or delete data from the memory it possesses. Because of this, it has the ability to learn about what data it needs to hold onto over time. Just as RNNs continuously adjust their weights and optimize for performance, LSTMs do the same thing by assigning levels of importance for what data to store or delete through its own weights.

LSTMs mirror our own ability to discard irrelevant or trivial information through time through LSTM cells, which have the ability to let the information come in as an input, be forgotten or excluded completely, or let it pass to influence the output. These categorizations are referred to as gates and they're what allow LSTMs to learn through backpropagation.

GANs

GANs are our favorite type of ANN because they're essentially made up of two neural networks that are pitted against each other, hence the name, and compete toward the goal of generating new data that's passable for real-world data. Because of this generative ability, GANs are used for image, video, and voice generation. They were also initially used for unsupervised learning because of their generative and self-regulation abilities but they can be used for supervised and reinforcement learning as well. The way it works is one of the neural networks is referred to as the generator and the other is the discriminator and the two compete as part of this generative process.

GANs were first introduced in a breakthrough paper that came out in 2014 by Ian J. Goodfellow, Jean Pouget-Abadie, Mehdi Mirza, Bing Xu, David Warde-Farley, Sherjil Ozair, Aaron Courville, and Yoshua Bengio, which states that GANs *"simultaneously train two models: a generative model G that captures the data distribution, and a discriminative model D that estimates the probability that a sample came from the training data rather than G. The training procedure for G is to maximize the probability of D making a mistake,"*

Citation

Goodfellow, I. J., Mirza, M., Xu, B., Ozair, S., Courville, A., & Bengio, Y. (2014). *Generative Adversarial Networks. arXiv.* https://doi.org/10.48550/arXiv.1406.2661

We can think of discriminative and generative models as two sides of the same coin. Discriminative models look at the features a type of image might have, for example, looking for associations between all the images of dogs it's currently learning from. Generative models start from the category itself and expand out into potential features a category in that image might possess. If we take the example of a category such as space kittens, the generative model might look at the example data it's fed and deduce that if it creates an image, it should create something that involves space and kittens. The discriminative model then takes the image the generative model creates and confirms, based on its own learning, that any images in the space kittens category must contain both kittens and space as features.

Another way to explain this is that the generative model maps the label to potential features and the discriminative model maps features to the label. What's most interesting to us about GANs is they effectively pass or fail their own version of the Turing test. How do you know whether you passed? If the GAN correctly identifies a generated image as a falsified image, it's passed (or failed?) its own test. It really depends on how you look at passing or failing for that matter. If it incorrectly labeled a falsified/generated image as a "real" image, it means the generative model is pretty strong because its own discriminator wasn't able to discriminate properly. Then again, because it's a double-sided coin, it means that the discriminator needs to be strengthened to be more discerning. This one is very meta.

The steps a GAN takes to run through its process first begin with a generator neural network that takes in data and returns an image, which is then fed to the discriminator along with other images from a real-world dataset. Then, the discriminator produces outputs that are numbered between 0 and 1, which it assigns as probabilities for each of the images it is discriminating, with 0 representing a fake and 1 representing an authentic real-world image. GANs also use backpropagation, so every time the discriminator makes a wrong call, the GAN learns from previous mistakes to correct its weights and optimize itself for accuracy.

DBNs

DBNs also have multiple layers, including multiple hidden layers, but the nodes in one layer aren't connected to each other, though they are connected to nodes in other layers. There are relations between the layers themselves, but not between the nodes within. DBNs are unsupervised learning layers of what are called **Restricted Boltzmann Machines** (**RBMs**), which are themselves another form of ANN. These layers of RBMs are chained together to form a DBN. Because of this chain, as data passes through the input layer of each RBM, the DBN learns and obtains features from the prior layer. The more layers of RBMs you add, the greater the improvement and training of the DBN overall. Also, every RBM is taught individually and the DBN training isn't done until all the DBNs have been trained.

DBNs are referred to as generative ANNs because each of the RBMs learns and obtains potential values for your data points based on probability. Because of this generative ability that they have, they can be used for things such as image recognition, capturing motion data, or recognizing speech. They are also computationally energy-efficient because each cluster of RBMs operates independently. Rather than data passing through all the layers in concert as with feedforward ANNs, data stays local to each cluster.

As a product manager, you won't need to have in-depth knowledge of each neural network because if you're building a product with DL components, you've got internal experts that can help determine which neural networks to use. But it does help to know what some of the most common types of neural networks out there are so that you aren't left in the dark about those determinations. In the next section, we will see how DL neural networks overlap with other emerging technologies for better context on the ability and influence of DL.

Emerging technologies – ancillary and related tech

ML and DL have been used heavily in applications related to natural language processing (**natural language generation (NLG)**, as well as **natural language understanding (NLU)**), speech recognition, chatbots, virtual agents and assistants, decision management, process automation, text analytics, biometrics, cybersecurity, content creation, image and emotion recognition, and marketing automation. It's important to remember, particularly from a product manager's perspective, that AI will increasingly work its way into more of how we live our lives and do our work. This is doubly true if you work in an innovative capacity as a product manager where you're involved with the ideation and creation of new use cases and MVPs for future products.

Over the passage of time, we'll see AI continue to augment our workforce both through the process of internal automation as well as through the adoption of AI-based no-code/low-code external products and applications that will boost job functions, skills, and abilities across the board. AR, VR, and the metaverse also offer us new emerging fields where ML will learn more about our world, help us learn about ourselves, and also help us build new worlds altogether. We will also continue to see ML employed through AI-powered devices such as self-driving planes, trains, and automobiles, as well as biometrics, nanotechnologies, and IoT devices that share streams of data about our bodies and appliances that we can increasingly use to optimize our security, health and energy usage.

There are, of course, other forms of AI beyond ML and DL, as well as ancillary emerging technologies that are often used in concert with the tech we've covered in this chapter. For instance, with all the innovation and fame that's accompanied the Boston Dynamics dog Spot, we were surprised to find out recently that they don't actually use ML to train these little guys. But even Spot will soon see AI updates to its operating system to help it with things such as object recognition and semantic contextualization of those objects.

AI in general, and DL specifically, might be getting an update of its own soon through quantum computing since IBM made its aspirations more concrete by publicly announcing a "road map" for the development of its quantum computers, including the ambitious goal of building one containing 1,000 qubits by 2023. IBM's current largest quantum computer contains 65 qubits.

Quantum computing can massively help us deal with the ongoing issue of storing and retrieving data, particularly big data, in cost-effective ways. Because so many DL projects can take weeks to train and require access to big data, ancillary developments in quantum computing can prove groundbreaking in the area of DL to the point where the algorithms both require fewer data to train on and can also handle more data and compute power more quickly. This could also allow us greater opportunities for making sense of how the models come to certain conclusions and assist with perhaps the greatest hurdle of DL – explainability.

Explainability – optimizing for ethics, caveats, and responsibility

Ethics and responsibility play a foundational role in dealing with your customers' data and behavior and because most of you will build products that help assist humans to make decisions, eventually someone is going to ask you how your product arrives at conclusions. Critical thinking is one of the foundational cornerstones of human reasoning and if your product is rooted in DL, your answer won't be able to truly satisfy anyone's skepticism. Our heartfelt advice is this: don't create a product that will harm people, get you sued, or pose a risk to your business.

If you're leveraging ML or DL in a capacity that has even the potential to cause harm to others, if there's a clear bias that affects underrepresented or minority groups (in terms of race, gender, or culture), go back to the ideation phase. This is true whether that's immediate or downstream harm. This is a general risk all of ML poses to us collectively: the notion that we're coding our societal biases into AI without taking the necessary precautions to make sure the data we feed our algorithms is truly unbiased.

The engineers themselves that build these ANNs are unable to look under the hood and truly explain how ANNs make decisions. As we've seen with the, albeit layman, preceding explanations of DL algorithms, ANN structures are built on existing ML algorithms and scaled, so it's almost impossible for anyone to truly explain how these networks come to certain conclusions.

Again, this is why DL algorithms are often referred to as a black box because they resist a truly in-depth analysis of the underpinnings of the logic that makes them work. DL has a natural opacity to it because of the nature and complexity of ANNs. Remember that ANNs effectively just make slight adjustments to the weights that affect each neuron within its layers. They are basically elaborate pattern finders using math and statistics to make optimizations to their weighting system. They do that hundreds of times for each data point over multiple iterations of training. We simply don't have the mental capacity or language to explain this.

You also don't have to be a DL engineer to truly understand how your product affects others. If you, as a product manager, are not able to fully articulate how DL is leveraged in your product and, at the very least, can't prove that the outputs of your DL product aren't causing harm to others, then it probably isn't a product you want to go all in for.

DL is still very much in the research phase and many product managers are hesitant to incorporate it because of the issue of explainability we discussed earlier in the chapter. So we urge product managers to use caution when looking to wet their feet with DL. We have plenty of examples of ML causing harm to people even when it involves basic linear regression models. Moving forward without a sense of stewardship of and responsibility for our peers and customers with something as complicated and full of potential as DL is a recipe for adding more chaos and harm to the world.

Do we always have to be so cautious? Not necessarily. If DL applications get really good at saving lives by detecting cancer or they work better when applied to robotics, who are we to stand in the way of progress? Be critical about when to be concerned with your use of DL. If your system works effectively and is better because of DL and there isn't some problem or concern springing from the opacity of the ANNs, then all is right with the world.

Accuracy – optimizing for success

When it comes to DL, we can only truly grapple with its performance. Even from a performance perspective, a lot of DL projects fail to give the results their own engineers are hoping for, so it's important to manage expectations. This is doubly true if you're managing the expectations of your leadership team as well. If you're a product manager or entrepreneur and you're thinking of incorporating DL, do so in the spirit of science and curiosity. Remain open about your expectations.

But make sure you're setting your team up for success. A big part of your ANN's performance also lies in the data preparation you take before you start training your models. Passing your data through an ANN is the last step in your pipeline. If you don't have good validation or if the quality of your data is poor, you're not going to see positive results. Then, once you feel confident that you have enough data and that it's clean enough to pass through an ANN, start experimenting. If you're looking for optimal performance, you'll want to try a few different models, or a selection of models together, and compare the performance.

The time it takes to fine-tune a DL model is also aggressively long. If you're used to other forms of ML, it might shock you to experience training a model over the course of days or weeks. This is largely because the amount of data you need to train ANNs is vast; most of the time you need at least 10,000 data points, and all this data is passed through multiple layers of nodes and processed by your ANN. Your ANN is also, most of the time, going to be an ensemble of several types of ANNs we mentioned previously. The chain then becomes quite long.

The nature of understanding ANNs is inherently mysterious because of the complexity of the layers of artificial neurons. We cannot see deterministic qualities. Even when you do everything "right" and you get a good performance, you don't really know why. You just know that it works. The same goes when something does go wrong or when you see poor performance. You once again don't really know why. Perhaps the fault lies with the ANN or with the method you're using or something has changed in the environment. The process of getting back to better performance is also iterative. And then it's back to the drawing board.

Remember that these are emerging tech algorithms. It may take us all some time to adjust to new technologies and truly understand the power they have. Or don't! Part of the disillusionment that's happened with DL actually lies in the tempering of expectations. Some DL algorithms can make amazing things happen and can show immensely promising performance but others can so easily fall flat. It's not a magic bullet. It's just a powerful tool that needs to be used in the proper way by people that have the knowledge, wisdom, and experience to do so. Considering most of the ANNs we went over together are from the 80s, 90s, and early 2000s, that's not much time.

So tread carefully here if you're building, managing, or ideating on DL products. When in doubt, there are other more explainable models to choose from, which we've covered in *Chapter 1*. It's better to be safe than sorry. If you've got lots of time, patience, excitement, and curiosity along with a safe, recreational idea for applying DL, then you're probably in a good position to explore that passion and create something the world could use in good faith.

Summary

We got the chance to go deep into DL in this chapter and understand some of the major social and historical influences that impact this subsection of ML. We also got the chance to look at some of the specific ANNs that are most commonly used in products powered by DL in order to get more familiar with the actual models we might come across as we build with DL. We ended the chapter with a look at some of the other emerging technologies that collaborate with DL, as well as getting further into some of the concepts that impact DL most: explainability and accuracy.

DL ANNs are super powerful and exhibit great performance, but if you need to explain them, you will run into more issues than you would if you stick to more traditional ML models. We've now spent the first three chapters of the book getting familiar with the more technical side of AI product management. Now that we've got that foundation covered, we can spend some time contextualizing all this tech.

In the next chapter, we will explore some of the major areas of AI products we see on the market, as well as examples of the ethics and success factors that contribute most to commercialization.

References

- Some Methods for Classification and Analysis of Multivariate Observations: `https://books.google.com/`

- K-Nearest Neighbors Algorithm: Classification and Regression Star `https://www.historyofdatascience.com/k-nearest-neighbors-algorithm-classification-and-regression-star/`

- Random Forests `https://www.stat.berkeley.edu/~breiman/randomforest2001.pdf`

- Decision Trees `https://www.cse.unr.edu/~bebis/CS479/PaperPresentations/DecisionTrees.pdf`

- Support Vector Machine: The most popular machine learning algorithm `https://cml.rhul.ac.uk/svm.html`

- Logistic Regression `https://uc-r.github.io/logistic_regression#:~:text=Logistic%20regression%20(aka%20logit%20regression,more%20predictor%20variables%20(X)`

- Logistic Regression History `https://holypython.com/log-reg/logistic-regression-history/`

- Bayes Classifier `https://www.sciencedirect.com/topics/computer-science/bayes-classifier#:~:text=Na%C3%AFve%20Bayes%20classifier%20(also%20known,use%20Na%C3%AFve%20Bayes%20since%201960s`

- Principal Component Analysis `https://www.sciencedirect.com/topics/agricultural-and-biological-sciences/principal-component-analysis#:~:text=PCA%20was%20invented%20in%201901,the%20modeling%20of%20response%20data`

- Galton, Pearson, and the Peas: A Brief History of Linear Regression for Statistics Instructors `https://www.tandfonline.com/doi/full/10.1080/10691898.2001.11910537`

- IBM promises 1000-qubit quantum computer—a milestone—by 2023 `https://www.science.org/content/article/ibm-promises-1000-qubit-quantum-computer-milestone-2023`

- Boston Dynamics says AI advances for Spot the robo-dog are coming `https://venturebeat.com/ai/boston-dynamics-says-ai-advances-for-spot-the-robo-dog-are-coming/`

- Convolutional Neural Network Tutorial `https://www.simplilearn.com/tutorials/deep-learning-tutorial/convolutional-neural-network`

- Generative Adversarial Networks `https://arxiv.org/abs/1406.2661`

- The Self-Organizing Map `https://sci2s.ugr.es/keel/pdf/algorithm/articulo/1990-Kohonen-PIEEE.pdf`

- Multivariable Functional Interpolation and Adaptive Networks `https://sci2s.ugr.es/keel/pdf/algorithm/articulo/1988-Broomhead-CS.pdf`

- Long Short-Term Memory `http://www.bioinf.jku.at/publications/older/2604.pdf`

- Learning Representations by Back Propagating Errors `https://www.iro.umontreal.ca/~vincentp/ift3395/lectures/backprop_old.pdf`

- The numerical solution of variational problems `https://www.sciencedirect.com/science/article/pii/0022247X62900045`

- The Perceptron: A Perceiving and Recognizing Automaton `https://blogs.umass.edu/brain-wars/files/2016/03/rosenblatt-1957.pdf`

- A Logical Calculus of the Ideas Immanent in Nervous Activity `https://www.cs.cmu.edu/~./epxing/Class/10715/reading/McCulloch.and.Pitts.pdf`

- AI Education `https://aiindex.stanford.edu/wp-content/uploads/2021/03/2021-AI-Index-Report-_Chapter-4`

4
Commercializing AI Products

Now that we're in the period of **artificial intelligence (AI)** integration, we're seeing many use cases of AI proliferating across industries. In our work managing AI products, we've certainly relied on AI consultants and PhD-level advisors to help us with modeling and orchestrating our data strategy to support a full-scale AI operation. However, as the rising tidal wave of AI continues to penetrate various companies and use cases, we're seeing less of a reliance on breakthroughs achieved through advanced degrees. What's most important now is familiarity with the use of even simple, reliable models. There's a time and place for specialization. Data science and AI are massive umbrella terms but, based on my experiences as a product manager, I see a real need for data and AI generalists that can understand the use cases themselves and how they relate to a business perspective.

In the age of AI breakthroughs, we didn't have a wide selection of use cases because the data wasn't as abundant as it is now. Now that data is abundant, we're seeing a profound shift. Instead of the focus being on researching and discovering the most leading-edge algorithms to choose in the first place, the focus is now on acquiring enough talent to use the tried and true models and algorithms. What we particularly like about this is the concept of AI democratization, or the idea that AI is becoming accessible to more groups of people outside research and MAANG companies.

As a product manager, your philosophy on this will really depend on who you ask. Some product managers believe that the way to create the best product is to conduct your own breakthrough research from an AI perspective. Other product managers believe you can actually get a lot done with models that have become commonplace or have been around a long time, such as regression models.

The goal of a product manager is to help the manifestation of a product that isn't just a commercial success but an industrial triumph as well. What exactly do we mean by industrial triumph? If we can influence you to bring a product to market that truly can offer something new, necessary, and useful to the world, we will have achieved the central goal of writing this book. We would also consider that a triumph. With that, let's explore the best examples of AI product management done well and see how this success impacts a business in all areas, expected and unexpected.

In this chapter, we will be taking a look at some examples of AI companies through the lens of differing business models and offerings including **business-to-business (B2B)** examples and **business-to-consumer (B2C)** examples. We will also be taking a look at companies thriving in unsaturated and underserved markets (blue oceans) as well as saturated and competitive markets (red oceans). The aim of this chapter is to highlight a few key areas in which businesses are thriving with regard to the AI products they bring to market.

The chapter will cover the following topics:

- The professionals – examples of B2B products done right

- The artists – examples of B2C products done right

- The pioneers – examples of blue ocean products

- The rebels – examples of red ocean products

- The GOAT – examples of differentiated disruptive and dominant strategy products

The professionals – examples of B2B products done right

The professionals are a good place to start with grouping products. AI will gravitate first toward use cases that can be profitable and allow for research and optimization. Because B2B products are products that are made for and used by other businesses, their use case is oriented completely toward the business world. This impacts everything from how they're marketed to how they're bought, sold, used, and negotiated. So many B2B products speak to the business impact that a product can satisfy for a customer across multiple levels. It's a great way to learn potentially helpful applications of AI.

Part of the challenge with the rising supply of AI companies is that they need data to train on. Specifically, one of the ethical challenges with this expansion in data and AI products is being able to offer large amounts of data without leaking information that can identify you as a person, also known as **private personal information (PPI)**. Hazy, a UK-based AI company, offers its customers just that: the ability to derive insights, understand signals, and share data using what's called synthetic data. Synthetic data is data that mimics real-world scenarios but is created in virtual worlds, and what it's mimicking is the statistical similarity with real-world datasets. Because of the nature of data-hungry deep learning models, synthetic data is preferred when training neural networks and because of that, Hazy has a bright future ahead of itself. The company's done a lot with its modest $3M in funding and has added a number of marquee customers to its roster in a short time.

The nature of a successful B2B company lies in its ability to create success for the businesses it supports, and though we're firmly in the data-rich era of big data, machine learning and deep learning still require massive volumes of data to learn and retrain from regularly. Hazy has done a fantastic job of alleviating businesses' pain points when it comes to data availability, and it's evident in the loyalty of their customer base. Another way Hazy maintains this loyalty is by educating its customers on the ethical and legal ramifications of traditional ways of anonymizing or masking existing real-world data.

Another great example of an AI company driving success in the B2B marketplace is a California-based gaming company called GGWP. While they don't create their own games, they use AI to reduce toxicity in the gaming culture and provide gaming companies with a dashboard where they can see how their users are performing from a moderation perspective. As gaming companies consistently take a more serious look at the safety and health of their gaming communities, they will come to rely on companies such as GGWP to ensure all their users feel safe. Moderation has long been a topic of discussion in social media companies and gaming companies alike, and it's really nice to find an AI company finding success in this field.

GGWP is also a positive example that reminds us of the importance of leveraging AI over human workers in specific fields. The biggest issue in employing human moderators is first and foremost the emotional toll it takes on their mental health as they go about their day. Scanning for hurtful or violent language isn't for the faint of heart, and finding depictions of graphic or hateful content on a consistent basis can deflate even the strongest of us. There's a strong case to be made for the ethical use of AI in helping us tackle the problems we, as human beings, would rather not be tasked with.

The professionals seemed most fitting for this bunch. When selling to other businesses in the B2B world, there's a standard operating procedure most businesses are comfortable with following. This includes everything from sales tactics to the approvals of budgets or statements of work to getting contracts approved through leadership, procurement, and all stakeholder teams in between. Because most B2B products are concerned with cost saving, productivity, or revenue generation, there are more structured interactions between all the players involved. The spirit of a professional is competence and integrity, no matter what arises in the moment, and B2B markets can be thought of in many ways as well-oiled machines. Much like the products they represent, these companies themselves are looking for ways to optimize productivity, generate revenue, and lower costs in their sales cycles and market interactions.

The artists – examples of B2C products done right

The artists are here to show us how AI can be leveraged in a way that allows expression for potentially billions of unmet customers. B2C refers to products that are built with the expectation that the product will be bought and used by individual consumers rather than other businesses. With B2C products, there's a feeling that you're looking for a way to satisfy the needs and tastes of many individuals. Upon further reflection, B2C companies are looking to satisfy the few common collective needs of millions. The more due diligence that goes into imagining solutions and understanding unmet needs that would help so many people, the more prepared these companies will be to satisfy unmet needs.

Hands down our favorite AI-powered consumer app would be TikTok. The Chinese giant uses three types of AI (`https://dev.to/mage_ai/how-does-tiktok-use-machine-learning-5b7i`) to optimize its experience for its users:

- Computer vision to track images in the videos
- Natural language processing to learn from sound and audio recordings
- Metadata from the captions to best deliver content users find most compelling

The biggest thing to remember with this example is it's a social media platform so we still see the inherent conflict between seeing compelling content and addictive behavior. This is still a problem area for them, judging by our own consumption. We're quite certain that we share this concern with our fellow one billion peers on the app. As far as B2C products are concerned, we struggled to find a better or more successful example.

Now, let's turn our attention to another addictive app. This time it's perhaps a healthier addiction: a thirst for knowledge! Pennsylvania-based Duolingo has leveraged deep learning in a way that helps people learn languages in a more efficient and specialized way for them. The gamified, personalized app reaches more than 300 million monthly active users and offers more than 30 languages. The main idea of Duolingo is it learns along with you and it offers you repetitions of words based on what it thinks you're just on the verge of forgetting. This repetition mimics the way we learn naturally and the gamified points-based behavior in the app gives you the emotional encouragement you need to keep going with your 15 minutes a day.

As a plus, Duolingo didn't start out as an AI company. It was founded in 2009, and once it started experimenting with personalization and A/B testing, it realized quickly that it ought to start testing with machine learning. Later on in the book, we will be discussing how to add AI features to an existing non-AI product. Duolingo offers us a successful example of a company that did just that.

We decided to call this group *the artists* because art captures the zeitgeist and varying energies coming from the social collective. It aligns pretty nicely with the idea of the invisible hand of the market. The concept of product-market fit is nebulous as well. The market wants what it wants and we all make up the market directly or indirectly, and the companies that create true art meet the market where it is. It's no wonder people are interested in learning languages. The world is increasingly global. The global job market supports people all over the world who can work remotely or locally, so the idea that someone could move or just learn a language out of curiosity seems like it would have increased within the last 10 to 15 years.

The idea that people would want to self-express in general, but particularly when sharing the collective retreat that was the COVID-19 pandemic, supports the idea of a global social media app that helps you create content almost effortlessly. TikTok and Duolingo captured the needs of the collective in a way that brought relief and ease to millions of people.

B2C apps are in the business of tapping into the collective needs of the masses. Consumers are different from those working with other businesses. There isn't an entire village of potential gatekeepers getting in the way of finding an able and willing sale. When selling a product to consumers, you've just got to win over one consciousness. You'd be tempted to be all things to all people in a way. We would imagine it would be hard to select and prioritize features. Catering your product to potentially millions of viewpoints would be unsustainable. But capturing an emotional need that would inspire and engage millions of viewers would ring like a bell, and everyone that hears its echo would feel its radiance. How so very artsy.

The pioneers – examples of blue ocean products

With pioneers, we wanted to focus on companies that were seeking new categories or use cases for their products. These are companies that are finding new paths to create demand for what they offer and these companies create demand for themselves in multiple ways. This is what's referred to as a **blue ocean**: a competitive landscape that's still being formed, that doesn't see a lot of competition (yet), and that has to advocate for its own demand. It's relatively straightforward to explore the market in a red ocean because so many pathways have been created. There is already a thriving ecosystem to learn and navigate. But pioneers have to work for this knowledge.

Partially, the companies themselves have to do enough research and development to warrant the pursuit of this industry they're helping build. Blue oceans also put a lot of onus on the early players in their industries to create thought leadership and evangelism to keep the potential competitors, investors, and customers curious in the first place.

Bearing.ai is a start-up that particularly caught our eye. Coming off the heels of a pandemic that has exacerbated the issues of an already strained supply chain crisis, we really loved the idea of a deep learning platform that was looking to not just streamline supply chain routes but also looking to solve the problem of maritime fuel consumption. We still find it shocking that we are so reliant on physically moving goods such large distances, and that labor costs and raw material availability fuel this highly inefficient global trade system we've built. We hope that, one day, we can create more efficient localized systems for managing global consumption, but in the meantime, there's Bearing.

What makes Bearing a good example of a blue ocean product? There really isn't much competition. A Google search for deep learning maritime route optimization products produced very few results, and this is the heart of the blue ocean landscape. You're not clamoring and infighting with your competitors for customers. The inherent challenge with blue oceans is that you have to create demand and justify the existence of your product. You have to essentially create a compelling story for why you should be in business, and why the world needs your product. It's a tricky game but if you do it well, you get your pick of customers. Right now, Bearing is in closed beta for a select group of customers. This is another advantage of the blue ocean: you can create an air of exclusivity. Only certain special ones get to know about this new, exciting venture.

We've talked about the ethics of using deep learning models and the issue of explainability. This is something that becomes more or less important to the success of a product based on the use case. With Bearing, the deep learning models are optimizing for the best routes, and for the company and its customers, the accuracy of the models is more important than their explainability. If it works, it works. Here, we see less of a reliance on explaining how the models come to certain conclusions because their customers are more concerned with whether the routes make sense and are indeed more efficient, and less concerned with how the inner mechanics are arriving at certain conclusions. This might not be the case if it were, say, a dating site or a property tech company optimizing costs for renters.

Speaking of explainable AI, our second blue ocean example is Fiddler.ai. We love that the rhetoric around explainability in machine learning has come to such a head that we're seeing companies emerge that partner with you to help create the transparency and trust needed to ensure that we continue to immerse AI in a responsible and ethical way. There aren't many companies doing this, and Fiddler allows you the ability to adhere to regulations and build models into your product at every stage of their life cycle. Fiddler does a great job of justifying itself: by bringing up the very real risks that might impact every company that's creating an environment for using machine learning models. They also do a great job of evangelizing their product. From the World Economic Forum, to Forbes, to CB Insights and Gartner, they're getting a lot of amazing press and they're using that to make a strong case for themselves in the blue ocean they find themselves in.

When we think of pioneers, we think of those that go into uncharted territories with curiosity and are rewarded for their bravery. Blue oceans are especially difficult to navigate because you are creating demand for a product and, in essence, creating a market. The belief and vision required to survive the uncertainty in this kind of market is something very few people can sustain for very long. The evangelism, experimentation, and mission-building make pioneers stand out from the crowd. The first path to be forged carries with it an inherent virtue. All subsequent paths have you to thank for laying the foundation.

Part of the evangelism being done on part of the pioneering companies also applies to the competitive landscape. When you're in a blue ocean, your competitors are your friends because they justify the existence of your product and solution. The more competitors you have, the more credibility you have as a business and the more you help create a supportive ecosystem with few key players. In many ways, pioneers are expanding and covering new ground in all directions.

The rebels – examples of red ocean products

Red oceans are markets that have become inhospitable environments with a full, mature, and developed competitive landscape. In this environment, many paths have already been formed and you have to choose one to live in and serve. You still have the option to create something new and you can employ many strategies to beat out the competition and specialize, but you're challenged with having enough intuition to see what the next step should be. Part of the challenge with having such a diverse and thriving ecosystem of competitors is that it's hard to know what direction you want to really go in, or which competitors are truly taking a piece of your business.

Lacework, a California-based cloud cybersecurity company, has shown a lot of promise, receiving a collective $1.9 billion in funding, according to Crunchbase. Cybersecurity is a blood bath when it comes to the competitive landscape. Between companies cannibalizing each other, new, innovative start-ups popping up consistently, and industry giants acquiring the most promising newcomers, it's a landscape that's often changing. Lacework has done a tremendous job of leveraging emerging machine learning use cases by having its own research lab (`https://www.lacework.com/labs/`) to test and train against new threats and attacks. This has allowed them to remain competitive and has given them the flexibility to inspire confidence in their investors. They now find themselves in their Series D round of funding and show no signs of stopping.

Lacework gives us another important point when it comes to ethical standards and practices of AI, which is to remain committed to the study of model optimization and diverse training data. Maintaining a lab has not only allowed them to continually refresh their AI applications across their product but it's also allowed them to maintain an air of responsibility in terms of how their product is coming to conclusions that impact their customers' most pressing problems in cybersecurity. This creates a lot of trust in their customer base, which is another primary success factor in a red ocean in particular.

We see this with another prime example in a red ocean competitive landscape, Lilt, a machine translation company also based in California. The localization and translation industry has also seen its fair share of infighting and this is a market that's full of translation service and tech providers and Lilt combines the two. From an AI perspective, what's special about Lilt is that it's *"the world's first and only interactive, self-learning neural machine translation system,"* according to their CEO, Spence Green. Its founders built Lilt as a response to the inadequacies they saw in machine translation while working at Google Translate and their work has paid off. The company finds itself in its Series C round of funding and has acquired more than $90M in funding so far.

When we think of rebels, we think of courage. It takes a lot of courage to compete in a highly crowded marketplace. With so many competitors, you can easily get distracted and burnt out. Every competitor represents a potential direction in which you can grow your product. Other opportunities can be elusive if you're focused enough, and companies that try to be all things to all people suffer from this lack of focus. Product managers and leadership will need to work together to ensure there is a clear vision for the product and that the company can rally behind that vision as a team. To us, rebels are fearless, and exploring this fear could be helpful to understand successful companies found in red oceans. Perhaps the fearlessness comes from the practiced courage of a company that's consistently facing so many adversaries in the market. Eventually, you sweat the small stuff and you gain the gift of having laser-focused vision.

The GOAT – examples of differentiated disruptive and dominant strategy products

Now, we'll turn our attention to the main market strategies and see some of the *greatest of all time*, or *GOAT*, examples for each strategy. A market strategy informs your go-to-market team's efforts. Will you be going after customers that have too many options or not enough? Will you create a product that effectively works better or worse than your competitors? These seem like obvious questions when putting together a business plan, but once things get going for your company and you start getting some customers, suddenly these decisions might not be as concrete as when the company was first formed.

One of our greatest lessons from the start-up world was about getting comfortable with asking questions that seemed so baked into the company mission and ethos that they seemed obvious. We've asked these questions reluctantly in previous experiences but we don't anymore. Companies can change their strategies if they're tempted enough, but every change poses a potential risk to the company. Market strategy informs everything from how you build a product to how you sell it. A lack of clarity into these aspects of your market strategy could result in building a product that isn't right. A lack of clarity in the communication and sale of a product could result in acquiring customers that aren't right for the company you are.

The following chart from Wes Bush's book *Product Led Growth* offers us a look at the four chambers of strategies companies can use in their growth strategies:

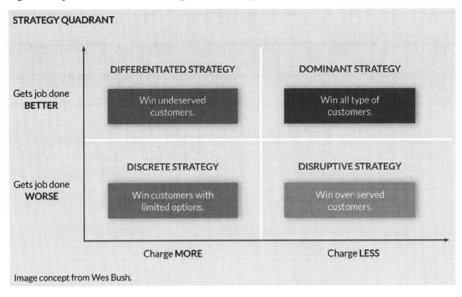

Figure 4.1 – The four chambers of strategies

This chart shows us the strategy quadrant that delineates the various areas of a go-to-market strategy and highlights the key areas between the discrete differentiated, dominant, and disruptive strategies. Every company will need to decide what its go-to-market strategy will be because this will inform how they sell, how they market its products, and the language it will use to reach its target customers.

In the following sections, we will be focusing on the differentiated, disruptive, and dominant strategies, and choosing one example for each that's using AI to fuel these growth strategies.

The dominant strategy

In the **dominant strategy**, you are looking to win customers of all types: those that are looking for a superior product as well as those that are looking to pay less. This increases your market share overall and is why this strategy is referred to as a dominant strategy because it's a winner-takes-all mentality. Let's take an example such as fast fashion, a highly competitive market if we've ever seen one. If you're a fast fashion retailer, it's not only important to have a cheaper product, but you must have operations to support the delivery of that product more efficiently. Think Netflix, a good example in its heyday, but today we struggle to find a better example than SHEIN. The Chinese brand manifests its dominant strategy by leveraging AI to better anticipate new trends and predict demand for certain products in the market and it marries that data with its supply chain to ensure that it can deliver on changes in demand to its customers' delight. This impacts everything from their marketing efforts to their in-app experience to the reviews of their products. The evidence is very telling as well.

Previously, a Spanish fast fashion company, Zara, had the fastest turnaround time of 3 weeks for creating and delivering a collection. SHEIN brought that down to a new best-in-class of 3 days. A truly admirable use of AI and machine learning.

A dominant strategy is one that undercuts the market they're competing with by getting the job done better and costing less. This is effective because it's maximizing its rewards on both ends. It gets to receive the customers that want the job done better as well as the customers that just want to pay less. That's quite a lot of the pie you win out on. When done right, companies employing these strategies can essentially print money.

The disruptive strategy

With a **disruptive strategy**, you're still selling a product for less money but it offers you less too. Who wants that? People who are overserved and bombarded with options, but who actually need relatively simple tools compared to the competing options they have to choose from. We can see no better example of that than Canva. You can edit photos and create anything from a social media post to a resume using Canva, and the tools to do so are incredibly user-friendly and simple.

The Australian creativity platform leverages AI to offer customers more of the kinds of templates and content they're looking for. While it offers *less* than Adobe's Photoshop or the Microsoft Office suite, it does offer what its users are specifically looking for and it's either free or cheap to use. It quickly rose to unicorn status for expertly meeting its customers where they were.

What's most interesting about disruptive strategies is the ability to influence your potential customers by showing them a different angle. Disruption changes the paradigm of the existing power structures in a market and a new tastemaker arrives to inspire their competitors and customers alike to try new things with regard to how they ask for and use a product. This change in paradigm offers the entire market the gift of novelty and specialization. Maybe the job gets done worse, but this is beneficial for a new group of proposed customers. Perhaps this new group is one none of the other competitors thought to try and serve.

The differentiated strategy

In a **differentiated strategy**, you may sell a superior product that specializes in some niche but you're also charging more for it to account for this specialization. My differentiated strategy example is a company that hits close to home: a British machine learning based property tech company I worked with named Beekin. Beekin isn't a property technology platform that was cheaper per se, but, at the time, it offered a next-generation platform no other property tech company was able to offer. We built a machine learning native platform that did everything from making market evaluations to predicting future behaviors to offer an optimal price for renters. Our customers didn't have many options for competing tools because their alternatives were property tech giants with antiquated rule-based engines, and the competitive landscape in property tech is newly being disrupted by AI.

Differentiated strategies flourish in environments where they can best communicate the strength of their products. Because the price tag is also higher, there needs to be a compelling reason why someone would pursue differentiators in a market. Unique products that differ greatly from their competitors thrive in this market strategy. In the case of Beekin, there weren't many other competitors using machine learning as the foundation of their product, and it was able to help many people with their jobs to be done. This is the greatest strength of a differentiated product: to satisfy a niche and advancing market. The need for differentiation is what furthers and matures industries. Once customers with more particular and pressing needs arise, differentiators pop up to show their competitors how they might begin specializing and rising to meet their customers where they are.

Let's take a moment to offer a round of applause for all the examples we have seen so far. The work and dedication that it takes to align a viable functioning product with a business model, a product strategy, and a loyal customer base is nothing short of a triumph, and success should be shouted out and celebrated. We learn so much from the successes of others and we had a lot of fun choosing fitting examples for this chapter.

Explainability is a big area of interest for a product manager. The idea that you can easily explain your AI product, how it comes to certain conclusions, and how the inner mechanics of how it works becomes very important when you're dealing with the public or sensitive subject matter, or if you have high-profile or enterprise customers that may be subject to risk later downstream. We don't want to convince you of what kind of product manager you should be; rather, we want to lay down the options for you to consider.

Whether you are trusting the brightest minds in AI or you're getting the help of a machine learning intern just out of bootcamp, know that a lot can be done with very simple models. Striving for algorithmic perfection and relying on simple tools that are commonly relied on and used are equally admirable. It's largely a question of preference and use case.

The purpose of this chapter is to highlight some promising developments in AI products in recent years to offer a variety of perspectives on how AI can be leveraged across a number of different business models. This isn't about emulating other companies but rather coming to appreciate how AI philosophy, behaviors, ethics, and practices can change from one business model to another. For us, this is vital to how the product is managed at the department level. As a product manager, you are tasked with the commercial success of the product, and understanding how AI relates to your business model is important to your risk management.

Summary

In this chapter, we covered some promising examples of AI done right in recent years for the purposes of finding inspiration in the successes and use cases of our peers in the space. As a product manager, having an understanding of your go-to-market strategy, business model, and the market you serve is crucial. We are firmly in the era of AI proliferation now. Many businesses are adopting AI within their products and within their businesses, and we hope you've enjoyed these examples as we continue to understand the particulars of managing an AI product.

In the next chapter, we will put our futurist hats on and understand a bit about what the emerging trends on the horizon in AI are. We believe all product managers need to have a streak of futurism in their composition. Having a grasp of where things are in the recent and present moments provides a snapshot with which to evaluate your existing strategy. But in tech, things evolve pretty quickly. In business, projections and future goals can change from week to week as well.

All of us will have to entertain future potentialities safely if we want to influence leadership, resources, and time toward the expansion of our AI products into areas that will inspire our customers and critics alike. Let's take a look and see what AI trends are in the forecast.

References

- *AI Helps Duolingo Personalize Language Learning*: `https://www.wired.com/brandlab/2018/12/ai-helps-duolingo-personalize-language-learning/#:~:text=The%20learning%20behind%20the%20lingo,data%20and%20make%20intelligent%20predictions`

- *Hazy Company Info*: `https://www.cbinsights.com/company/anon-ai`

- *GGWP Company Info*: `https://www.crunchbase.com/organization/ggwp-65c2`

- *Lacework Labs*: `https://www.lacework.com/labs/`

- *How does TikTok use machine learning?*: `https://dev.to/mage_ai/how-does-tiktok-use-machine-learning-5b7i`

- *Canva*: `https://www.lifeatcanva.com/en`

- *Lilt Company Info*: `https://www.crunchbase.com/organization/lilt`

5

AI Transformation and Its Impact on Product Management

As I look to the future and imagine what's to come regarding AI products, I feel tremendous inspiration and optimism about AI's ability to help us out of some of the greatest challenges that face humanity. I moderate a monthly talk with Women in AI called *WAITalks*. Many of my questions during these monthly talks are recurring questions, largely centered on how the speakers broke into the field, what excites them most about AI, and what they wish others knew about their area of AI. There's a lot of beauty and insight from how the various women working in AI, from research to corporate to entrepreneurship, answer the same set of questions.

One of our March 2022 speakers worked in AI policy at Meta. Because so much of her work involves ethics, we spent a great deal of time discussing the risks and inherent problems AI poses. After some time on that, I wanted to know what someone in her position looks forward to regarding AI. We hear so much about the promise of AI, and it's always nice to get a sense of what diverse sets of people believe AI will help us with. Her answer blew me away. She said that because her work focuses so much on the legalities, risks, and biases AI poses, it would be easy for her to take on a pessimistic view of AI and its effect on humans across the world. But this wasn't the case with her. She said she felt, more than ever, that AI will be foundational in helping us with the greatest problems humanity will face, from cancer to climate change to the social biases that plague us and keep us apart.

In this chapter, we will be discussing a few waves of AI transformation and cover ideation, building **minimal viable products** (**MVPs**), and how to leverage AI for the common good as well as for commercial success. Firstly, we will take a look at how AI will revolutionize our economic systems and how we relate to money and value. There will be broad brushstrokes here. Then, we will take a look at the commercial level and how AI is fueling growth in MVPs. This will be an exploration into the kinds of integrations AI will enable at the goods and services level. The expansion of AI in how we're governed will be the subject of our third section, particularly the intersection of public citizen data and how governments will choose to use data on their own citizens. Our fourth section will explore the use of AI in healthcare, and finally, our fifth section will offer some insights into how AI is being used for the good of all and the fulfillment of basic needs worldwide.

We will go into these macro-level trends to offer insights to product managers out there interested in creating their own products, or to those looking for opportunities to expand within the existing suite of products they currently represent. We will also be looking at these macro trends from the perspective of product managers that aren't necessarily overseeing a product, platform, or a suite of products, but who are product managers over their area of business or stakeholder teams. There are many manifestations of product managers, and the following sections will offer paths and inspiration to all levels of product managers out there that are interested in keeping an eye on the future, to expand on how AI is being leveraged within their organizations. Every product manager has the ability to influence their business, their product roadmap, and the ideas that come forward as their organizations evolve.

Remember that, as a product person, you are an agent of change. You have tremendous influence no matter your level. You are responsible for overseeing the commercial success and growth of your product, and you have a tremendous ability to inspire your business to evolve and embrace the technologies of the future. Use your power wisely and keep an ear to the ground to stay up to date on new ways to use your influence.

With that, in this chapter, we will cover the following topics:

- Money and value – how AI could revolutionize our economic systems
- Goods and services – growth in commercial MVPs
- Government and autonomy – how AI will shape our borders and freedom
- Sickness and health – the benefits of AI and nanotech across healthcare
- Basic needs – AI for Good

Money and value – how AI could revolutionize our economic systems

AI has been no stranger to fintech as well as our greater economic systems. We've seen the rise of cryptocurrencies develop in concert with this change in how the financial industry is operating. Smart contracts specifically have been a huge motivator for crypto and blockchain adoption. This isn't a book about crypto, but it does signal a change in how financial industries and economic systems are fundamentally operating.

Artificial intelligence (**AI**) and **machine learning** (**ML**) are excellent tools for optimization, and there are few more compelling use cases for AI/ML than the optimization of profits. The financial industry has been leveraging quantitative analysts or *quants* for a long time. Quants do statistical and mathematical modeling for financial and risk modeling problems and, in many cases, it has been a profitable career for those that were interested in *the sexiest job of the 21st century*, aka data science, even before this term was made famous by *Harvard Business Review* in 2012.

Modeling and risk minimization have been pushed into overdrive with AI and, considering the financial industry as a whole is people-heavy, the adoption of AI has been competing with human jobs. Let's take the example of trading and the use of algorithmic trading. This is the ability to program a set of instructions to account for different variables, such as volume, price, and time of day. In comparison to a human trader, an AI or algorithm can optimize for the purchase of certain shares and learn from successful past behaviors much faster. Deep learning can also be leveraged here, and the output of its performance can be used as input to further train the algorithmic trading platforms, which means that these complex systems can start to see patterns and recognize opportunities almost infinitely better than a human trader.

There are, of course, other use cases of AI that have been helpful in the financial sector. Things such as detecting fraud, optimizing accounting, processing customer reviews, and assessing risk are all areas of financial services that have seen AI transformation. In looking toward the future, we also see tremendous investment allocated specifically for AI expansion. A 2021 report by the **Organization for Economic Co-Operation and Development (OECD)** predicts that by 2024, global spending on AI will reach over $110 billion. In 2020, it was about half of this predicted amount, and given the impact of the COVID-19 pandemic, this trend toward AI adoption has been accelerated.

Though there are often concerns about the *black-box* nature of deep learning models, we do want to note that in performance-driven environments such as trading, this isn't so relevant. Assessing bias and making sure algorithms are not autonomously making decisions that would impact disparate groups of people will always be relevant, and we have governmental bodies that are looking into the fairness of financial exchanges and market regulation. These governmental bodies themselves are embracing AI as well – toward the end of improving regulatory activities, surveillance, and compliance more easily and faster.

There are still limitations to the use of AI/ML, and modeling is currently being used in a capacity that still requires significant input from human staff. Scott W. Bauguess, acting director and acting chief economist of **Division of Economic and Risk Analysis (DERA)** at the US **Securities and Exchange Commission (SEC)**, recently gave us a collective sigh of relief when he said, "*While the major advances in machine learning have and will continue to improve our ability to monitor markets for possible misconduct, it is premature to think of AI as our next market regulator. Science is not yet there. The most advanced machine learning technologies used today can mimic human behavior in unprecedented ways, but higher-level reasoning by machines remains an elusive hope*" (`https://www.sec.gov/news/speech/bauguess-big-data-ai`).

From financial transactions to the exchange of stocks, to the regulation of financial activities, we've seen a few examples in this part of how AI is impacting the industry as a whole. We'd like to end with a more philosophical view of what AI adoption means for the very concept of value, worth, and money from a product perspective. If you work in fintech and you support financial products, you're likely concerned with not only the value this will deliver to your customers, but you're also keeping an eye out for risks to the commercialization of your product. The financial examples in this section remind us of the importance of ideating use cases and products in a way that delivers value first and foremost.

Whether you work in Web3 and blockchain tech, traditional banks, or in the regulation of financial products, you're looking to harness AI/ML in a capacity where your product is helping someone improve some outcome. Help comes in all shapes and sizes. As you're in the throes of ideation and looking to offer something the market needs, consider products that are helping someone to arrive at conclusions in a faster, easier, or otherwise more efficient way. Maybe it's making your customers more profitable or minimizing their costs. Maybe it's helping your customers predict future uncertainty. Maybe it's offering them a way to expand their generational wealth and gain financial independence. Maybe your offering is using AI/ML to best understand your customer through personalization. There is immense value in this too.

If you're thinking about how to best leverage AI/ML for your products, think in terms of how you can best deliver revenue and value to your end users and your business. We find it best to think in terms of reverse thinking, which is imagining the final result your product will provide its users and working backward from that to craft a solution that fits that final result. Another great technique is using divergent thinking in your brainstorming during the ideation process. Whether your product is predicting, optimizing, or personalizing an experience for your customers, try to imagine other scenarios and use cases in which your product might be helpful. Now is the time to be experimental with your ideations in a way that most influences your customers to see AI/ML's value most prominently.

Once you have a few good ideas, you're ready to test. You can build MVPs that test out the effectiveness of those ideas in a way that communicates value and aligns the collective benefits of the target market you're serving, bringing commercial success. We will explore this in more detail in the following section.

Goods and services – growth in commercial MVPs

Now the fun stuff! One of the great blessings of AI/ML is seeing just how creative we humans can get with it. In the previous section, we wanted to start with finance and business because this is the heart of the capitalist free market – everyone is in the business of making money at the end of the day, and product management is, once again, an inherently commercial role. Let's take one step away from that and briefly explore the world of AI commercialization. What we mean by this is that various AI use cases are appearing across various industries and sectors. There are many to choose from, and we have no doubt someone out there will have all the fun in the world writing a book about all the creative and fun new ways you can use AI/ML across a wide variety of commercial industries, but here, we will only use a few key examples that we find particularly inspiring as promising, early MVPs.

In keeping with the theme of this chapter, we would encourage all product managers to keep up with promising developments in AI/ML products because this phase of AI adoption we're in is all about inspiration. This is the golden age of the entrepreneur, and nowhere is that more evident than in the start-up world. Technologists from all ages would relish the opportunity to be alive today in the era of big data and AI. As we've mentioned previously, the earlier phase of AI was research-heavy and we were starved of data. Now that we have loads of data and a pretty good understanding of the models and languages we can leverage to make the most of it, we can actually apply it and do what humans do best – create!

I had the privilege of being part of the Women in AI Accelerator (WaiACCELERATE) in 2021, and after seeing all the candidates going through the program and the applications going through the process, from ideation to building an MVP, I found myself inspired by the creativity going into these nascent ideas. From optimizing building materials to scanning the internet for fake news, to robotics, to AI assistance advocating for women, **BIPOC (Black, Indigenous, and People of Color)**, and other marginalized groups, it seems like the sky's the limit for AI adoption.

Earlier in this chapter, we briefly discussed personalization and ideation. One company that's leveraging reinforcement learning to better understand the tastes of its customers is a London beer company called **IntelligentX** that's brewing *the world's first beer brewed by AI*. Or perhaps you're more interested in food; IBM's Chef Watson can already whip up a recipe for you using only the ingredients you have in your fridge. We're sure they can inspire you with a gourmet meal using only the pickle juice, mayonnaise, and leftover Chinese food floating around in there.

Moving onto a different kind of recipe, AI is now being used to create perfumes with the help of a company called Symrise. Though a bit of a departure, taking the theme of personalization further, we are also seeing the rise of visual AI start-ups that will find items for you to purchase based on photos you capture, such as CamFindApp. And let's suppose you want the ultimate personalization – for that, there's Replika, AI that gets at the deepest part of what makes us relate, an AI companion and friend who "cares."

Now, let's move onto a topic we think of as being uniquely human – the idea of AI making art. It's a worthwhile philosophical topic to ponder. Can we consider something art when it doesn't come from the tortured soul of an artist? We think we will come to find, increasingly in the future as well, that indeed we can:

"Sunset Memory

by Poetry Potty

One in clothes

She wears destruction

As a female

It compounds daily

Confusion

That is impossible to deny"

The preceding poem was written with a neural net through a literary magazine, written by a machine called CuratedAI (http://curatedai.com/poetry/she-wears-destruction/). Take a moment to think about this. If you didn't know who it was written by, would you have doubted its artistic integrity? Does it matter in the end? Philosophical debates aside, we would be remiss if we didn't mention GPT-3, the most powerful language model we currently have, which was released in 2020 by OpenAI, who recently released ChatGPT and is actively working on the next generation of GPT-3 – GPT-4. ChatGPT itself has been the latest sensation, springing its own network of new start-ups that harness its vast capabilities. OpenAI's current evaluation is at $29 billion and its ChatGPT functionality is being added to Microsoft's Bing search engine, launching a search engine war with Google.

We will likely see new language models popping up to empower more creative applications of AI in poetry and writing. Another thing to note is the ability of AI to effectively *convince* you. What these powerful language models offer us as technologists, product managers, and customers is the ability to interact with a machine that doesn't feel like a machine. The use of these new language models and abilities will become more prevalent in the future as AI applications become more social. The ability of AI models to generate long-form text is huge. As language models get better and better, they'll be changing how we interact with all kinds of tech, simply because they're making it easier for us to interact with it. If people have the option to use natural language and effectively speak to a piece of technology in their own native language, they'll gladly take it.

To sum up the arts, maybe it's music you want to create. There's a whole slew of music apps using AI to generate new music, such as SOUNDRAW, Jukebox, and Boomy, or lyrics, such as Audoir. Or maybe we can explore the myriad ways AI has been changing how we optimize film schedules, promote films, predict the success of films, edit films, and even produce films. There is virtually no creative industry that's going to be untouched by AI in the future, which also brings up the importance of finding ways for AI to coexist with human artists. Will we see AI art rise to such prevalence that humans are left out in the cold? Or will human artists start to incorporate AI into the art they themselves create? Will there be a pushback on the part of consumers that then places a premium on human-made art and will we see them get paid more for it? Time will tell.

All these products started with an idea to create a product that could bring the richness of life to consumers, and these product teams built MVPs out of these seminal ideas. An MVP should be released to market quickly so that you can start the process of collecting feedback on how your users are resonating and working with it, allowing you to iterate further through the production process. In many of the examples in this section, these companies built MVPs that they then tested, and they found an overwhelming willingness and curiosity from their target markets to the point where there are now many competing products for each aforementioned area. Building an MVP that you can test and improve quickly not only helps your own business but also creates an even bigger market that attracts more competitors.

Building an MVP is a tool to give you an early signal that you've got the right idea, market, and target customer base. This helps you to quickly and successfully balance the needs of your customer with your own commercial success. We can also call this product market fit. However, how does this change when applied to governmental sectors? We will explore that in the following section.

Government and autonomy – how AI will shape our borders and freedom

It's not all fun and games. The immense availability of data and AI simultaneously opens us up to the risk of authoritarianism and the rise of oppression, and the collective empowerment to combat threats to democracy across the world. At the moment, we have some striking contradictions of power and protection being exerted in very different ways, based on a system of shared societal values. In this section, we will be looking at how AI will be leveraged in governmental capacities and what it means for all of us as consumers and makers alike.

Governments will increasingly need to focus on preserving their country's ecosystems and the fallout from climate change, and with that focus, there will need to be some degree of investment as well. The private sector can only do so much, and we hope that governmental bodies will use their influence for the betterment of their citizens. Let's take an issue such as voting, which, at least in the US, has seen many headlines during the last few presidential elections. Companies such as Microsoft are developing electronic voting systems, such as ElectionGuard, as part of their Defending Democracy Program to allow for safe, secure, and verifiable voting processes in the future.

AI also has a role to play in policy-making itself. There are several stages in which AI and big data can be leveraged to facilitate the process of legislating. We see a range of use cases where AI can be helpful at the legislation and policy levels. Pattern detection and identification of topics that constituents most want to address, the creation of analysis and forecasting at a granular level, the generation of data to support findings, the implementation and diagnostic feedback for how certain policies are performing, and ultimately, the evaluation of the ultimate effectiveness of certain policies are all ways AI can be immensely beneficial. If governments choose to partner with the private sector or invest in their own development of AI applications to address policy-making, we will likely see an expansion of the democratic process.

On a broader societal level, we can see some novel applications of AI that will likely continue into the future. The alleviation of bias is something AI can help address at the governmental level, where policies are impacting varying demographic groups' intersectionality. Companies such as PwC are doing just that with their Bias Analyzer product. Part of the ethical conundrum of using AI resides with the issue of bias in algorithms, a topic made famous recently by M.I.T. Media Lab researcher Joy Buolamwini in the Netflix documentary *Coded Bias*. Joy has taken her work forward by building her own organization (and effectively her own movement), the Algorithmic Justice League, to continue this advocacy for algorithmic bias further. We're also starting to see companies such as Pipeline Equity that advocate for pay transparency and equity across demographics to minimize the pay gap and give organizations sound business proof for why they should invest in pay equity as well.

By far, where governmental bodies are concerned, AI is the elephant in the room. Particularly, the use of autonomous weapons and mass surveillance are most controversial for understandable reasons. People want to feel safe, but they also don't want their privacy abused. I had the honor of speaking with Colonel Dave Barnes, chief AI ethics officer at the US Army Artificial Intelligence Task Force and professor and deputy head of English and philosophy at the USMA, at a virtual conference I participated in with Women in Trusted AI in 2020. The greatest insight from that conversation was the acknowledgment that every country is still grappling with how to most responsibly and effectively use AI and understand the potential harms and risks.

There's much to be done across governments to set limits and understand the full capacity of how AI is leveraged, and we see more conversations about how to limit the negative externalities of AI in defense. Regarding autonomous weapons, the US Department of Defense's principles of AI are as follows: responsible, equitable, traceable, reliable, and governable. This sentiment is perhaps best expressed by Air Force Lt. Gen. Jack Shanahan, director of the Joint Artificial Intelligence Center: "*The complexity and the speed of warfare will change as we build an AI-ready force of the future. We owe it to the American people and our men and women in uniform to adopt AI ethics principles that reflect our nation's values of a free and open society.*" Societies aren't free or open if they're being controlled and oppressed.

The same could be said for mass surveillance. AI can be used to empower governments to oppress and control their citizens, and it can also be used to keep them safe. Mass surveillance is also bleeding into the private sector, with many private companies choosing to use facial recognition, which is very difficult to opt out of, for something as simple as going to a theater or a bar. The recent **AI Global Surveillance** (**AIGS**) Index shows an increase in AI surveillance being used worldwide.

The following is an extract from *The Global Expansion of AI Surveillance* by Steven Feldstein (https://carnegieendowment.org/files/WP-Feldstein-AISurveillance_final1.pdf):

> "*The index shows that 51 percent of advanced democracies deploy AI surveillance systems. In contrast, 37 percent of closed autocratic states, 41 percent of electoral autocratic/competitive autocratic states, and 41 percent of electoral democracies/illiberal democracies deploy AI surveillance technology. Liberal democratic governments are aggressively using AI tools to police borders, apprehend potential criminals, monitor citizens for bad behavior, and pull out suspected terrorists from crowds. This doesn't necessarily mean that democracies are using this technology unlawfully. The most important factor determining whether governments will exploit this technology for repressive purposes is the quality of their governance – is there an existing pattern of human rights violations? Are there strong rule of law traditions and independent institutions of accountability? That should provide a measure of reassurance for citizens residing in democratic states.*"

What does this mean for product managers? Well, for one, if you're in the *authoritarian tech* space, business is booming, no matter your politics! More importantly, it means that we as product managers have a responsibility to support and create products we believe in. Our input and involvement in building these products has massive repercussions, depending on the audience and whether you have your eyes set on governmental or military aspirations. You should think critically about the products you bring to market to see how you can combine the common good with your own success. These governmental examples also went through the process of ideating, from building an MVP to releasing it and getting feedback. The only difference is these products are being administered in areas that affect public citizens, and we would say the responsible use and development of these products is the hardest area to get right when the potential impact is so high.

Sickness and health – the benefits of AI and nanotech across healthcare

AI continues to be incredibly successful when applied to the medical and healthcare industry. Drug discovery and development companies such as CytoReason, DeepCure, and BullFrog AI help their customers find and analyze new molecular compounds to create novel drugs for some of the most pressing illnesses that plague humanity, shorten time to market for these new drugs, and assist with the patenting process. Companies such as Standigm enable AI workflows to leverage AI through the journey of highly customizable target identification and lead generation. Before AI, the journey to discovering a new drug, conducting clinical trials, and bringing the drug to market might have taken upward of 10 years.

We also see personalization and prediction being applied to personal care through the use of AI, which is particularly exciting when you consider the doctor shortage we're experiencing worldwide. Wouldn't it be nice to see a personal health dashboard, where you can check your vitals on a regular basis through the use of nanotechnology and the analysis of data streams of your own personal data? Companies such as Biofourmis are investing in this and are also providing patients and doctors alike with the power to detect illnesses and potential health-related issues early, with their FDA-cleared Biovitals Analytics Engine (`https://biofourmis.com/`). We can easily envision a scenario where companies start to build similar dashboards, customized for people with a specific illness or within specific demographic groups.

Necessity is the mother of invention, and disability is also a huge area of healthcare that AI has been serving for some time. With the combination of robotics, computer vision, voice assistance, audio assistance, speech-to-text, and smart home tech, we have been applying and will continue to apply AI in contexts that can help individuals with disabilities related to sight, sound, smell, taste, touch, mobility, mental health, understanding, communication, and learning.

A company called Parrots has created a medical assistive AI called Polly that's assisting people with neurological conditions. Polly helps its customers physically see the world around them better with 360-degree vision and navigate within their home or outside, offers real-time prediction by analyzing eye-tracking technology to anticipate needs, and facilitates the communication of needs, thoughts, and desires to the people around them. Essentially, it's a whole suite of products in one platform for a specific use case. Wheelmap is a crowdsourced navigation app that helps you find wheelchair-accessible routes, building on its knowledge through a community of users that participate in a feedback loop. Biped, a company that makes smart harnesses, has developed a product that fits like a backpack to assist blind and vision-impaired people with potential collision risks as they navigate the world.

Mental health and suicide prevention are also areas we've seen tremendous investment in with the use of AI applications. I teamed up with a colleague from my data science program to create my dream product in 2020. It was a mental health-focused conversational AI that got to know you, established goals with you, and recorded your mood. We were interested in using AI to serve as a real-time journal and dashboard for self-reflection, with the option to share this data and dashboard with a therapist if you chose to work with one.

Through the process of building the idea and MVP, we did our research and discovered other companies that were tackling mental health and suicide prevention in their own ways. Companies such as ResolveX are using AI to work with suicide hotlines to eliminate manual and administrative tasks so that the workers can focus on the human on the other end of the line. Woebot developed a chatbot using cognitive behavioral therapy techniques to help people battling depression and anxiety.

In healthcare, we see a similar mission-driven element to the ideation, MVP, and release cycle, but the good of all is once again the main focus because, as is often the case, these products can have significant repercussions for users and customers if the products themselves haven't been thoroughly tested, and if the downstream effects of using these products haven't been studied. While it's always important to get the right idea and a working version of your idea out there to test with users, in healthcare use cases, it's imperative that all areas are strongly accounted for because you're dealing with people's health and safety.

Basic needs – AI for Good

One thing that really struck me about the data science and AI/ML community when I first joined was how communal it was. My prior career was in sales and account management, and I took how competitive it was for granted. I was struck by the benevolence of the community. There were so many open source projects you could get involved in. You could put your projects up on Kaggle and win competitions. You could find an almost infinite supply of solutions to problems on Stack Overflow. I found a lot of success reaching out to people, who shared their perspectives on their area of AI. Never was this more apparent than when I reached out to potential speakers to host a panel or a workshop to teach others. It makes this field all the more compelling because if you do want to focus on a particular AI solution, you can find lots of friends along the way to join your cause and support you.

You'll likely see the term *AI for Good* used by organizations that look to use AI for some social or humanitarian cause. Many of them work with other companies, schools, governments, and NGOs collaboratively to address certain causes. AI4Good.org has worked on smart cities, workforce diversity, AI ethics, and Economists for Ukraine projects alongside the United Nations Sustainable development goals. The UN itself has the **International Telecommunication Union (ITU)**, a specialized agency for information and communication technologies that has its own AI for a good year-round platform to host volunteers and serve their communities as well. There are more ecosystems, such as Omdena, DataKind, and Teamcore, that look to collaboratively address humanitarian causes as well. Microsoft, H2O.ai, Google, and IBM also have their own AI for Good initiatives.

Saving ourselves from ourselves is big business for AI, and there are many companies that put humanitarianism in their business model, using a combined passion and entrepreneurship to bring products to market that also benefit society on some level. Companies such as Peat are able to help farmers in insecure areas better maximize their yields with their product Plantix. Ad hoc collaborations such as the one Lokai made with Facebook to create a pop-up water charity are appearing more and more. Sustainable food distribution and urban farming projects are being powered by AI, where companies such as Square Roots and Bowery Farming can *"dream of a world where agriculture gives back more to the people and planet than it takes."*

Bringing products to market that affect people's access to basic needs is one of the greatest expressions of AI products we see out there, and we want to remind you of the importance of divergent thinking here with regard to ideation. Where AI for Good is concerned, we are barely scratching the surface of what AI can do, and we would recommend people who enter this realm as product managers focus most of their attention on the ideation phase. Practice the use of divergent thinking, hone in on the end result you're looking to achieve with AI, and use this as your guide in your ideation phase. Building an MVP will come with its own considerations, and you're already crafting this offering for the benefit of all and combining it with a way to create commercial success with your tool, so you can really take your time with ideation.

This is by far not an exhaustive list in terms of the future of AI, but I believe it's representative enough of where we're heading to offer those in AI product management a few insights into a few major sectors that shape our world through AI. I honestly could go on and on. My hopes were to offer a window to the future for the technologists and builders reading this to better conceptualize how AI can be leveraged in varying capacities across industries. The strategic side of product management requires big-picture thinking. I'm a firm believer in the interconnectivity of ideas. One use case in one industry can birth new ideas in another. The elegance of tech lies with those that can apply technologies in new, faster, easier, and better-leveraged ways.

The biggest contributor to my interest in building a career as a product manager was the big-picture, strategic element. I don't want to be an entrepreneur. I'd rather leave the fundraising, pitching, and administration to more entrepreneurial types. I first and foremost want to build products that help people, and it is my deep belief that technology enables us to do this most efficiently.

Summary

This concludes *Part 1*. We started with an introduction to AI and the infrastructure required to support it, went into the weeds of model maintenance and the particulars of ML and deep learning, saw a mix of applications and business model examples of AI products, and concluded with a glimpse into where AI is going next. *Part 2* will expand on the AI native products themselves by focusing on what it takes to understand, ideate, create, and productize AI. We will also explore how AI products can be customized and how performance can be optimized, as well as going into some examples of common pitfalls and successes a product manager can run into with the AI native product.

In the next chapter, we will be looking at what areas are essential when you're building an AI-native product. We will be looking at the particulars of managing a product from the ground up, with certain AI considerations and what product managers will need to account for as they begin the process of ideating, building an MVP, and ultimately, launching an AI product. The chapter will be primarily for those that are entrepreneurial and are looking specifically to ship products that will meet the needs of their market using AI.

AI is often discussed as an integral part of the fourth industrial revolution, but when we consider just how many facets of our world and our businesses AI will impact, it's easy to see why we are constantly returning to the gravity of these terms. We know that we will continue to see more novel ideas of how to harness AI, and that's what makes this period of AI implementation so exciting.

Additional resources

If you're in the US and at risk of self-harm, please check out the following resources:

- Crisis Text Line: Text *CRISIS* to 741741 for free, confidential crisis counseling
- The National Suicide Prevention Lifeline: 1-800-273-8255
- The Trevor Project: 1-866-488-7386

For those outside the US, check out these resources:

The International Association for Suicide Prevention lists a number of suicide hotlines by country. You can find them by going to their website (https://findahelpline.com/i/iasp). Also, check out Befrienders Worldwide (https://www.befrienders.org/need-to-talk).

References

- The Role of Big Data, Machine Learning, and AI in Assessing Risks: a Regulatory Perspective: https://www.sec.gov/news/speech/bauguess-big-data-ai
- Artificial Intelligence, Machine Learning, and Big Data in Finance: https://www.oecd.org/finance/financial-markets/Artificial-intelligence-machine-learning-big-data-in-finance.pdf
- Data Scientist: The Sexiest Job of the 21st Century: https://hbr.org/2012/10/data-scientist-the-sexiest-job-of-the-21st-century
- Bowery Farming: https://boweryfarming.com
- Square Roots: https://www.squarerootsgrow.com/
- Plantix: https://plantix.net/en/
- Peat: https://peat.technology/en/
- IBM AI for Good sponsorship focuses on AI in service of the planet: https://www.ibm.com/blogs/journey-to-ai/2021/11/ibm-ai-for-good-sponsorship-focuses-on-ai-in-service-of-the-planet/
- Google AI FOR SOCIAL GOOD: https://ai.google/social-good/
- H2O.ai AI 4 Good: https://h2o.ai/company/ai-4-good/

- Microsoft AI for Good: `https://www.microsoft.com/en-us/ai/ai-for-good`

- Harvard University Teamcore: `https://teamcore.seas.harvard.edu/`

- Omdena: `https://omdena.com/`

- DataKind: `https://www.datakind.org/`

- AI for Good: `https://aiforgood.itu.int/about-ai-for-good/`

- AI for Good: `https://ai4good.org/what-we-do/`

- Woebot: `https://woebothealth.com/`

- Resolvex: `https://resolvex.com/`

- Biped unveils an AI copilot for blind and visually impaired people at CES 2022:

- `https://www.designboom.com/technology/biped-ai-copilot-blind-visually-impaired-people-ces-2022-01-10-2022/`

- Wheelmap.org: `https://wheelmap.org/?locale=en-us`

- Parrots: `https://www.flyparrots.com/`

- Biofourmis: `https://biofourmis.com/`

- Standigm: `https://www.standigm.com/about/company`

- Bullfrog AI: `https://bullfrogai.com/`

- Deepcure AI: `https://deepcure.ai/technology/`

- Cytoreason: `https://www.cytoreason.com/company/`

- The Global Expansion of AI Surveillance: `https://carnegieendowment.org/files/WP-Feldstein-AISurveillance_final1.pdf`

- DOD Adopts 5 Principles of Artificial Intelligence Ethics: `https://www.defense.gov/News/News-Stories/Article/Article/2094085/dod-adopts-5-principles-of-artificial-intelligence-ethics/`

- Pipeline: `https://www.pipelineequity.com/how-it-works/`

- Algorithmic Justice League: `https://www.ajl.org/`

- Coded Bias Netflix: `https://www.netflix.com/title/81328723`

- Bias Analyzer PWC: `https://www.pwc.com/us/en/services/consulting/cloud-digital/data-analytics/artificial-intelligence/bias-analyzer.html`

- New cyberthreats require new ways to protect democracy: `https://blogs.microsoft.com/on-the-issues/2019/07/17/new-cyberthreats-require-new-ways-to-protect-democracy/`

- How Artificial Intelligence Is Used in the Film Industry: `https://smartclick.ai/articles/how-artificial-intelligence-is-used-in-the-film-industry/#:~:text=Promoting%20movies,highest%20interest%20from%20the%20audience`

- AI Lyrics and Poetry Generator: `https://www.audoir.com/`

- Boomy: `https://boomy.com/`

- OpenAI Jukebox: `https://openai.com/blog/jukebox/`

- Soundraw: `https://soundraw.io/`

- OpenAI's new language generator GPT-3 is shockingly good—and completely mindless: `https://www.technologyreview.com/2020/07/20/1005454/openai-machine-learning-language-generator-gpt-3-nlp/`

- CuratedAI Sunset Memory: `http://curatedai.com/poetry/she-wears-destruction/`

- Replika: `https://replika.com/`

- CamFind App: `https://camfindapp.com/`

- Breaking new fragrance ground with Artificial Intelligence (AI): IBM Research and Symrise are working together: `https://www.symrise.com/newsroom/article/breaking-new-fragrance-ground-with-artificial-intelligence-ai-ibm-research-and-symrise-are-workin/`

- Chef Watson: `https://researcher.watson.ibm.com/researcher/view_group.php?id=5077`

- INTELLIGENTX: AI BEER: `https://weare10x.com/portfolio_page/intelligentx/`

Part 2 –
Building an AI-Native Product

Understanding what it takes to manage an AI program is a prerequisite when it comes to AI product management. Now that we've covered the basics of that in *Part 1*, we can move on to contextualize the outputs of that AI program in your AI- native product in this second part.

This part consists of five chapters addressing the various relevant areas when going to market with a new product built with AI from the very beginning. We will cover the basics when it comes to creating an AI-native product, productizing the AI/ML service that powers it, positioning that product for various groups, AI/ML options you can take when building, and how that all relates to performance benchmarking, costs, and growth. We'll understand both tactical and strategic considerations when launching an AI/ML- native product by the end of this part.

This part comprises the following chapters:

- *Chapter 6, Understanding the AI-Native Product*
- *Chapter 7, Productizing the ML Service*
- *Chapter 8, Customization for Verticals, Customers, and Peer Groups*
- *Chapter 9, Macro and Micro AI for Your Product*
- *Chapter 10, Benchmarking Performance, Growth Hacking, and Cost*

6

Understanding the AI-Native Product

In this chapter, we will go over the essential components for creating a strategy for building an AI product. This strategy will allow companies a process that will help them succeed in building an AI native tool. In *Chapter 2*, we briefly introduced the new product development stages, and in this chapter, we will build on that structure by focusing on the most important phases of introducing a new AI/ML native product: ideation, data management, research, development, and deployment. We will also address the main contributors to your AI/ML product team, as well as the tech stack that will empower them. AI native products begin and end with your data, and the roles you fill to support the team responsible for their creation will be critical to their success. When building an AI native tool, do your due diligence so that you aren't being wasteful of your company's finances and resources. A bad hire or incorrect tech investment can be costly in both time and resources.

This chapter is primarily for **product managers** (**PMs**), technologists, and entrepreneurs coming into the AI space that want to inherently build AI tools. In this chapter, we will cover the following sections:

- Stages of AI product development

- AI/ML product dream team

- Investing in your tech stack (further expanding on concepts from the preceding infrastructure section)

- Productizing AI-powered outputs—how AI product management is different

- Customization for groups—considerations for verticals and customer groupings

- Selling AI—product management as a higher octave of sales

By the end of this chapter, you'll have a firm understanding of the most important considerations for every stage of your AI product development life cycle, as well as the development of your product team and the tech stack that will support them. You'll also be able to think about some of the differences between traditional product management and AI product management, as well as some of the relevant elements when customizing your product for different audiences and how to craft a message that resonates with them.

Stages of AI product development

Whether your organization is robust enough that you're supporting multiple product teams for various stages of your AI product development or lean enough that you're running on a skeleton crew that will see your product through each stage, you'll want to be cognizant of what these different stages are so that you can define success through each phase. There are various schools of thought on what product management is or should be. We'll do our best here to summarize the various phases in a way that best summarizes the core aspects of AI product development.

Either way, as an AI PM or leader of an AI product, you'll want to consider how your product relates to each of the phases described in the following subsections so that you can identify the phase your product is currently in and what you need to do to bring it to full maturity.

Phase 1 – Ideation

Just as with the traditional software product life cycle, as a PM you'll be involved in the ideation phase. You might see this referred to as the innovation or design phase as well. Whatever you call it, this is the phase where the brainstorming on features is happening, and as a PM, you're a key stakeholder in influencing the direction of the product. This is the phase where you're also weighing the cost/benefit of incorporating various features, as well as the phase where you're identifying what are the non-negotiables for your product.

One differentiator between traditional software development and AI product development in this phase is that the focus on ideation is paramount before continuing because the costs of investing in an AI product are great. Therefore, you want to be heavily focused on this phase before you move on in the product development life cycle. You don't want to be going back to the drawing board after you're in the thick of it with your product only to realize halfway through that you have a better idea of how to leverage AI for your product and have to lose months of work, time integrating a specific tech stack, storage, and expensive headcount.

Ideally, the work in the ideation phase results in getting a picture of what the product will look like using UX mockups/wireframes and surveys, as well as gathering the requirements you need to have in order to properly scope out your MVP. As a PM, perhaps the most important part of your role is understanding what the actual opportunity or problem is you're addressing. This is true from the market perspective as well as the ML perspective.

Where ML is concerned, you're using AI to address six main types of problems:

- Anomaly detection

- Clustering/peer grouping

- Classification

- Regression

- Recommendations

- Ranking

Getting clear on which capital-P problem you're addressing in the market, as well as which ML problem you're solving based on the six competencies will be your most important task as a PM. Everything else is secondary.

As a PM, you'll want to bring everyone together here. Your UX, data architects, data engineers, data analysts, data scientists, ML engineers, backend/frontend/full stack engineers, and leadership team will make up the key stakeholders that you'll want to be involved in this phase so that every voice has a chance to be heard.

By the end of the phase, you should have the following decided:

- What are the outcome/requirements you must have to have a working MVP

- How this MVP will be delivered

- Who will use this MVP

- How they will use this MVP

- A clear understanding of the problem/opportunity you're addressing

Phase 2 – Data management

Once you have a clear idea of what you're building and why, you invest in setting up your product for success. Throughout this book, we refer to AI, ML, and **deep learning** (DL) products, but it's important to remember the original colloquialism for any of these products is this: data product. At its core, any product that leverages AI/ML in any way is a data product first, and no data product can be good at anything without lots of quality, clean data. Organizing and expanding on the infrastructure needed to support all your data is the first applied step post-ideation. You'll want to understand the requirements, constraints, and vocabulary required for a system that supports the data gathering and data processing that will be required to make your AI product function properly because you'll be central in helping make decisions about this.

In this phase, you're also defining the best features to use in your AI/ML models. We discussed feature engineering in previous chapters. As a refresher, this is the idea that you're looking for facets or *features* in your dataset that you're primarily going to use for training your model. You can think of features as the individual columns of data elements that will be most important to include in your model preparation and training. You won't want to leave this up to your data scientists, engineers, and architects either. As a PM, you'll want to be intimately involved with and understand the various features that will be selected as the most relevant and final inputs in training the models that will make up your product.

Once that's been decided, this is the phase where the data pipelines to support this data feed will be put in place. Having a good grasp on how you're setting your organization and product up for sound data collection and preparation, data storage, and data pipeline practices will be crucial in this step as well. These data practices will allow you to leverage data for internal use cases and traditional analytics, and they will also serve as the true foundation of your AI product.

Phase 3 – Research and development

So, you've got your plan, you've got your data organized, and you're ready to start building. In this phase, you're **researching and developing (R&D)** the actual structure and substance that will make up your AI product. R&D can be synonymous with experimentation. You aren't going to build a product around one model, and no matter how intuitive and talented your data scientists or ML engineers are, they likely won't go with the first model that occurs to them either. We've gone over the various ML models in previous chapters, and we've mentioned a few times that most of the time, ensembles of models are what get used in products.

In the *Deployment strategies* section of *Chapter 1*, we introduced the concept of **A/B testing**, which is sometimes referred to as split testing. Essentially, the process is relevant here as well because there will be a fair amount of A/B testing and evaluation in this process, so you'll want to understand the basics of A/B testing as well as data distributions, cohorts, confidence intervals, and other probabilistic concepts. A/B testing is a common testing method used in ML, and if you'd like to get into this topic as it relates to AI/ML products, we recommend this resource: `https://mlops.community/the-what-why-and-how-of-a-b-testing-in-ml/#:~:text=An%20A%2FB%20test%2C%20also,guesswork.`

This phase also means there's a fair amount of experimentation that needs to take place before a model is selected for your specific use case. If you're hiring the most experienced data scientists and ML engineers and you see them going back and forth with different models, seemingly unable to choose and wanting to further experiment until they see performance they can get on board with this is normal. Hiring a talented, knowledgeable, and experienced headcount is only one side of the coin with AI products.

Sure—they have the know-how, but they aren't business experts. They're experts in modeling and creating algorithms that will fit the use case the business experts outline for them. Use the R&D phase as a way to give your data scientists and ML engineers the proper direction, and manage expectations with them. You'll want to properly set these hires up with the proper tools, stakeholders, and resources to make them successful. There are other considerations as well. Let's take the notion of performance.

As a PM, it could be up to you, rather than the data scientists, to decide what level of performance or precision level would be most acceptable for the customers you're trying to serve. Establishing these thresholds and expectations is something you, as the AI PM, will be regularly doing with your team.

Phase 4 – Deployment

We're using deployment as an umbrella term here for everything that comes after the R&D phase. At this point, you've settled on a model or a collection of models that satisfies your products' ideation and MVP requirements, is supported by your data infrastructure, and has been thoroughly tested. Now, you're ready to build the supporting infrastructure to make sure this model and its outputs can be integrated into the broader product that your end users will experience. This is the deployment phase where you're marrying the work of your data scientists and ML engineers to the work of your full stack developers and actually integrating it into the greater product that will support these AI/ML outputs.

Your product may have many *features*, and only a couple of them may be *AI features*, or the very heart of your product could be ML. Regardless of how rooted in AI your product is, you will need to deploy the ML findings from the models you've invested time in building in the context of the greater UI/UX. Because of this integrative dance that has to happen between your AI/ML code and your production code, you might go through your own R&D phase with deployment as well. Selecting the proper ML model and technique is a separate process from selecting the proper way to showcase and use the outputs of that ML R&D and how to maintain those outputs.

The broader context of the deployment phase is really to create continuity and delivery of the substance of your ML outputs. This is also where you'll be creating processes and structure around the continuous maintenance and delivery of your product that were outlined in *Chapter 2*.

Now that we've covered the various phases of the AI product development life cycle, let's focus on the folks that will make the magic happen in the first place: the AI product team. Building a new team for a new AI product is tricky, and it can be tough to adequately hire for the needs your product will have. Every product and company will have different needs, so we will try to remain as objective as possible in this section.

AI/ML product dream team

In this section, we will be spending some time understanding the various roles that will empower your AI product team to maximize success. We'll also be grouping these functions across the stages we outlined in the preceding sections so that we can get a sense of when these roles come into play. Note that not all these roles will be necessary in your organization. Every organization is different and will have different needs. Use your discretion when building your AI teams. You may include other stakeholders in your AI program, but the following is a relatively complete list of the main stakeholders you will want to include in your hiring process as your AI/ML product team grows.

We'll now look at a cumulative list of roles that will likely apply to your ideal AI dream team. We have listed the roles in order of common appearance.

AI PM

Here, we start on our journey of creating a dream team. All organizations are different. Some won't hire PMs until they're further along with building an MVP. Others might hire *founding* PMs. Others might already be mature organizations and are just ready to launch their first AI product. No matter where your organization lies, you will eventually need all the activities required to support an AI/ML product to be centralized into one person.

A product is a living breathing ecosystem in and of itself, so having a point person to go to that can be responsive to and responsible for the needs of various parts of that ecosystem will be important. Because of our own bias, we will place the AI PM firmly at the beginning of this list. Finding someone that's worked with or specialized in AI/ML products in the past will serve as your due diligence for making sure your product is properly set up for success. We consider it ideal to hire for this role before you start hiring for other roles to maintain a cohesive vision across your product. Having an AI/ML PM on board before you begin the implementation of your product means that person is aware of the historical discussions and market influences to support your product best.

AI/ML/data strategists

This will be more of a consultative role for most companies. Ideally, this person would help with the acquisition of talent, along with developing methodologies and workflows that would support your AI/ML function/team in its entirety. This might be a role that you hire for at the start of your AI/ML journey to help with key decisions about who to hire for various roles in your AI program or product team, what should be included in your tech stack, and how certain workflows should be set up with regard to experimentation and deployment.

This may be someone that stays on for the planning and initial phases of your product development (first 6-8 months) or someone that you keep on staff as a PM in more resourced environments. This person will also ideally be well versed in AI ethics principles. If you're a start-up and you're creating a company and a product from scratch, this might be your technical cofounder who is able to act as your technical decision-maker. This role could also be referred to as a data architect role.

Data engineer

We have an architect for how the AI product/program team will function; now, we start laying down the foundations for our data pipelines with a data engineer based on the blueprint that's come out of our collaboration with an AI strategist. If you're setting up an AI product from scratch, look for a data engineer that can help support your team's choices of data engineering philosophies.

Will you be using a data mesh, a data fabric, a data lake, or a data warehouse? Because you're starting this function from the beginning for an AI/ML native product, you'll want to hire someone with the confidence and experience to help guide you with a proper setup. Migrating and changing your data architecture can be expensive and time-consuming. If you get the help you need properly at the beginning, it will save you potential headaches later and give you a sustainable, scalable infrastructure to grow with confidence.

Data analyst

A path for many companies will be to build on an already established foundation of data analytics before they start expanding on those analytics with ML. The traditional order of operations is gaining clarity and control over your data by hiring amazing data analysts first that will quickly figure out what's interesting and worth exploring in the data you already have. In this role, you're looking for someone that's able to quickly analyze your swathes of data with curiosity and exploration.

This is the person that might be your expert query maker, working in concert with your data engineer to feed queries through the workflows you establish to power your AI/ML product. These will also be the hires that will improve on the analytics you use internally to improve internal processes as well as the analytics you pass on to your customers through your product or platform's dashboard UI/UX.

Data scientist

Once you have the ability to generate and move data, you're ready to start experimenting with that data, and you'll eventually need to collaborate with someone that's an expert at model building. In order to be an expert at model building, you have to also be an expert at ML algorithms, big data, statistics, and programming. Most companies are coding in Python, so unless you're serving academic circles, we recommend sticking with Python. This role doesn't just need technical skills—it also needs soft skills because it's a collaborative role, and it also communicates heavily with leadership.

At this point, you're hiring a data scientist to execute the business goals you've established early on. This person should have a strong business acumen and must be able to understand the impact and purpose of their work. They should also have the expertise to technically and functionally realize the algorithmic solution that best fits your organization, data, and product. This role is inherently elusive to fill because finding someone with competence and experience in all these areas proves to be difficult for most organizations, particularly when you're in the early phases of creating a start-up or a product from the beginning.

ML engineer

At this point, you've got a firm handle on your strategy, your data architecture, the capabilities of your customer/product data, and the models you'll be using in your product. Your goals and objectives have been outlined and confirmed by the technical stakeholders on your leadership team. Taking a cumulative approach, by this point you can outsource the execution of this planning-heavy part of establishing your AI/ML product or program. ML engineers are able to use the models and algorithms whipped up by your data scientists by incorporating (coding) them into the workflows or code repository for your product.

Again, because this is a role that will support the AI native product, this role will have the burden of getting in the weeds with your data and algorithms to see what comes out. This person can expect to do a lot of trial and error as they feel their way toward acceptable performance. Your ML engineer will use the data that's been vetted by your data analysts and marry it with the algorithms your data scientists have selected in their work. Nothing really matters until you actually deploy something into production. The act of putting it all together and ultimately deploying the code that supports all the prior functions falls on the applied ML engineer that makes the dream team. Depending on your organization, you might have to make a choice between a data scientist and an ML engineer.

Frontend/backend/full stack engineers

Various manifestations of the preceding five roles exist in many capacities. Your particular organization might not need them all, all at once. But one thing's for sure: no matter how you navigate the previous five roles, you will always need full stack engineering to support the AI/ML work that needs to be done before it's time for deployment. ML engineers are able to add the AI/ML functions to your code base, but you'll need built-out engineering teams to be supporting your product end to end. Your frontend, backend, and full stack engineers will collaborate with your ML engineers and data scientists often for the AI/ML native product.

Structuring these teams so that they're working intimately and have deep trust built between them will be important. Most of the time, any AI/ML product will have plenty of features and needs that don't have anything to do with the AI/ML aspect of your product. You'll need a built-out engineering team that manages the tasks and epics in your sprints outside of the AI/ML function. These are the folks that are going to get you set up with a working MVP of your product that you can iterate on as you continue in your product management journey. You don't have a working product until you're in this phase.

UX designers/researchers

The manifestation of your MVP is your product's starting point. You can't iterate a product that doesn't yet exist, and reaching MVP level allows you a confident start. Depending on your organization and philosophy, you may already have leveraged UI/UX feedback during the planning phases. Perhaps you did have a product designer on board early on, or perhaps you worked with a UX researcher when you were doing your early market reconnaissance. But once you have a working product MVP, you're able to establish a baseline with your users (or beta users) and get a sense of how they're receiving value from your product.

UI/UX is all about how to most efficiently deliver value to your end users. Minimizing sources of frustration and inspiring moments of delight is the primary focus of this function. A good UI/UX designer or researcher will guide the visible changes of your product that your end users will experience. We recommend having this function be an ongoing engagement so that you can learn from your users as you build further iterations of your product that align most closely with what your users—and, by extension, their buyers—will approve.

Customer success

Having proper channels for listening via UI/UX design and research is important, but eventually, your customers will want you to talk back—and not just through the product itself. You might not have a huge need for a customer success team if you're creating a B2C product, but if you're selling an AI/ML product to other businesses, you certainly will. The customer success team exists to make sure your customers are properly using your product and receiving the intended value from it.

They're also a great source of feedback for your data and AI/ML functions. The customer success team offers the feedback loop that an AI/ML product will need to build and improve over time. They're also incredibly helpful at helping to expand on product features and collaborating with products on which potential new features end users might really love to see. If you're an AI/ML PM, make sure you have a warm and open relationship with the customer success team because they're your biggest source of knowledge on the ground. They're the ones actually talking to your customers!

Marketing/sales/go-to-market team

This is another one that will likely be involved at the beginning and throughout your product development journey. We're lumping in sales and marketing as **go-to-market** (**GTM**) because this is essentially what this function does. It communicates out to your market: the entire landscape of your potential customers. This is where you'll combine your skill sets to optimize your product language fit or the message your market will see about your product. You'll be using your GTM meetings to decide on the following:

- Terminology about your product

- How you're going to position it in the market

- How much of your proprietary tech and algorithmic magic you're going to allow your salesforce to discuss with potential customers on demos

- How much explainability you're going to offer

- How you're going to communicate about technical decisions you've made about your product

- How much information about your product you're going to shield from the world in the spirit of competition

As you build and improve your product, your GTM team will stick with you, and you'll be regularly in the flow of discussing how you're going to communicate about upcoming features or releases.

Investing in your tech stack

Understanding the tech stack and languages that will give you the most flexibility is the most important part of beginning your tech stack journey. In this phase, you'll work closely with your data science and data engineering teams to create the proper channels for delivering the relevant data to your models in a reliable way so that all the other stakeholders involved in building your product can trust the infrastructure in place.

Managing ML experimentation is a formidable undertaking in and of itself, and we've seen tools such as MLflow and Weights & Biases used for managing versions and experiments. You can also use tools such as Cloudera Data Science Workbench, Seldon, Dataiku, DataRobot, Domino, SageMaker, and TensorFlow to support your data scientists with a workstation for building, experimenting with, deploying, and training ML models.

As a PM, you're regularly thinking about the value of building something compared to the cost or effort required to build it. This is why you can't ignore your tech stack. It might be tempting to say, well, a CTO can decide on which tech stack to invest in, but it's not so easy to outsource if this tech stack is directly involved with the building of your product in any way. Empowering your stakeholders impacts the effort and cost that goes into your AI product, so you'll want to make sure you're involved in the making of these key decisions.

The biggest consideration in your tech stack is paying attention to properly setting up your infrastructure to handle the scale of your data as your business grows. Building the right tech stack to handle the cleansing, storing, securing, preparing, and monitoring of your data will be the foundation for supporting your AI program or product team. This goes hand in hand with building your data strategy. Beyond this, you'll seek to create a collaborative environment for the many roles in your AI program to participate in. Between the analysts, data scientists, ML engineers, broader engineering team, and any leaders and consultants you include in the formation of your AI team, you'll want to create channels for all these various members to communicate and collaborate.

As is the case with many AI programs, you'll also be looking for ways to automate your processes and workflows. AI/ML technologies are consistently changing and improving, so you'll make a lot of traction when you invest in applying automation for your AI program itself. Use the brainpower of your talented staff to make higher-level decisions and use their complex problem-solving abilities. Anything that can be automated, refreshed, or standardized should be. This aligns with the precepts of agile and lean development. Refactoring and making elegant improvements in your code should be done proactively, so make sure to plan this into your springs responsibly and use the advantages of your tech stack in your favor to set your team up for success.

Having the right process, talent, and tech stack to power your AI product is just the beginning. You're bringing all the necessary elements together to create AI-powered outputs. Those outputs will be integrated into your product somehow in the form of features that your customers will experience the benefit of. The next section will be about understanding how to orient the outputs of your AI/ML program and team in a way that's most evident to your customers.

Productizing AI-powered outputs – how AI product management is different

In this section, we will be exploring the difference between product management for traditional products and product management for AI/ML products. At first glance, it may seem that AI/ML products aren't that different from traditional products. We're still creating a baseline of value, use, performance, and functionality and optimizing that baseline as best we can. This is true for every product as well as for the greater practice of product management, and this won't change just because our product works with AI.

The true differentiator when it comes to AI products is you're essentially productizing a service. Think about it for a moment. In order for AI to work, it has to learn from your (or your customer's) data. Different models might work better on different kinds of data. Different datasets will require different hyperparameters from your models. This is the nature of AI/ML. In a way, this means that you could find yourself in a situation where the way you build and structure your product could even change fundamentally from one customer to another, especially at first when you have very few customers.

What this effectively means is you're understanding how all your customers are benefiting from the AI/ML *service* you're providing your customers and establishing a standard procedure for recreating that process so that all your customers are able to experience the highest benefit. The general advice when productizing a service is first to find a niche or a specific cohort of customers to reach. If you can understand how AI is most helping your customers through your product and you're able to focus on what value means for your customers' success, you've begun the first steps of productizing.

The main focus will then be on how to best structure your product and internal processes so that you're not starting from scratch with every customer. This will be exploratory at first. Perhaps certain models are working better with some customers' data than others. Perhaps there are specific use cases that didn't arise until one of your customers asked for them. The basic idea of productizing is finding something that has value and brainstorming to understand where else you can leverage a previous project, output, or process for the betterment of all. Waste not, want not. If you can recycle something for the benefit of your collection of customers, it will add to the success and collective love your product receives.

Productizing services is a familiar concept in consulting where consultants are working project to project and often have to create new engagements with clients with an almost blank slate. But given that our own minds are pattern detection machines, eventually, we start to see similar requests come in or similar use cases pop up. Creating a repeatable process for certain types of customers, verticals, profiles, or use cases is the very essence of productizing. This is exactly what we're doing with AI/ML products. This is also a way to better anticipate how and why your customers are coming to you and your product specifically so that you know how to share successes and case studies that apply directly to them. The act of productizing will also immensely empower your marketing, sales, customer success, and broader GTM teams.

As we have seen in this section, AI/ML product integration is about finding the balance between the outputs of your models and the use cases or groups those outputs are trying to serve. Many PMs come out of the experience of building with AI/ML finding they may need to customize their product for certain cohorts. In the following section, we're going to address the need for AI customization should it arise.

AI customization

Through the act of productizing, you'll likely start to create groupings or cohorts for your product. You might find that certain models work best for certain kinds of customers and build a structure around that. The act of grouping your offering into use cases and communicating differently or optimally to those cohorts builds on the wisdom gained from productizing. Taking that a step further, you'll then naturally start to verticalize.

Understanding the various considerations for business models, verticals, and special customer groupings will be an important part of how you go to market with your product. For instance, if you're supporting a B2C or consumer product, you'll want to invest more in information gathering by acquiring more of your end users' direct feedback for your ideation phase. Because you'll be creating a product that's going to be experienced by potentially millions of users, you will want a strong handle on the preferences and desires of those end users so that your product is most aligned with the *voice* of your customer. A product such as this could also benefit from experimenting and iterating fast so that you can get a product out and start gathering feedback on it before you're even getting your desired level of performance from the AI/ML models themselves.

If you're supporting B2B or business-facing apps, you might spend more time on the ideation and deployment of that product so that you can zero in on the specific set of customers you're hoping to win over. With business applications, you might be creating a very complex product that does a number of overlapping operations but for a very niche group of users. You might also have a wide variety of well-documented tools that offer similar solutions to your customers, so maintaining feature parity with the market could be more of a factor for this line of products.

The size of your business will also impact how you show up in your organization as an AI PM. For instance, if your organization is large enough, there might be a separate PM allocated to every version of the product cycles mentioned previously. There could also be various PMs that support various aspects of the functionality of your AI product. There could also be a PM that's devoted only to the AI features of the product with a higher-level PM or product director overseeing the entire suite. In a smaller organization, there might be only one AI PM overseeing the entirety of the product throughout all the phases of the life cycle or ideating to continuously maintain that product.

Another differentiation between the sizes of companies lies in the data itself. Depending on how large your company is, the access or quality of the data you have can have varying degrees of difficulty. As a PM, making this data available and in a usable condition could prove more difficult and take up more of your time than it would at a start-up because of having to get access to siloed groupings of data that require administrative governance permissions. Even getting that data to fit together could be tough, depending on the conventions of each silo. Conversely, a start-up might have a hard time even amassing enough users and have issues with data volumes. Data availability and quality are notorious issues for companies big and small.

If you have a highly verticalized product, this could also impact how your work shows up as an AI PM. For instance, having a product that's specialized for healthcare, fintech, or education might necessitate a PM that has domain knowledge and expertise in these different verticals. Even if it's the same PM that's supporting this product for those verticals, you'll likely see it as three different versions of your product because the weights, thresholds, and performance metrics for these specific verticals will likely be drastically different. Depending on the type of product you're offering, you might even see a hyper-specialization to the point where the product is customized heavily even for every customer you have! This might be the case for highly tailored ML products that have to be fit to your clients' data.

Ultimately, the work of building products and crafting them for specific audiences is all about creating a product that sells. We need to be able to understand our audience—the buyers and users of our products—in order to build something that will truly serve them. In the next section, we will discuss the notion of selling and what that means from a product management perspective.

Selling AI – product management as a higher octave of sales

With AI product management, you're selling in a number of ways. There's the traditional sense of selling, which is this: creating a product that your market wants to buy. This is inherent in any traditional PM role. Your understanding of your market, your product, and your salesforce is one where you're confident in the solution you're bringing to market, your solution's performance, and your salesforce's ability to articulate the value of the solution you're building. Then, there's the opportunity and challenge AI presents: the ability to sell the AI functionality itself.

Earlier in this book, we mentioned the difficulty AI/ML projects have in being deployed into production; this happens for a number of reasons, but among the top reasons is the inability to sell the value of AI to the broader organization. This will be incredibly relevant to any PM that's looking to work with AI products because you will have to develop this intuition and ability to sell your product to the outside market as well as to your internal stakeholders and leaders. This is the case whether you work at a large organization or a small start-up.

Part of the work of selling AI within your organization is going to directly correlate with how you empower your teams. If you want to be successful in evangelizing your AI product, we have the following advice:

- Make sure there's alignment on the data strategy and data architecture side. Remember: AI products are data products, and if you don't have sound practices on the data end, you'll have to reverse engineer your data pipelines, and that's not fun. Part of this is also making sure there is a sound data strategy that will grow as your business and product scale to support more users and customers.

- Make sure that you are not focusing so much on the technology and tech stack that you're forgetting about tying the use of that technology to impact. Remind yourself why you want to use AI for your product. What value is it providing your product and, by extension, your organization and customers? No sale is successful without perceived value. People that work in sales understand they need to be successful in communicating the value of their product before you'll open your wallet. You'll have to have the same mentality if you're working in product management. This isn't just relevant for your customers but for your leadership team as well.

- Make sure you're embracing experimentation. As we've said countless times: AI/ML is a highly iterative process. You can't load up your practitioners and the models themselves with expectations and results without first allowing them the space to experiment. Beautiful, miraculous things can happen with AI/ML but first they need to be coaxed through iteration. Flexibility and curiosity will also be important when you're considering various ML models that will support your product as it scales as well.

As with other product roles, the role of an AI PM is vast and requires knowledge and competencies in several areas. Having an understanding of how an AI product is created and brainstormed allows you to meet your market's needs with leading-edge technology. Knowing how to best support the data end of such a product means you are setting up the most integral members of your AI team for success. Allowing your hands-on AI practitioners the space and ownership to experiment and report their findings to you and your leadership creates the proper feedback loop between tech and leadership to see your product flourish. Finally, creating the proper deployment tech stack and process ensures your end users are benefiting from your product in the way you originally intended and gives you the perfect board with which to dive into the day-to-day of iterating on your product until its sunset days.

Summary

The work of a PM is never done. There are always more voices, perspectives, and considerations to take in. Coordinating all the stakeholders, technology, leadership, market analysis, customer feedback, and passion for a product isn't an easy task. In this chapter, we covered the stages of the AI product development life cycle and the various roles that can make up your AI product dream team. We also covered the tech stack that can help that team build a product, and various focus areas to help that product stand out and resonate with the cohorts of groups that will be buying and using your product. Hopefully, this chapter has helped you understand what the most important factors are when you set out to build an AI native product.

As long as you're hiring the right people for the roles you have open in your AI program, doing your due diligence to uncover the right strategy for tech stack adoption, structuring your product in a way that benefits your customers according to their verticals, and working with your leadership and greater GTM team to build a product that meets a need in your market, you'll be set up for success. You're likely to do better than you think.

References

- The What Why and How of A/B Testing in Machine Learning: `https://mlops.community/the-what-why-and-how-of-a-b-testing-in-ml/#:~:text=An%20A%2FB%20test%2C%20also,guesswork`

- TFX: `https://www.tensorflow.org/tfx`

- Seldon: `https://www.seldon.io/`

- Dataiku: `https://www.dataiku.com/`

- DataRobot: `https://www.datarobot.com/`

- Domino Data Lab: `https://www.dominodatalab.com/`

- Cloudera Data Science Workbench: `https://www.cloudera.com/products/data-science-and-engineering/data-science-workbench.html`

- Weights and Biases: `https://wandb.ai/site`

- ML Flow: `https://mlflow.org/`

Productizing the ML Service

In *Chapter 6*, we briefly touched upon the notion of productizing and what that means for AI outputs in the *Productizing AI-powered outputs – how AI product management is different* section. We will be expanding on that concept in this chapter by exploring the trials and tribulations that may come up when building an AI product. Rather than thinking of AI products as traditional software products, it helps to think of them as a service that you're learning to productize. What this refers to is the ability to create a consistent workflow that you can rely on to deliver consistent results in the way traditional products demand.

We will be going more in depth into product management principles and aligning them to the idiosyncrasies of AI/ML services.

By the end of this chapter, we will have an understanding of the following topics:

- Understanding the differences between AI and traditional software products
- B2B versus B2C – productizing business models
- Consistency and AIOps/MLOps – reliance and trust
- Performance evaluation – testing, retraining, and hyperparameter tuning
- Feedback loop – relationship building

Understanding the differences between AI and traditional software products

There are a number of differences between traditional software products and AI/ML products. In the following subsections, we'll first go over how they're similar, and then we'll note the differences between the two to give us a well-rounded sense of what to expect when you're product managing an AI/ML product. This will help us establish a baseline as well as a deviation from traditional PM work. When you're a PM, you're often tasked with being the person to maintain an intuition about your product and how it will grow and evolve through the process of building and shipping the product and working with your engineering team.

Part of that intuition will relate to how you will market and sell your product, what kinds of customer needs and issues your product can anticipate, as well as potential problems that might arise as you start to get into the weeds with building and marketing your AI product. Many PMs might not be aware of the demands AI/ML products will place on them, and this section is primarily aimed at helping PMs build this intuition as they start to navigate the world of AI/ML products.

It's also important to note that traditional software products and AI products are increasingly blurring together. This is because most software companies have already started to integrate AI/ML into their existing products or launched AI native products. PMs that cover a wide variety of products will want to deepen their knowledge of AI/ML as a way to stay competitive within their own fields, whether they plan to go deep into AI or not. Understanding the differences between traditional software and AI products isn't so much about comparing two disparate groups of products. It's helpful in this case as well, but this is a macro trend, and the biggest reason for understanding the two is to anticipate how all products will evolve with AI. Let's begin by checking out how traditional software products are similar to AI.

How are they similar?

There are a number of similarities between traditional software products and AI products because, fundamentally, AI products are traditional software products with a productized AI/ML service built in. For this reason, the similarities we will outline here involve agile product development as well as data. Native AI products, along with the outputs from the AI pipelines that support them, follow the same building process most traditional software products use. They are also built with a heavy focus on the data that powers them. This is still true for traditional software products.

Agile development

In traditional software development, you're going to follow some methodology to ideate, keep track of your work, and stay consistent with some framework or schedule. Most software companies these days don't use waterfall methodology anymore and have instead opted to use some version of agile, scrum, or lean methodology. This means most software companies are using an iterative and experimental approach to building and shipping products. They're taking large overarching business goals and translating those goals into specific tasks that will then amount to deliverables by the end of any given sprint. Once they have these deliverables done, they undergo a process of evaluation to make sure they meet varying expectations through testing.

The heart of this approach is agility. When you're building out features of your product over time, you have time to test those features both functionally and conceptually. This is an economical way of spending time, energy, and resources on a product or a feature to then see how it's received by your customer base and greater market. The agility this offers is what allows tech companies to be successful: they are able to make changes and adjustments as they build if they're seeing that their product or feature isn't resonating with their audience of users. This will be true whether or not your product supports AI/ML features.

We'd even go a step beyond this and say AI/ML takes the heart of this agility to the next level. Because AI/ML products are consistently building from prior manifestations, they're constantly evolving and adapting to new demands on performance, accuracy, or speed. You can't build an AI product in a vacuum. Over time, AI products will have many transformations, and because of this, they're always in a state of being updated or upgraded to meet the expectations of their outputs.

Data

Then there's the similarity of data. Even if certain software products aren't heavily dealing with your personal data, they are often built as data products in the sense that they are leveraging and storing some data about you or the entire user base to some degree to make certain determinations. Traditional software development will have some feedback loop to a database or be built upon a data pipeline of some kind that is passing information back and forth from its UI to some centralized (or decentralized) repository of some kind.

This means that software engineers are working with massive volumes of data in addition to working with source code. We've discussed the data demands AI/ML products have at length over the course of this book, but it's important to note that this is inherently true of most software products out there. Software products are consistently using and accounting for data, whether or not it's a "data" or an "AI/ML" product. Acquiring this data from your initial customers if you're launching a new product is going to be true whether or not you're building an applied AI product. Now that we have looked at how the two are similar, let's check out what differentiates traditional software products from AI.

How are they different?

While AI products are built on a foundation of traditional software development for the most part, they do have a number of key differences you should be aware of as a PM. AI is able to evolve a traditional software product, and you'll hear this referred to as *applied AI* in product circles. What this means is applications of AI outside of a research setting or lab that are used in the building of tech products. Essentially, the concept of putting AI/ML to use, testing and optimizing the models for accuracy and precision, and evolving it over time through feedback loops is what constitutes applied AI.

The following sections will cover the biggest differences between traditional software products and AI products, which surround scalability, profit margins, and uncertainty.

Scalability

One of the major differences between applied AI products and traditional software products is in the area of scalability. Because AI is so specific and sensitive to the quality and peccadilloes of the training data, you're likely going to have issues with scaling this kind of product because you're likely to encounter so many edge cases that you have to go back to the drawing board or start to create cohorts within your user base. This has led to what *AI Forum* (`https://ai-forum.com/opinion/why-commercial-artificial-intelligence-products-do-not-scale/`) refers to as a **collective AI fatigue** from people that are working directly on developing AI but also with leadership and the market at large itself that all stems from the issue of scalability when applied for commercial uses.

This issue lies not just in the challenge AI poses with accuracy; indeed, you need a lot of data for advanced ML and DL models to work well and give you good performance, but you also need those models to be robust enough to work with a generalized population of users, situations, contexts, and locations. In traditional software products, you might not need this level of granularity to see success, but with applied AI products you might get the sense that in a perfect world, you might need a highly personalized model for every user or use case.

This sense might not be that far off from an optimal reality. What this also means is that AI is particularly sensitive to the idea of edge cases, and the threshold for what even constitutes an edge case might be lower for AI products compared to their traditional software counterparts. While edge cases impact all software products, traditional software companies do have an inherent advantage in that they're iterative, so once you build and ship a product, you're able to sell it to virtually all your customers without having to do a lot of customization.

We will go over the differences in business models later on in this chapter, but this issue of scalability is doubly affected by your choice of business model. For instance, if you're a B2B company, your AI product might behave wildly differently when compared to other customers because their training data differences might be too great. If we contrast this with a B2C company, you might be training your models on really representative and diverse data, but then the way your individual consumers interact with your product might vary wildly.

Whether an issue with the training data or the way end users work with your product, the issue is the same: you're having to account for so many perspectives and demands on your product from outside influences that it makes the scaling of the models used almost impossible while keeping with one consistent product build. Even the issue of agreeing on an acceptable level of product performance will likely be time, cost, and energy inefficient, let alone actually acquiring those levels of accuracy you'll need to end up with a product that's consistent enough to sell as an MVP.

Getting to a level of trust where your earliest customers will see the value in your product enough to consistently use it will require a lot of initial work, and you don't have guarantees that this intensive customer acquisition will necessarily dissipate as it might with traditional software products. With applied AI products, the process of acquiring and keeping your customers may stay at a consistently grueling pace, which further contributes to this issue of scalability up to a certain point. Strides are being made, however, to build and discover ways to improve models that are less reliant on massive hoards of data.

According to *AI Forum* (`https://ai-forum.com/opinion/why-commercial-artificial-intelligence-products-do-not-scale/`): *"Data can be expensive to collect, requiring annotation and labelling (by clinicians in healthcare), cleaning, and preparation which can contribute 50% of AI training costs. Consent from data owners (e.g. patients) is needed to use their private data, and additional incentives are sometimes required for data custodians to share the data. Data privacy and security laws can introduce barriers to sharing, storing, accessing and handling the data."*

This reinforces the idea that the quantity of data itself is secondary to the commercial success of scalable AI products compared to the quality and diversity of the training data. It doesn't just need to be standardized in a way that's uniform across your data sample, it also needs to have enough representative data points that encompass the diversity of users as well—the idea being that the more diverse your data is, the more it will be able to anticipate the needs and uses of the general users that will experience it once it is deployed to the greater public.

Access to clean data is easier said than done. Most real-world datasets are riddled with data hygiene issues. Tableau (`https://www.tableau.com/learn/articles/what-is-data-cleaning#:~:text=tools%20and%20software-,What%20is%20data%20cleaning%3F,to%20be%20duplicated%20or%20mislabeled`) offers a great summary of how to solve this: "*Data cleaning is the process of fixing or removing incorrect, corrupted, incorrectly formatted, duplicate, or incomplete data within a dataset. When combining multiple data sources, there are many opportunities for data to be duplicated or mislabeled. If data is incorrect, outcomes and algorithms are unreliable, even though they may look correct. There is no one absolute way to prescribe the exact steps in the data cleaning process because the processes will vary from dataset to dataset.*"

AI/ML products are particularly sensitive to the quality of data, and this is further exacerbated by the issue of deliberate tampering or data poisoning in which end users attack AI/ML systems to intentionally manipulate the training data that powers them.

Profit margins

We've discussed the costs associated with building out an AI organization, which you'll have to do if you're building applied AI products. These costs are some of the biggest differentiators between traditional software products and applied AI products. Because these costs can be so high, they will impact your margins. KeyBanc Capital Markets' 2021 survey of 354 private SaaS companies found that the profit margins for most companies were seeing gross profit margins of 80%, and those margins fell to between 68% and 75% when accounting for customer support/success (`https://onplan.co/blog/what-are-the-net-profit-margins-of-a-saas-company-startup/#:~:text=Based%20on%20a%20KeyBank%20Capital,between%2068%25%20and%2075%25`).

This number falls dramatically for AI products even in the best of circumstances, when companies are running optimally. To paint a picture of what can go wrong, the best example we were able to find came from *Harvard Business Review* (`https://hbr.org/2022/03/how-to-scale-ai-in-your-organization`), which mentioned "*...one financial company lost $20,000 in 10 minutes because one of its machine learning models began to misbehave. With no visibility into the root issue — and no way to even identify which of its models was malfunctioning — the company was left with no choice but to pull the plug. All models were rolled back to much earlier iterations, which severely degraded performance and erased weeks of effort.*" Imagine losing that much money in such a short time and still not being able to know where the problem was!

With that said, there are aspects of applied AI that are more profitable than others. According to *Forbes* (`https://www.forbes.com/sites/forbesfinancecouncil/2020/09/01/ past-the-ai-hype-when-is-ai-actually-profitable/?sh=3fdab9b81fb4`), the area where we see the fastest return on applied AI is when it supports customer behavior, which makes sense because it directly impacts sales and is one of the highest revenue drivers. This would be use cases of applied AI such as product recommendations, scaled pricing algorithms, or advertising personalization/optimization that are bringing in more traffic to your website or helping customers with choosing more products based on their specific spending and purchasing habits, cost consciousness, or tastes and preferences.

The more medium-term payoff of applied AI is when AI is used to improve a product or make a user's experience better in some way. This could look like product automation that boosts users' productivity. For most of this book, we've been talking about these applications of AI because they directly impact an individual product and its performance. As a PM, this is likely the primary area you are focused on when it comes to applied AI and where the best place for it to fit is as far as your product's performance and standing with customers and with your greater market is concerned. Because this essentially poses a medium-term payoff, and because your AI costs will be front-loaded for the most part, you'll have to manage expectations with your engineering, leadership, and customer-facing teams from both a revenue and performance perspective.

Finally, the most long-term payoff of applied AI is when it affects the reputation of the company. This means AI is applied in a way that boosts a company's trust reputationally, particularly when compared to its competitors and peers in the same space. But acquiring this level of AI supremacy is time intensive, and it sheds light on the double-edged sword of AI. Eventually, your competitors will catch on and will pay to play in your arena as well. This is the nature of competition, and as PMs, we understand that our products are scrutinized in the market, and rightly so.

That being said, these areas of profitability aren't exactly siloed. The short-term advantages of AI that we just discussed can also bleed into this area if your product specializes in marketing, recommendation systems, or advertising, for instance. The long-term advantages of AI that we discussed next can also apply to integrating applied AI into your product if what the premium AI offers your product is so great that it impacts your reputational standing in your chosen market or vertical. As a PM, technologist, or entrepreneur, you're going to have to grapple with the costs AI poses as well as its advantages and create a plan for how you want to start leveraging applied AI.

As you're getting started, one of the best ways to do this is to first understand the benefits AI can offer your product and company at large and then draft your own version of this plan and pitch it to your leadership. Communicating the effectiveness of AI and your understanding of how it will impact profitability will help you gain credibility in your own organization, and it will offer an avenue for your stakeholders to be able to understand the challenges and opportunities and ultimately contribute to the plan.

Once you have this plan, you can start keeping track of the relative profitability of the various areas AI is applied to and have champions/supporters within your organization that help keep visibility of AI. If you can all agree on a specific appetite for AI spending and margin threshold tolerance, it will be easier to navigate the AI waters as you continue down your applied AI journey because it will force you to invest in AI in cases where there's data, economic returns, and excitement to keep it going. And it will keep your finance team happy.

Uncertainty

The last big difference is conceptual. AI introduces a whole lot of uncertainty to the work of product management. With traditional software products, the deterministic qualities of a product are hardcoded. Algorithms still exist, but they're not improving or learning over time. They are static. With AI products, these qualities are more fluid. There's a level of expectation setting and performance that has to be agreed upon, expressly or intuitively, by the builders and users. If that level of performance doesn't happen because the models aren't trained enough, they have to be trained more. If performance doesn't come no matter how much training you throw at it, you might not have a product to sell at the end of the day! This level of uncertainty is cushioned in traditional software because your performance goals aren't quite the moving target they are when you're building an AI product.

Where ML is concerned, you're bound to have some level of error because, as we know, no model is going to be perfect. You will always need more data to get better performance. Collectively with your leadership, customers, and engineering team, you will come to understand where the threshold of accuracy needs to lie. It will be different for every product and every use case. The output from one model based on a certain training dataset might be great one day, but if you diversify the training set and retrain, it's probable you won't get the results you're expecting. It's very hard to exactly recreate and test these products, and keeping an experimental attitude when it comes to managing how you are testing, deploying, and maintaining versions will be essential. It's also hard to know whether your models will most improve because of the type of model you've chosen, the training data selected, or the features you've selected.

You also don't know how much time, how many resources, and how much data you need, which makes it really difficult to actually plan your roadmap and keep a sense of time in the way you might be used to if you've worked with traditional software products. If you've been a PM before, that last sentence might raise some eyebrows. Yes, indeed: AI products are even more difficult to forecast! Finding the right balance of factors might take days, weeks, or months. With AI, it might not be until you're well within the weeds of building that you start to grasp the complexity of your scope. This poses a great challenge to your leadership team, which might be interested in more concrete answers about the length of time you need. AI introduces so many factors of uncertainty to keep track of, which is why it's so important to find a leadership team that gets this and supports you because the journey is riddled with doubt.

All in all, AI is here to stay, and it's going to be a surrounding theme as we head into the 2030s. The promise and opportunity of AI continue to grow as we see companies applying AI in new and innovative ways, and our guess is as the decade continues, we will see more inspired ways for companies to benefit from AI adoption. Companies investing in and building AI native products today will be setting themselves up for success for decades to come if they survive. The key is surviving.

We bring up the differences between AI products and traditional software products here because we want everyone that has the investment and will to create AI products to be set up for success. If you can anticipate potential hurdles as you're building a novel product, you can better prepare your teams for surmounting them as well. PMs will always be tasked with managing product stakeholders, mapping problems to solutions in their products, scrutinizing their data analytics and insights, communicating, and deciding on acceptance criteria that will hold their products' performance, as well as the accountability, explainability, and ethics of their products. These areas need to be nurtured whether you are supporting an AI product or not, and it's all part of your evangelism work as a PM.

Now that we've discussed some of the similarities and differences between traditional software products and AI products, let's turn our attention to how AI/ML products are positioned and built according to their business models. Creating products for a B2B business model is different from creating products for a B2C business model. Let's get into some of those differences in the following section.

B2B versus B2C – productizing business models

When it comes to building and shipping products, some of the biggest differences between B2B and B2C business models include domain knowledge and the degree of experimentation. In this section, we'll be focusing on those two areas because they have the biggest impact on what productizing looks like for AI/ML products between these two business models. If we expand on the notion that AI/ML products behave more like services, the desired end result of both these business models will be different because they serve different kinds of customers and different overall needs.

With B2B products, there's a strong need for these products to demonstrate a high degree of domain knowledge and a focus on that. Since B2B products are often serving a proven business niche, they must often prove they have expertise in this niche and have studied it thoroughly enough to be able to deliver on a need. With B2C products, we see a focus on experimentation because rather than tapping into a business need that already exists, these products are looking to tap into a more collective need that their own customer base may not yet be aware they have. This requires a high degree of experimentation. In the following sections, we will build on these ideas further.

Domain knowledge – understanding the needs of your market

For starters, in B2B products, domain knowledge reigns supreme. This is because the use cases are incredibly specific, and the products themselves solve niche business problems that are specific to certain industries and domains. In order for a PM to be effective in the B2B space, they need to be intimately connected to their customers' needs, workflows, and major pain points because their products solve very specific use cases. This isn't to say PMs in this space have to come from the specific industry they're serving, but they do need to invest a significant amount of time in building empathy with their user base in order to be effective.

This time-intensive process can look like a number of things: conducting customer interviews, keeping up with industry trends, and understanding the competitive landscape and the benefits and features their competitors are serving their own customers are all part of this work toward building credibility in the space their product is competing in. This is all preliminary work of understanding the various types of users their product will serve as well. You're setting yourself up for success if you're a PM in this space and you're spending time on establishing clear buyer and user personas and making sure you have a handle on what their individual needs, problems, and "jobs to be done" are.

The expectation threshold of B2B customers is high because this space is likely riddled with a large number of competing products to choose from. In many cases, these customers are undergoing various rounds of **Requests for Proposals (RFPs)** and in-depth **Proof-of-Concept (PoC)** processes to make sure they are purchasing the right product for their use case. For an AI/ML product, these PoCs can be costly for your organization because you'll need to acquire a large enough sample from your customers, use that data to train your models, and present your product and its capabilities to them once its performance is at an acceptable level to be able to show to your prospective customers.

This means there are often many eyes on these products, and each of those pairs of eyes may come with its own set of expectations and objections to your product, so you really need to be aware of multiple perspectives when building B2B products. This also means that as you build, you're planning your release schedules with the idea that every release may include features that could impact your customers' individual workflows, so you often have to be mindful of how often and how loaded your release rollouts into production are.

This domain knowledge is then built up to the point where you as a PM and your broader organization as a whole then become thought leaders in the space they're serving. Because the professional landscape is a small world, once a product—along with its leadership team—does make a splash, it will trickle across the professional world. Building credibility internally and externally is foundationally proportional to the level of industry expertise that's acquired.

This further reinforces that the expectations of an AI/ML B2B product are quite high. Your users and buyers will scrutinize you on the tech stack that's supporting your AI product as well as its performance and accuracy and will want to have evidence of explainability and why your product works. This will all be happening in conjunction with them testing and trialing other AI/ML solutions that are out there to compare them. This also means that you will have to be incredibly intentional about your releases to make sure there aren't any lags in performance when you do make your push to production, with the full knowledge that other businesses are relying on your product.

Expectations are to be managed at every stage of the customer journey. B2B products exist in a massive ecosystem, and companies that use one product might pass outputs from that product to other workflows or to their own customers. This places a premium on B2B companies to maintain their company's and product's reputation and be more transparent about their marketing efforts, and introduces a lot more strain on AI/ML product teams to shy away from black-box algorithms and sell products that can stand by their determinants. B2B company customers have a tremendous amount of leverage because the stakes are high all around, and B2B products benefit from having engaged customers that want to see a certain level of performance from their products.

Experimentation – discover the needs of your collective

With B2C products, because there isn't such a hyperfocus on the domain you're serving, the pressure on the market you're serving is a bit more relaxed, but this creates another kind of pressure: the pressure to build a product that appeals to a much wider audience universally. Casting a wider net brings other areas into focus. As a PM building in a B2C environment, you're going to approach your product and the market it serves more experimentally and derive insights about what's most useful to your customers by tracking how they use your product. You can conduct focus groups, nurture beta testers, or interview your customers through in-product surveys, but because you can't conduct customer interviews in the way you might for a B2B product, you're left with understanding your customers' impressions of your product through their in-product behaviors.

This business model also consolidates all your user and buyer personas in one because, typically, the person that's using your product is also the person buying it. Understanding the main drivers, desires, hopes, and dreams of your customer base becomes a very nebulous task because what you're trying to capture are underlying needs, pain points, and moments of delight that will apply to all your users at once. This complicates a PM's ability to empathize with their end users. Because most of these users aren't signing the kind of year-long contracts you see with B2B products, the pressure to keep these consumers charmed is constant because they can leave at any point. This puts pressure on product, leadership, and development teams to consistently be providing their customer base reasons to stay and choose them.

Because of the bird's-eye view B2C products enforce on their builders, this means PMs have to be very discerning with their data analytics and metrics. Investing in understanding their customer lifetime value and customer acquisition costs and tracking those metrics is an important part of staying profitable and sustainable in the B2C landscape. B2C offers PMs an easy outlet for applying AI/ML toward the acquisition and retention of customers since they have such few touchpoints with the end users of their product. PMs in the consumer space also need to hone in on the demographic and individualistic qualities of their consumers to better understand what to build. If you see that it's mostly people within a geographic area, gender, generation, or subgenre that appeals most to your product, you might start to build future features and releases in your roadmap with them in mind.

We've mentioned many times that AI/ML products are experimental in nature because you want to leverage AI/ML in ways that will impact your product most obviously for it to be worth the top-heavy investment it requires. This is doubly true for B2C products because you're building and using AI to deliver something that saves your consumers money or delights them, as well as using the data your product produces to decide on how to pivot your product. B2C PMs are reliant on data and analytics to make global decisions about their products on a regular basis. Although this is changing for the most part, traditionally in the B2B space, your marketing efforts are most oriented toward your buyers because they're the ultimate decision-makers. This is sharply contrasted in the B2C space because your marketing efforts are directly linked to collective information you can derive and infer from your data.

Experimentation is fun to a point, but at the end of the day, it has to deliver. By far the greatest pressure this places on AI/ML consumer products is the pressure to perform well, maintain their enormous user base, and keep their consumers happy. This means that consumers want to use an app that does what it says it's going to do in a way that's visually appealing. Because they aren't as concerned with the downstream risks of using your product as B2B customers are, consumers don't particularly care why it's working, just that it does work. This means that the issue of explainability is minimized in the B2C space, and the use of black-box or DL algorithms is less scrutinized.

B2B and B2C business models come with their own blend of challenges, but at the end of the day, players in both business models must understand their customers enough to create products that actually bring them value. Once you've built something of value for your customers, you enter a new phase. This next phase is about delivering that value consistently enough to not only win customers but keep them in the long run. In the following section, we will take a look under the hood to understand the necessary elements of delivering value consistently with the help of **ML operations** (**MLOps**) or **AI operations** (**AIOps**). Both will be used interchangeably in this book.

Consistency and AIOps/MLOps – reliance and trust

Maintaining trust, reliance, and consistency within your internal product teams as well as with your customer base is an act of committing to a specific ritual. Ritualizing the acquisition of clean data, tracking the flow through your infrastructure, tracking your model training, versions, and experiments, setting up a deployment schedule, and monitoring pipelines that get pushed to production are all part of the necessary work that needs to be done to make sure there's a handle on the comings and goings of your AI/ML pipeline. This ritualizing is what's referred to as MLOps or AIOps. In this section, we will explore the benefits of AIOps/MLOps and how they help you stay consistent.

If you're managing an ML pipeline, you will need to learn how to depend on an MLOps team and set up your team for success. You don't want to get caught losing $20,000 in 10 minutes (as we saw in our *Profit margins* section earlier in this chapter) and have no leads for where the problem is stemming from. At the very least, you should have some idea where the problem is stemming from. MLOps is able to help with creating and managing the ML pipelines themselves, scaling those pipelines, and moving sensitive data at scale. Ultimately, the risks of compromising your customers' reliance on and trust in your product are great. MLOps' greatest contribution to your business is maintaining the consistency needed to build an AI/ML product that lasts.

We've spoken at length in this chapter about productizing and what that looks like in different contexts of AI product management, but MLOps is actually where the productizing functionally happens. Taking a service and splitting that service apart into smaller pieces that are managed and standardized into reproducible and regulated segments is the work of "productizing," and in that vein, MLOps is really the vehicle we use to truly productize AI/ML. In order to build the consistency and credibility customers can expect from your product, the ritual of MLOps needs to be cemented into your process. You never know when you'll need to revert to a specific version of your models or zero in on an experiment that had the right mix of factors. MLOps creates the organization and focus your team needs to have in order to have a handle on such a wide variety of experiments.

Now that we've covered some of the benefits of creating an MLOps organization to help keep track of your AI/ML pipeline, let's explore how to build on that pipeline and evaluate the state of the models used. In the following section, we will reiterate some concepts around testing, retraining, and hyperparameter tuning to ensure your AI/ML pipelines are routinely being refreshed and optimized for performance.

Performance evaluation – testing, retraining, and hyperparameter tuning

MLOps helps us with accentuating the importance of retraining and hyperparameter tuning our models to deliver performance. Without having a built-out AI/ML pipeline that validates, trains, and retrains regularly, you won't have a great handle on your product's performance. Your MLOps team will essentially be made up of data scientists and ML and DL engineers that will be tasked with making adjustments to the hyperparameters of your model builds, testing those models, and retraining them when needed. This will need to be done in conjunction with managing the data needed to feed this testing, along with the code base for your product's interface as well.

In addition to testing and validating the models and working to clean and explore the data, MLOps team members also traditionally do software testing such as code tests, unit testing, and integration testing. In many cases, your AI products will effectively be traditional software products that incorporate AI/ML features in a subset of a greater ecosystem that's in line with traditional software development. This means that MLOps may, in many cases, ensure your greater product is working functionally along with the AI/ML deliverables and outputs.

Another major area MLOps is well suited to minimize the risk of is the concept of data drift and system degradation. We covered a few different types of drift in earlier chapters of this book, but we'd like to reiterate here that this is a risk that can sneak up on you. Model degradation can happen for a number of reasons. Perhaps there are differences between assumptions that are made with the data in training and in production. Perhaps there's been a change to the data itself. Perhaps there are unseen biases in your training data that were never picked up on. Whatever the reason, continuous monitoring of models in production by MLOps will be your best defense in picking up on these nuances and changes in AI/ML outputs so that the risks from any number of issues within the ML pipeline are minimized as much as possible.

In *Chapters 1* and *2* of this book, we covered the concept of continuous maintenance, which consists of **Continuous Integration (CI)**, **Continuous Deployment (CD)**, and **Continuous Testing (CT)**. These basic areas of MLOps are mirrored in DevOps, which is common to traditional software development. The main differences are that in MLOps, CI isn't just about testing and validating code—it's also about validating and testing the models, data schemas, and the data samples themselves. Another difference is that CD isn't just about deploying a software package but about nurturing an automated ML pipeline deployment process that's optimized for deploying the model prediction service or for automatically scaling back to an earlier version if there is trouble ahead. Finally, CT isn't just about testing software packages themselves but about retraining and testing the models that are actively being relied upon.

In this section, we've built on the idea of building consistency in how we manage our AI/ML pipelines and reinforced the importance of maintaining high standards in the performance of our AI/ML pipelines. This shouldn't be viewed as a nice-to-have but rather a need-to-have. The performance and quality of AI/ML models can suffer for many reasons, so this consistent practice of scrutinizing performance is meant to ensure your product's performance doesn't come at the risk of the trust you've built with your developers and customers. In the following section, we'll be discussing the importance of maintaining strong relationships, whether they're internal or external.

Feedback loop – relationship building

Continuously monitoring and reinforcing the legitimacy of a complicated system such as an AI/ML pipeline is all in service of the ultimate goal of building relationships that last. Relationships between your company and customers, your development team and your sales team, and your MLOps team and your leadership team are all forged through this work of building and going to market with your AI/ML native product. In AI/ML products, the feedback loop is everything. Nurturing a strong relationship with the builders of these products and the customers they serve is the underlying work of the PM. **Productizing** is the process of taking a service, process, skill, or idea and finding a way to present that to the greater market. Many layers of work go into accomplishing this well, but at its most basic level, this work is really just an elaborate feedback loop.

We haven't discussed marketing much in this chapter, but this will also be an integral part of maintaining this feedback loop. Finding the right words to use to describe your product and reach your audience (also known as product language fit) will be a big part of productizing. You will have to create marketing collateral, advertisements, and sales scripts that will all convey the value the product you're building with AI/ML will have for your customers and end users. Building product collateral and expressing that through your various marketing and sales channels will go a long way toward level-setting expectations with your customers.

As we've seen earlier in this section, customers come with expectations, whether they're business users or consumers, and it's the task of the AI/ML PM to take those expectations and deliver something that aligns with them. Understanding the risk and promise of AI/ML and how it compares and contrasts to traditional software development, understanding the challenges and opportunities in your business model, translating all that to reproducible, repeatable tasks internally, and demonstrating consistency with your product's performance in a way that aligns with your customers' expectations is the work of productizing the AI native product. You'll know you've successfully done this when you have a loyal customer base that wouldn't dream of parting with you.

Summary

The act of productizing involves taking a concept, a service, or a piece of technology and developing it into a commercial product that's suitable for the customers you're looking to attract. As we've seen throughout this chapter, this work isn't just a matter of getting your product up and running and creating a landing page for your potential customers to magically find. Productizing involves critically understanding the business model you're working in and the ultimate audience you're building for. Remember that AI products can be thought of as AI/ML services that are being built into traditional software products. This means that another big part of productizing for AI products involves the standardization and ritualization of the AI/ML service in a way that's repeatable and predictable for the internal operations teams as well as the customers that will come to rely on your product.

If you're able to understand your market, build internal structures to make sure there's consistency with the outputs of your AI/ML pipelines, and communicate that consistency through your marketing efforts, as well as the ongoing performance of your product, you've successfully productized. But productizing may not be enough. Depending on the specifics of the market you're serving, you might have to customize your product even further for specific use cases, verticals, customer segments, and other peer groups. Because AI/ML model performance is so dependent on training data, there might be collections of data that perform differently when run against one model. Further specialization might be in order. If you find this applies to your product and market, read on to *Chapter 8*, where we will build on the concept of customization.

References

- Past The AI Hype: When Is AI Actually Profitable?: `https://www.forbes.com/sites/forbesfinancecouncil/2020/09/01/past-the-ai-hype-when-is-ai-actually-profitable/?sh=3fdab9b81fb4`

- How to Scale AI in Your Organization: `https://hbr.org/2022/03/how-to-scale-ai-in-your-organization`

- What are the net profit margins of a SaaS company/startup?: `https://onplan.co/blog/what-are-the-net-profit-margins-of-a-saas-company-startup/#:~:text=Based%20on%20a%20KeyBank%20Capital,between%2068%25%20and%2075%25`

- Guide To Data Cleaning: Definition, Benefits, Components, And How To Clean Your Data: `https://www.tableau.com/learn/articles/what-is-data-cleaning#:~:text=tools%20and%20software-,What%20is%20data%20cleaning%3F,to%20be%20duplicated%20or%20mislabeled`

- Why Commercial Artificial Intelligence Products Do Not Scale: `https://ai-forum.com/opinion/why-commercial-artificial-intelligence-products-do-not-scale/`

8

Customization for Verticals, Customers, and Peer Groups

In this chapter, we'll understand how products evolve and segment themselves across **verticals**, **customers**, and **customer peer groups**. The purpose of this analysis is to understand how you can start to think of product management's role in orienting **artificial intelligence** (**AI**) products for specialized groups and, ultimately, what AI allows you to do for those groups. **AI** and **machine learning** (**ML**) are powerful tools but have a general power that needs to be applied specifically in order for their value to be fully understood. In many ways, the work of a **product manager** (**PM**) is to make that value as obvious as possible to everyone, from customers to developers.

The role of a PM incorporates a lot; it's multifaceted by nature. You're involved with designing the product, organizing the workflow as that product evolves, analyzing feedback from your customers, incorporating that feedback into your overarching business goals, researching new methods and improvements, building the greater product strategy that aligns with your company's strategy, and, ultimately, communicating across all levels to all your stakeholders, developers, and leaders. This requires a lot of understanding, intimacy, and commitment to your product and its success!

When you incorporate the role of a PM into an AI PM, you've got a few more areas to consider. You'll want to understand the options you have in terms of ML algorithms and data models, as well as understanding how AI will move the needle as far as your acceptance criteria and key metrics are concerned. You'll also want to have an understanding of data privacy and AI ethics to make sure you aren't building something that might cause harm to any of your customers or the greater business down the line.

Above all, the role of an AI PM will require a level of data fluency and literacy. Gaining an intuition about how to use data, how to apply data to specific use cases, and understanding a bit about statistics and the data models themselves will be crucial to making sure you've got enough of an understanding to be confident as an AI PM. This area is, in many ways, a prerequisite to being able to start your AI PM career. As an AI PM, you'll be working with data heavily. Critical thinking and complex problem-solving will be necessary to build a successful product that best aligns with the specific use case for your AI product. As the chapter continues, we'll be exploring the most common use cases, domains, verticals, and peer groups that AI is leveraged in.

The topics we will cover in this chapter are as follows:

- Understanding domain spaces and how AI can be optimized for these domains

- Fluency with various verticals that are seeing a high saturation of AI products

- Understanding user behavior analytics

- Optimizing value metrics for AI products

- Learning from peers in your space through thought leadership and consultancy

Domains – orienting AI toward specific areas

When discussing **domains**, there are really two major domains you'll want to invest significant time establishing credibility in. The first is in *understanding AI concepts* themselves, which we've already covered extensively throughout this book so far. The second is in *understanding how AI is helping certain domains achieve success*. Considering that the part of the book we're in is focused on building an AI-native product, we will focus on how an AI PM can achieve this as they're setting out to build a new AI product.

Depending on the industry you're in, you're going to want to understand your space well enough that you have an understanding of who your direct and indirect competitors are. This might be more straightforward or not, depending on the space you're working and competing in. Gartner has a great tool called **the magic quadrant**. The four areas of the quadrant are as follows:

- **Leaders**: Established players in a market that have been most reliable and prevalent. They demonstrate the most complete vision as well as the highest ability to execute.

- **Challengers**: Newcomers that are threatening the dominance of leaders in a given market. Their completeness of vision isn't quite where it is for leaders, but they are able to compete on execution.

- **Visionaries**: This group has a lot of vision but their ability to execute is limited, so they're competing with leaders but they're not able to execute quite as quickly or comprehensively.

- **Niche players**: This group is able to focus on a limited amount of use cases and serve that select group quite well. They're not expanding their product suite to meet a higher vision, nor are they aggressively trying to execute to gain a higher market share. They're happy in their niche.

As an AI PM building a novel AI product in your space, you'll want to have an understanding of all four kinds of competitors in your chosen space or domain. The four quadrants themselves are built on an x axis based on the completeness of vision, and a y axis based on the ability to execute. We're not able to share the visuals of this here in this book but we encourage you to use Gartner's magic quadrant as a resource when evaluating your organization's placement in your own market, as well as the placement of your biggest competitors. Your ability to gauge where you fall along these fault lines will best prepare you for coming to market with a new AI product, particularly now that so many AI products are still in their early days.

When building the AI-native product, a lot of initial work needs to go into ideating and positioning your product because it's so new and it's entering a new market. In the following sections, we will be focusing on the work of positioning a product appropriately for your market, understanding how your product design will actually serve that market, and how to build an AI product strategy that will make the most sense for your market.

Understanding your market

For any specific domain, the leaders are demonstrating a proven history of executing based on the most complete vision. These guys can show you what's been working and what needs the main market players in the domain are predominately addressing. This will be valuable for you to get a sense of what the addressable market actually wants out of the companies that serve them. Leaders are also great for showing their domains what a sustainable execution of domain pain points looks like, as they've been around for a long time and fellow PMs can learn from the products they've released and how the greater market has received them over the years. Leaders offer a great foundation for research when you're in a new domain as a PM.

Though challengers in the quadrant show less of a complete vision, they're able to address the needs of their market well enough to take some of the market share away from leaders. This is a helpful dynamic to understand when you're thinking about your own product. If challengers are able to take a market share from the leaders in their domains, it means there are potential fault lines to tap into. Those fault lines are areas where leaders are not addressing the needs of their market adequately and the most successful challengers are able to find opportunities in those fault lines.

At this point, the leaders and challengers may or may not be suiting up their products with AI capabilities, but understanding these two major groups will help you see where there may be potential opportunities as you're ideating or thinking about building a product to address some common issues or persisting areas of weakness in your domain.

Niche players are not overachieving in the completeness of their vision nor their ability to execute, but it's exactly what gives them their superpower, as the niche players are able to show you where the edge cases might be. This could help you potentially identify features or use cases for your product as you're building and designing that have some proven success. These edge cases might be so niche that the challengers and leaders themselves don't find them strategic to build into their existing product suites, but for an emerging product, this knowledge could be valuable. Getting an understanding of what niches exist within your domain will show you where there might be latent areas of growth that are currently untapped or underserved.

In the final category, we have the visionaries. These are the players that have a robust vision for their product suite and, likely, their entire domain. Visionaries are able to show you what's possible from a product in your chosen domain and will likely include some of the most cutting-edge features you're likely to find in your space. As an AI PM, you'll see most of your direct competitors here because AI features are still slow to adopt in most domains, and we would wager that most of these players are starting to experiment with AI capabilities.

If you're getting started in AI in your domain, and you have the privilege of being involved with your product strategy from the very beginning, understanding the emerging visionaries in your domain will be a great place to start. Today's visionaries may be tomorrow's leaders, so you'll want to get cozy with the names in this category for your chosen domain.

You can do your own market research but either way, you're going to want to have some sense of the landscape that makes up your domain so that you understand your competition, the problems they're trying to solve, and the customers that are in your domain as completely as possible. Working with your marketing team or building a comprehensive understanding of your competitive landscape is a crucial layer to building your AI-native product. In order to build something of value, you have to build something that addresses the deepest customer pain points you're trying to solve with AI.

Beyond the pain points themselves, your product will also begin to collect customer data. This means that you're not just building a product that addresses your customers' problems; you're also improving how your product functions with the data your product is collecting from your customers. We will talk about this specific point further in our UEBA section, but for now, keep in mind that understanding how much and what kind of customer data to collect, in addition to how to use that customer data, will be part of the work you need to do while doing the market research to fully understand the market you're looking to serve.

Again, this will be a prerequisite for ideating on the early stages of your product design and strategy.

Understanding how your product design will serve your market

After you feel like you understand the domain, the major players, the way they're leveraging AI, and some of the main customer pain points you're looking to solve in your chosen domain, you're going to be ready to start to ideate on your product. This will come with a whole slew of activities. Before all the wireframing, building version one of your product strategy, and coming up with a roadmap, you're going to want to be really clear on why you're using AI to address this market. Building an AI product to address your market without having a clear understanding of why it takes AI to solve this problem is an easy way to waste the money you worked hard to raise.

Yes, there's a market splash and many start-ups embrace AI for the funding alone, but this alone will not have enough substance to get you through the stages of responsibly building an AI product that will perform well in your market. Before you go out and build an amazing product that solves all your customers' problems with the power of AI, you will need to solve the fundamental question of *Why AI?*

Once you have a clear idea of why you're using AI to solve your customers' issues, you have the building blocks of your marketing message. Because we're at an integral time for AI products, just coming to market with AI features is enough to put you in the position of having to evangelize AI in your domain. Sure, some industries and domains are seeing lots of AI features already, as we will cover in the next section, but by and large, you'll likely be among the first so this question of *Why AI* will keep coming up from your customers, from your competitors who insist their product is superior, or from your design and building team internally.

As you begin to ideate, you will need to keep this answer, along with your customers' major problems, at the front of your mind so that you're remaining customer focused and dedicated to your message. As you build through the initial versions of your product, always keep asking how AI is helping you solve your customers' most frustrating and integral needs. As a PM, you're an energy-generating force within your company. This means that your work of ideating and building a solution that works for everyone is also meant to stimulate your leadership team. Keeping your focus on *Why AI*, as well as the primary problems of the customers you're serving, means you're keeping your leadership team focused as well.

Keeping your leadership team, **go-to-market** (**GTM**) marketing/business development/sales team, and development team aligned toward your customers and the AI solutions you're bringing to the table means you're helping your entire stakeholder team focus on your main goal, which is to build an AI product that best addresses your market's needs. This seems like an obvious point, but as many PMs know, once you get started with the day-to-day work of building and evolving a product through your various sprints, losing sight of your main goal is easier than it seems. There are so many specialized skills that an AI PM needs, so keeping this focus is important when you start getting into the weeds with your design, choose which AI algorithms to go with, and so on.

Building your AI product strategy

Once you've done the work on designing a product that addresses your customers' and the market's major pain points you want to solve with AI, you're then in a position to start to build out your overarching product strategy. Obviously, your product MVP will start somewhere but after that, there needs to be a course for your product vision to grow toward. Remember that completeness of vision was one of the *x* axes in the Gartner magic quadrant? The reason for this is that an addressable market has a variety of needs ranging in complexity. Your product MVP will only solve a small fraction of these needs. Your leadership and company goals will likely not be to solve all the needs of your market, but you will need to work with your leadership team to define what you're looking to do for your market at large, as this will directly inform your product strategy.

Remember, building a product strategy falls on the PM but creating company goals falls on leadership, so in many ways, you can consider your leadership team as offering you the crucial outputs (the company goals) you need to build a robust product strategy, vision, and roadmap that aligns with your company's business objectives. Once you can take these overarching company goals and turn them into a product vision, strategy, and roadmap, you're able to communicate this to your development team and start the work of building the actual product, which will result in an MVP all the stakeholders involved can be proud of that satisfies the minimum solution needed for your company to go to market with your product.

In order to build a product strategy and vision that can grow with your market, you will need to see how your market has been changing and have as complete an understanding as you possibly can to look at where this market is headed. Countless articles come out every day about the trends for particular industries and domains. As an AI PM, it's even more important for you to keep ahead of these articles so that you have a clear picture of how your market is changing and evolving. Many of your internal stakeholders, along with your customers, will be looking to you for thought leadership and communications about how your company or product suite is growing with the market. Staying aware of these market trends, particularly as they align with your AI strategy, will be necessary for you to keep maturing your product strategy responsibly in a robust, evolving, unpredictable world.

Nowadays, specific domains can have hundreds or thousands of competitors in the space. Particularly now that so many start-ups can erupt and work remotely first, we're seeing a growing number of companies coming into virtually every domain. Being able to communicate your company's offering in a way that meets your customers where they are, using the technical language or jargon they're familiar with, and being able to show them why your product is the best choice through AI will be your challenge and opportunity as an AI PM.

While we will be going over some of the common use cases as we continue with this chapter, we do want to stress one important point before we complete this section: AI is incredibly customizable. Its basic building blocks are data, and what you choose to do with that data is really what gives AI the power it possesses. If you're an eager, talented PM in the AI space and you're passionate about solving your customers' major problems through a novel product you're helping build, you can build something highly customizable to your customers' specific needs.

That's what the next decade will show us as we look toward new ways of applying AI in a way that addresses specific domains perfectly. If a great solution doesn't yet exist, see whether you can dream it up yourself. If you can pull it off, your domain can reward you with thought leadership bragging rights, an ever-growing customer roster, and the knowledge that you were able to forge something memorable in the wilderness. Many still think of applied AI as the Wild West because many of us technologists know that by 2030, we will be looking back on some amazing breakthroughs and use cases of AI that we haven't even thought of yet. It's important to keep this spirit of curiosity and creativity alive in such a nascent field.

For many AI PMs, you likely already have some familiarity and credibility built in your domain. It is possible to grow your reputation in your chosen domain by bringing something novel to your company, organization, or industry. AI offers a vehicle to do this but again, you first must have a clear answer to why you want to be using AI that goes beyond the marketing fluff so that you can stand out from the competition. Making sure that you're understanding your market needs, understanding how your product will specifically address those needs, and building and communicating a product strategy that aligns all that into one path forward will be a great way to make sure AI is properly oriented toward your chosen domain.

This is agnostic, no matter which domain you're in. Some domains will be more advanced as far as AI adoption is concerned and this will make your work as an AI PM more and less difficult because each level of advancement of AI has its own slew of challenges and opportunities, but the process will be the same regardless. If you're in a domain that is more advanced as far as AI adoption is concerned, you'll be more interested in which AI features your competitors are using to address certain needs and decide whether that's a direction you want to go in as you refine your product strategy. If you're in a domain that's less advanced, you'll have to look to other industries for inspiration for AI adoption and you'll be able to make a more eye-catching splash with your own product in your market.

Either way, you will be able to successfully reach a market when you're able to apply all you've learned in a way that offers your domain something that's currently missing from the offerings that already exist. As an AI PM, you don't need to be an expert in all areas of AI but you do need to have enough of an understanding of your market and AI capabilities/strategies/algorithms that will best serve the exact use cases you're trying to apply AI toward.

Once you're able to see progress in this area, you're then looking to make sure your market receives the message that your product has arrived. Whether it's through your customers, conferences and trade shows, ads, marketing messages, or your own efforts of evangelism, your goal is to make sure your domain sees you because you're ready to spread the word about the problems in your domain and why your AI product is best suited to solve them!

Now that we've spent some time seeing how to best position a product for your market and the considerations of building an AI strategy that serves the customers you're trying to attract, we can take a look at some of the most popular verticals for AI. Each vertical will have a series of popular use cases that we see time and again, and this can shed light on some of the greatest benefits AI can give certain verticals.

Verticals – examination into four areas (FinTech, healthcare, consumer goods, and cybersecurity)

We discussed general domains in understanding how AI is to be oriented in your chosen domain in the previous section. In this section, we will be looking at four specific verticals – that is, **fintech**, **healthcare**, **consumer goods**, and **cybersecurity** – that have seen increased AI adoption in order to best demonstrate trends within major areas of AI development through these examples. Getting an understanding of how and why AI was adopted in these verticals can give us promising examples of how AI can be applied in other domains as well. Let's explore the adoption of AI in these four verticals.

FinTech

Perhaps the swiftest and most substantial AI transformation has been in the fintech space, and it's not surprising to see why. AI applied toward specific use cases can bring about significant revenues saved or generated when done right. According to a recent report by UnivDatos Market Insights, *"The AI in Fintech Market is expected to grow at a steady rate of around 30% owing to the increasing demand for fraud detection, virtual helpers coupled with easy transactions, and chatbots for quick and instant query solutions."*

Let's take a look at some of the most compelling use cases of AI for the fintech space that have contributed to its quick adoption.

Chatbots

Chatbots or **conversational AIs** use **natural language processing** (**NLP**) to handle more of the customer service through what's referred to as **sentiment analysis**. NLP is made up of two components – **natural language generation** and **natural language understanding** (**NLG** and **NLU**, respectively) – and these language models are used to find patterns in what end users are asking for to inform things such as a centralized knowledge base, a frequently asked questions page, or to help the company understand more about their customers and what they're looking for. Where ML and deep learning work with data points, in NLP, the data points are the words themselves and it's their orientation and arrangement that gets optimized.

Players in the fintech space are able to use chatbots to also optimize for other things, such as customer feedback with their fintech apps, process automation, and lowering wait times. They're also great for capturing generational sentiments, such as not wanting to jump on a quick call, something that's increasingly prioritized by the younger generations that prefer to interact with a brand digitally. For instance, the Bank of America has seen its Erica chatbot reach 1 million users and plans to increase its AI capabilities because of how accessible Erica has been to its users. Outside of fintech, chatbots are often used to assist with call centers and customer service departments as well.

Fraud detection

This is a big one, particularly because so many financial institutions are left with a risk when there is fraudulent activity on an account. Therefore, it makes sense that one of the primary use cases for AI that caught on heavily within fintech has to do with catching fraud more efficiently. In this use case, AI is being used for anomaly detection within accounts so that banks and other financial institutions can be alerted faster when an activity that's outside an existing customer's pattern of behavior is identified. This is also used for money laundering and other illegal activities.

Fraud detection as a use case isn't quite as straightforward as building a chatbot because there are likely multiple layers of AI tools working together to make it happen. It's more likely to be a combination of things. First, some version of continuous data mining is at play to discover whether there are overarching, easy-to-detect patterns in the customer data. There's also likely to be a rules-based system that's used to mine as it's scouring the data and looking for anomalies. On top of this, there are likely unsupervised ML models used to look for patterns beyond the mining and to group activities into clusters to be analyzed later, and there are often neural networks used as well to learn from established suspicious patterns that do turn out to be fraudulent.

Because of the level of sophistication that's out there now in the cybersecurity space, fraud can come from multiple sources. Fraud can come from the customer themselves, someone impersonating them, an adversarial bot attack, phishing attacks, and other scams. Fintech institutions need to find a way to address all these potential cybercrimes through the help of various layers of AI. Setting up this kind of in-depth operation is expensive, but the cost to run a system like that is nothing in the face of the $51M fintech loses to fraud every year. With regard to fraud detection, there are also temporal qualities to it, so fintech is often looking at finding fraud that has occurred, finding fraud as it's occurring, and finding and stopping fraud before it happens.

Algorithmic trading and predictive analytics

AI is helpful when it comes to the fast trading speeds and improving accuracy that's needed to compete with things such as **high-frequency trading** (**HFT**). ML models are used to effectively predict market movements more quickly to help algorithms make their bids, anticipate the best times in the day to make trades, and use historical data for prediction models to understand when the prices might go up. Apart from the main motivator being to make better, more fortuitous trades for their customers, another big driver of the adoption of this AI use case is that algorithmic trading also helps limit mistakes coming from emotional or psychologically stressed traders to limit trade volatility.

Though algorithmic trading relies on a set of instructions to execute decisions, and there are a number of solutions out there that do just that, the underlying technology that supports it is based on predictive analytics. Fintech players are able to crunch so much data and they're so committed to improving their ML models that even small percentages of improvement in their accuracy or precision could result in millions of dollars of saved revenue or maximized profits. Whether they're a start-up that's looking to convert a lead or a bank that's looking to offer a loan based on a credit score, fintech is using predictive analytics to constantly learn from new and historical data to power most of their decisions so that they know how much a potential customer transaction is worth to them in the long run.

Healthcare

We're constantly hearing about the staffing shortages that plague most hospital and health networks, and healthcare is another reasonable vertical that's embraced the capabilities and help of AI with open arms. Staffing shortages aside, AI has been able to help with one of the most costly impediments to perfection: human error. Because of the increased demand for personnel and the life-and-death urgency that comes with a lot of the medical activities that go on in the name of our well-being and health, AI has been a great contender for fighting some of the most important battles in the healthcare space. We've seen AI applied in a range of beneficial ways, from image recognition and diagnostics to drug discovery.

Imaging and diagnosis

Supervised and **unsupervised** ML models are used to identify, group, and orient medical images to better understand, for instance, which cells in an image might be cancerous and dangerous. Also, because of the digitizing of medical records, there's a large amount of data that needs to be analyzed and learned from. Mountains of pieces of data in the form of images from MRIs, CT scans, cardiograms, and ultrasounds are all available to be analyzed en masse. AI is able to help make sense of these images that exist, as well as learn from new graphics and images that are produced as people continue with their medical activities. The more examples it gets, the better it gets at detecting anomalies. As time goes on, we should be seeing improvements in the models optimizing further, to the point where most diagnoses will be coming from AI-assisted doctors.

Because so much data is being analyzed and the use cases for these models are so specialized, the patterns and relationships that the algorithms are looking for are getting refined for accuracy and speed over time. This means that AI apps such as *IBM Watson Health* are increasingly getting involved in helping patients diagnostically. This is doubly true when we consider the rise of diagnostic and treatment apps themselves. Cameras are getting really good at picking up even small blemishes and abnormalities that human eyes can't pick up, so as doctors and patients continue to use apps to assist them on their journey together, and as that data is collected and centralized further and further, we're likely to see more accurate diagnoses over time as well.

Drug discovery and research

Drug discovery and research have historically been notoriously time- and energy-consuming. A process that might have taken years or decades in the past can be sped up today with the help of AI. We all collectively saw AI applied in this way to address the COVID-19 pandemic and speed up vaccine discovery, and according to the National Library of Medicine, "*AI is being successfully used in the identification of disease clusters, monitoring of cases, prediction of the future outbreaks, mortality risk, diagnosis of COVID-19, disease management by resource allocation, facilitating training, record maintenance and pattern recognition for studying the disease trend.*"

Moderna's chief data and AI officer offers us the best insight into the use of AI in the drug discovery and research phase. As he's detailing the process for using algorithms across a wide range of opportunities in drug discovery, he's highlighting that there are countless processes, it's a very complicated process to bring something to market, and there are just numerous opportunities along the way. Even within a specific use case, you're rarely using one AI algorithm. It's often, "*For this part of the problem, we need to use this algorithm, and for this, we need to use another.*"

Cybersecurity

Cybercrime is up, and cybersecurity continues to be one of the most prevalent sources of AI/ML adoption that we see most regularly because of the persistence and sophistication of cyber criminals. The nature of cybersecurity is ever-changing, which means that, over time, companies need to keep step with their potential adversaries. It feels like we hear about a new data leak every day, and perhaps the most alarming part of cybersecurity is the number of attacks you *don't* hear about.

In the next section, we will discuss two popular use cases used in cybersecurity: anomaly detection and **user and entity behavior analytics** (**UEBA**).

Anomaly detection and user and entity behavior analytics

Uncovering patterns and changes in those patterns is at the very heart of anomaly detection. In cybersecurity, this established baseline and deviation from it are what create the use case of anomaly detection. Once there's been an anomaly and an action is required from the system, we can then move toward rectifying it somehow. Often, cyber attacks come from within networks and have clever ways of hiding their tracks, but with advanced pattern recognition that's used for anomaly detection, AI systems can see when some actor/user is behaving in ways that don't make sense for a normal user.

As we went through some of the use cases for various verticals, you're likely seeing patterns of your own emerge in terms of some of the underlying tech used to power those applications of AI. One of these overarching use cases is encapsulated in UEBA, which is, in many ways, an undercurrent for many of the use cases we discussed. As an AI PM, it will be really helpful if you can understand the power of UEBA and how to apply it within your product and beyond, particularly as you're in the operational phase of building out increasingly powerful features over time.

You can think of UEBA as a network of insights that are gathered by basically pooling all your users' actions and subsequent data that is generated from those actions on a daily basis. Once all this data is centralized and analyzed, it's able to offer you profound insights by giving you a baseline for not just individual users but for all your users all at once as well. This makes things such as finding anomalies or new patterns, no matter what the change is, easier because you can establish triggers or actions that alert your user or your internal workforce when something that requires attention has happened.

Companies these days need to stay more vigilant than ever, and many don't have the headcount or allocated budget to truly stay on top of this potential risk, which is why the breaches keep coming. This is a big part of the reason cybersecurity has adopted AI so readily: it's ripe for it. When use cases are notoriously underfunded and understaffed, AI has an opportunity to get adopted and truly shine.

Value metrics – evaluating performance across verticals and peer groups

No matter what domain, vertical, or peer group your AI product is in, you're going to need to establish some way of communicating the success of your product through a combination of value (business) metrics, **key performance indicators (KPIs)**, and **objectives and key results (OKRs)**, along with a number of technical metrics that might be required when you're communicating about the efficacy and success of your product to a technical audience. As with anything, if we can't establish a baseline and see how we've grown from that baseline, we won't know whether our performance is improving (and if it is, by how much) unless we track it.

In the following section, we will be looking at the various types of metrics we will start to collect on our products' efficacy. For AI products, deciding on which metrics you will track, how you will talk about them, and what kinds of audiences you'll tailor certain metrics for will be an important part of your product strategy, as well as your marketing.

Objectives and key results

When you're defining success for your AI product, you'll want to set some OKRs from a technical and business level so you can track how your AI product is building toward the performance you want to see. OKRs are used heavily in product management to track progress toward higher-level business goals. You'll want to choose two or three objectives to start with, and you'll want a group of three to five key results for each objective.

The purpose of this is to show which direct results are impacting the greater overarching business goals your product might be tasked with. Let's say you're supporting an AI cybersecurity product. An example of this might be that you want to reduce the number of false negatives for your fraud detection algorithm with a number of key results from the work your product has been able to achieve toward that goal.

You'll want to set these quarterly and reference them often because these will be the highest focus of your product as you build through each release. The establishment of new OKRs will arise in your product planning sessions and will be informed by the features you have planned in your roadmap, your customers, and customer success and marketing feedback, as well as the ever-evolving goals from leadership in order to best align your product's objectives with the feedback loops you have in place to make sure you're building something that's valuable to your domain and market.

Key performance indicators

KPIs are used more generally and also tend to grow over time as new indicators are discovered as important. Some of the most common KPIs have to do with measuring customer or employee satisfaction, measuring time or accuracy, calculating the cost efficiency or return on investment for purchasing something, or agreeing on a metric that aligns with the company's goals somehow. There are also categories of KPIs ranging from strategic to operational to functional, which means they're either affecting the entire company as a whole or are high-level metrics, relating to a specific time frame operationally across the entire company, or relating to specific departments.

If you've been working in the business world for some time, you've likely heard of KPIs or value metrics in a number of contexts, but in this section, we're going to specifically cover some common KPIs that are likely to help you when you're deciding on how to best track and communicate your AI product's success.

Whether you're running an AI program agnostically in your business or running an AI program as part of your AI product feature stack, the following KPIs will help with maintaining the health and progress of your AI infrastructure. Being aware of the following metrics will help communicate the success of your AI activities, which is a common part of **AI operations (AIOps)**:

- **Mean time to detect (MTTD)**: This is calculating the average time it takes for your product to identify a potential issue. You'll want to demonstrate that this is minimizing over time.

- **Mean time to acknowledge (MTTA)**: This is calculating the average time to acknowledge the problem and identify who will resolve it. You'll want to demonstrate that this is minimizing over time.

- **Mean time to resolve/repair (MTTR)**: This is calculating the average time it takes to actually address the problem. You'll want to demonstrate that this is minimizing over time.

- **Mean time between failures (MTBF)**: This is calculating the average time between failures to give a sense of how long the AI program is working optimally. You'll want to demonstrate that this is growing over time.

- **Ticket to incident ratio**: Recognition that one incident may create multiple tickets so this metric seeks to minimize the number of tickets or logs that are created by customers when one issue is being experienced. You'll want to demonstrate that this is minimizing over time.

- **Service availability**: The uptime where your AI program is running optimally without issues. You'll want to demonstrate that this is growing over time.

- **Automated versus manual resolution**: This is essentially labeling which response was manual or automated so that your ML program can optimize for strategies in the future and learn from past remediations. You'll want to demonstrate that this is growing over time.

- **User reporting versus automatic detection**: This is the ratio between how many customers reported an issue versus how often your own product detected the issue. You'll want to demonstrate that this is minimizing over time.

Technical metrics

The following list includes some of the common technical KPIs that are used to communicate the accuracy of ML models:

- **Classification accuracy (precision or specificity, recall or sensitivity, and F1 score)**: There are a number of formulas that try to derive how often your models are correct, whether by the rate of true and false positives, the rate of true and false negatives, or some combination of the two (an F1 score)

- **Root mean square error (RMSE)**: The root of the average rate of error for regression models

- **Mean absolute error (MAE)**: The average rate of error

There are a number of other metrics you might want to keep track of. Perhaps you will have categories of all your metrics that pertain to the volume or amount of data sources or availability, perhaps you'll want to quantify or qualify the strength or robustness of your AI/ML organization somehow, or have metrics related to your product marketing outputs or the availability of models. Perhaps you'll have adoption metrics beyond just your users to understand how certain teams are using your products internally. Defining business goals is a highly selective and customized activity that should, first and foremost, serve the highest ideals of your business: to best serve your customers and market.

Thought leadership – learning from peer groups

At the start of this chapter, we discussed the idea of building a foundation in your domain and understanding (as much as possible) what the specific pain points in your domain are with the aim of building an AI product that will serve the space for years to come. Building a product that works well, aligns with what your customers need, and employs modern technology is a fast way to build the credibility that's necessary to spread thought leadership across your domain.

You might choose to take on a leadership role in your domain in order to be positioned as a leader in your industry. With all the knowledge hubs and white papers and product one-pagers that are out there, it's common to see companies adopt the role of an industry thought leader for a number of reasons. Maybe this is for marketing, inbound leads, glory, or simply because they're generous with their knowledge and success.

Choosing how open and transparent you want to be with your company's choices and major roadblocks will be up to you and your leadership team. Will you choose to be an example for the other players in your field? Or will you choose to keep quiet and hold your algorithmic secret sauces, dirty laundry, and success stories close to your chest? Companies are constantly learning from each other, and being a true thought leader in an industry may come at a financial and design cost if you're not careful of how much information you do let out. As with all risky endeavors of the heart, sometimes we need to open ourselves up to risk in order to also accept the gifts that come with transparency.

As we've mentioned so many times, this period of applied AI products is still new. We have yet to understand the future use cases that will allow companies the greatest growth and success. The spirit of innovation and technological advancement is fed through example. Every use case and applied example has the ability to inspire us to discover a new use case. The newness of AI brings with it a kind of excitement about what's possible.

Particularly in a time when so many are apprehensive about whether AI can and should solve all our biggest problems, maybe it's up to companies, PMs, technologists, and entrepreneurs to embody the collaborative quality of this spirit. AI products bring together science, data, technology, and humanity in a way that has shown so much promise already. Should you choose to open up and share the examples that do come up in your experience, whether directly or indirectly, the gifts that come along with that won't just benefit you or your organization. They will benefit us all.

Summary

This chapter was geared toward markets, positioning, and common use cases of AI/ML products. We've been able to look at how AI can be optimized for certain domains and markets and how AI can commonly be leveraged in various verticals that are seeing a high saturation of AI products. Through those use cases, we've been able to see how companies leverage AI to be able to make the most of the data they have. As an AI/ML PM, you won't be building your AI-native product in a vacuum. You'll regularly be studying your market and your competition to make sure you're bringing use cases for AI that truly set you apart.

In *Chapter 9*, we will be building on use cases of AI products by getting deeper into the landscape of AI technologies, both at a high level and at the feature level. We'll get a chance to see how various types of AI can be built collaboratively, and we'll see examples of products that have done this successfully. We'll also get into some of the common challenges that have impacted the success of products and some of the common factors when things go wrong.

References

- *AI and the COVID-19 Vaccine: Moderna's Dave Johnson* `https://sloanreview.mit.edu/audio/ai-and-the-covid-19-vaccine-modernas-dave-johnson/`

- *The role of artificial intelligence in tackling COVID-19* `https://www.ncbi.nlm.nih.gov/pmc/articles/PMC7692869/`

- *Merative* `https://www.ibm.com/watson-health`

- *FinTech Execs Expose the Real Costs of Fraud* `https://www.pymnts.com/money-mobility/2022/fintech-execs-expose-the-real-costs-of-fraud/`

- *One Million People Are Now Using Erica - BofA's AI-Powered Chatbot* `https://netfinance.wbresearch.com/blog/bank-of-america-ai-powered-chatbot-strategy`

- *Artificial Intelligence (AI) in Fintech Market is expected to display a steady growth by 2028 due to the Increasing Demand for Process Automation Among Financial Organizations |CAGR: ~30%| UnivDatos Market Insights* `https://www.yahoo.com/now/artificial-intelligence-ai-fintech-market-143000099.html?guce_referrer=aHR0cHM6Ly93d3cuZ29vZ2xlLmNvbS8&guce_referrer_sig=AQAAAIa4n2Vt4bMuwrpKI6BWtwyr6Xa0kjjl1XMLqnCLcCuxa3ti_1t5pj3wNNZAbYRvBVpa1mzptsnLfeiFKUu_CoyFEiDihfPPoRh1vPY0d44aGe-t-YuEiR2YAgB_1mqn3O-ofRU1l6vh5EJus9ddy6RKgR-hlQq2U5_Fo7rlAsf9&guccounter=2#:~:text=Advertisement-,The%20AI%20in%20Fintech%20Market%20is%20expected%20to%20grow%20at,quick%20and%20instant%20query%20solutions`

- *Gartner Magic Quadrant* `https://www.gartner.co.uk/en/methodologies/magic-quadrants-research`

9

Macro and Micro AI for Your Product

The term *AI* is often used as an umbrella term that encapsulates the idea that a machine, whether physical or not, is mimicking the way humans either think, work, speak, express, or understand. This is a pretty big concept to wrap up in one term. It's hard to embody not just the diversity of models and use cases but the implementation of these models and use cases themselves. This chapter will serve as a handy recap of the various types of AI that products can absorb as you begin to explore the various ways you can leverage AI, as well as some of the most successful examples and common mistakes that can arise as PMs build AI products.

It's important to note that the application of AI has seen many iterations and will continue to do so as we build into the next decade, but it's hard to understate the importance of what this technological wave can offer PMs and companies. This is a substantial wave of innovation that's showing no signs of going away, and having a clear picture of the options that are ahead of you will help in building something that will have self-evident value to offer the market.

Though we've touched on the complexities and types of engagement with various ML and DL models, we will use this chapter to cover our bases with regard to the greater umbrella of AI to offer a comprehensive macro example of what AI is and how it can most bring value to product creators and users alike. In the *Macro AI – Foundations and umbrellas* section, we will understand how AI can be used in ways that help a product perform more optimally and evolve over time at a high level. In the *Micro AI – Feature level* section, we will go over common, accessible uses of AI at the more detailed feature level. Then, we will use the successes and challenges sections to point out a few examples of applications of AI that embody the concepts in the previous two sections.

Any PM will know that, as we discussed in *Chapter 8*, understanding what their product needs to be successful will require their own domain knowledge, as well as knowledge of what the competitors in their space are offering their markets. There is a third piece that we hope to bridge in this chapter, and that's in understanding what the baseline for AI adoption looks like so that you can tailor this baseline to your own domain and find success in the design, promotion, and performance of your product. This is where the fault line lies between domain knowledge and the foundational understanding of what AI can offer your audience. We want to empower you to be able to apply these general concepts to your particular domains in a way that feels accessible and exciting.

To achieve the goals we set here, we will cover the following topics in this chapter:

- Macro AI – Foundations and umbrellas
- Micro AI – Feature level
- Successes – Examples that inspire
- Challenges – Common pitfalls

Macro AI – Foundations and umbrellas

So far, we've talked a great deal about ML and DL models in the previous chapters. This was intentional because most of the time when we see AI advertised to us through various products, this is what the underlying technology employed is—for the most part. It's either a DL or an ML algorithm that's powering the products we've discussed. But as you've seen in the previous chapters, AI is a great umbrella term that can actually mean more than just an ML or a DL model is being used.

There are a number of major domains in AI that don't involve ML and DL. We've minimally touched on the other areas but haven't given them their due in their impact and contributions to the AI landscape. Focusing only on ML and DL makes sense from a practical perspective to offer AI technologists, entrepreneurs, and PMs the best chance to pitch their AI products to investors and users, but it also leaves holes in our greater tapestry of AI options that are out there. It's also important to understand that as we carry on and evolve through AI adoption in the coming years and decades, new domains within AI could emerge that may perform better than ML or DL, and there are a number of prominent voices out there that offer this perspective.

For now, the following is an inclusive macro screenshot of the various categories of AI. Since we've focused on ML and DL for most of this book, we wanted to offer a holistic view of all current concentrations of AI. As this section goes on, we will be addressing each area of AI in an effort to broaden your understanding of the other options you have when building AI products:

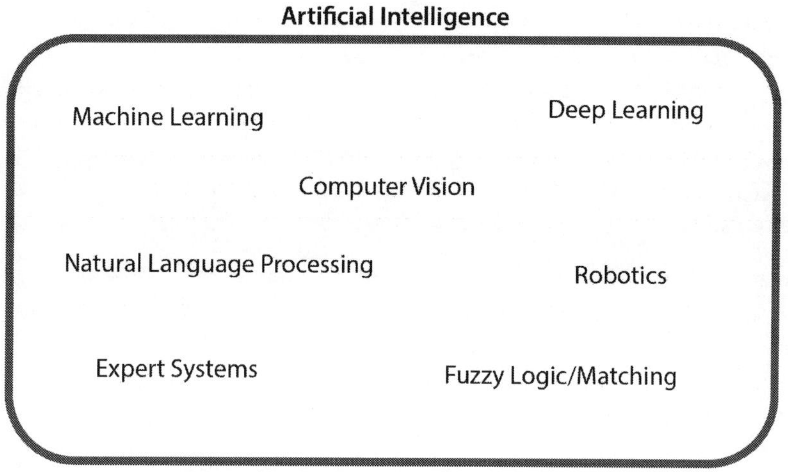

Artificial Intelligence

Machine Learning

Deep Learning

Computer Vision

Natural Language Processing

Robotics

Expert Systems

Fuzzy Logic/Matching

Figure 9.1 – Categories of AI

So, let's dive into these various domains of AI and offer a thorough overview of what each of these domains is, what they offer their products and users, and how they've impacted their greater markets! We will end this section with what new, further domains in AI might look like to catch a glimpse of future manifestations of AI before we start to discuss the use and implementation of these domains at the feature level in more applied terms in the following *Micro AI – Feature level* section.

ML

ML is a general concept that gives us the basic thinking and organizing power that gives machines the ability to reason with data in a way a human might. You can think of this as a way for a machine to mimic how a human can think, understand, and work. It dominates the market, and it serves as its own umbrella term of sorts because within it we can break down ML into the models we associate with traditional ML, along with their specializations such as **computer vision**, **natural language processing** (**NLP**), and DL as further subsets of ML.

We've gone over the specific models and algorithms that are used in ML in *Chapters 2* and *3* of this book, so we won't go into those in detail here, but suffice it to say this is where there are major categories in the kind of learning these machines do. To jog your memory, those learning types are **supervised learning**, **unsupervised learning**, **reinforcement learning**, and **deep learning** (**neural networks**). All these types of learning can be applied in generalized ways, either together or separately, to make up an ML network in what's considered ensemble modeling.

Generally speaking, you can see the term *AI* used so often because of the confusion and ambiguity that plagues the market now. In many cases, companies opt for it because their audiences may have the familiarity to appreciate more specificity, or because they don't want you to know what methods they actually employ in their products. This will start to change but for now, this is likely due to AI still being new in its market adoption and to end users still being unclear on what to call the underlying tech. As we see more and more adoption of AI, we will also start to see more clarity in what kind of AI a product is using.

Even ML can perhaps be too broad of a descriptor. We may even see the term *AI* or *ML* fall off entirely, giving way to more exact descriptions of the tech. If you aren't sure what's considered ML and what isn't, it might be convenient to break down the terms themselves. ML presupposes that the machines, or models, are learning by training from past examples. This learning and adaptation from the past is not an explicitly programmed action. Let's get into the various learning methods of ML further.

In supervised learning, we humans are giving machines a clue as to what the data points mean. To put it simply, we label the data for the machines to understand. But the pattern recognition and optimization that goes on to predict a future value, let's say, is not something we tell the machine to do. In unsupervised learning, we're not giving the machines any indication of what the data means or whether it's correct in its prediction. So, in unsupervised learning, the machines are not just coming up with their own conclusions, but they're assembling the patterns they see based on no input from us at all. They are *learning* and deriving insights based on their own ability to see patterns. In reinforcement learning, we are doing a combination of the two, so when the machines do perform well, we offer them a *cheat code* to be able to recreate that good performance again to reinforce their learning. Finally, in neural networks, we let the machine's hidden layers derive meaning; it is left to its own devices.

The last major aspect of ML to keep in mind is that data is the major input that impacts its success. Unlike other domains of AI mentioned next, ML relies on the quantity and quality of the data it's fed on for its success and performance. Though there are innovations being worked on now to move ML to be less data-reliant, we still haven't gotten there. ML still requires massive swaths of data that needs to be stored, used, and learned in order for us to see its value. The foundational intelligence that powers how it does this at the model level is based on underlying mathematical foundations, so it's trying to understand and correct how wrong it was from the correct answer even incrementally so that it guesses or predicts more correctly with each wave of *learning*.

Computer vision

Computer vision is the underlying tech that powers everything from agriculture and climate change tracking to autonomous vehicles, facial recognition and surveillance, and medical imaging and manufacturing. Basically, it's ML for images and dynamic video. Much like what we discussed in the previous section, it's learning by example, and its models are optimized in much the same way but for visual content. Whereas the ML umbrella term is for recognizing, understanding, and predicting words and numbers, computer vision does the same but for visual data. We still consider this ML because the basic principle of ML from previous examples and optimizing for correcting its own mistakes is still present with computer vision models.

Perhaps what's most interesting about computer vision is that it's in essence using mathematical foundations to basically split up an image into what it can understand: a matrix of numbers. Then, in some cases, it's learning from that breakdown in order to reassemble it back into a new image. Computer vision models look for ways to recognize objects and images and translate an image based on various factors such as edges, frames, textures, and 3D shapes to distinguish between what's a static or moving object. They try to understand motion as it progresses through time.

Computer vision is a translation of how a machine might see, but a more exact description is that it's processing data in a way that mimics how we see. It's translating data from something a human eye can understand to something a machine can understand, and it's able to do so much more quickly than we humans can. If you doubt that, you should see the human versus self-driving car crash records.

NLP

If computer vision is how a machine might see, **NLP** is how a machine might hear and speak. It's a machine processing human language and all the specifics that come along with that. NLP is used heavily in translation, speech-to-text, and speech recognition. It dominates the market in terms of products that work with human speech, personal assistants, conversational AI, and chatbots, and it's a huge domain within AI as these markets continue to grow.

NLP is made up of two components, **natural language understanding** (**NLU**) and **natural language generation** (**NLG**), so the entire system together is called natural language processing. But do keep in mind these two major components that have their own expertise. A machine needs to fully understand what's being asked of it before it can create a response, and given the popularity of massive language models such as OpenAI's GPT-3 and GPT-4, Google's BERT, and IBM Watson, NLP is only going to grow in adoption and reliance.

NLP is truly a tremendous innovation when you consider all the world's languages that exist and even the disparity in how much variety exists in the way people express ideas and speak. It's not just about the words people will choose to use and the inherent variety within that but also the speed, inflections, and accents in the words they choose as well—the mood of the person speaking, how much they enunciate, how lazy or fast they are with delivering their words. There's so much nuance in the world of language, and advancements in NLP have proven to triumph against these nuances. They aren't perfect, and we sometimes do have to repeat something when we're communicating with a personal assistant, but those cases are increasingly rare because the more we interact with them, the more they can anticipate and understand our inquiries and offer thoughtful, correct responses.

Deep learning

Finally, **DL** is a subset we've discussed at length throughout this book, and it relies on neural networks to arrive at insights and predictions. You've likely seen the term *black-box models* thrown around often throughout the book, and this is your reminder that this likely means DL models are involved because hidden layers are opaque structures that the humans that program DL neural networks can't see into. The reason for this is that within each hidden layer there are nodes that make computational decisions, and these decisions are happening essentially all at once, so it's not a matter of not wanting to offer transparency into the models—it's a matter of really not being able to in the first place.

Considering that a lack of transparency is one of the major issues with using DL models, particularly in applications that require explainability, seeing advancements in how DL models can be applied in ways that are more transparent would be a big win for DL. Current market applications of DL thrive when there isn't a huge need for explainability because there are minimized negative downstream effects or because good performance is reason enough to use them. So, if your product uses DL and this lack of transparency isn't hurting any of your customers, users, or your own reputation, you can carry on. For those that want the performance of DL but can't move forward until there is less opacity, you'll sadly need to wait for the models to catch up to themselves. Perhaps a day will come when they will explain themselves!

Despite the naming conventions, explainability, and neural aspect of the models, DL is still ML in the sense that the models are still learning from prior examples, they're still optimizing and predicting for future values and checking against that performance to see how *correct* they were so that they can mimic the performance later, and they still follow the learning types we discussed prior. There are still supervised, unsupervised, semi-supervised, and reinforcement neural networks. They are still finding patterns within the data you feed them and learning from past examples with every new training they receive.

The major difference between ML and DL is in the data needs DL has. With traditional ML, you might be OK with—say—hundreds, thousands, or hundreds of thousands of data points, but with DL, even those scales might not be enough. We don't want to offer specific numbers because the data required is always going to depend on the models you're using, what you're doing with them, and how diverse the datasets are in terms of the variety of examples they offer. The more diverse your data, the better chance you're offering your models to understand more and more so that they're optimized for success and performance. This data hunger for DL is another barrier to entry for a lot of folks that want to be working with neural networks in their products. They may not have the data luxury to offer them, even if the performance is high, and currently, investments are being made in researching ways to make DL models less reliant on data.

Robotics

If AI is considered an umbrella term for machines mimicking how humans might work and reach conclusions, this is perhaps most visibly obvious with robotics, which is physically trying to reproduce the work of a human. The term *robot* is in and of itself a generic term that encompasses a lot of nuances, much like the term *AI*. ML is considered as powerful as it is because of the ability of machines to learn from past actions and behaviors. In that sense, perhaps they are considered more advanced than the underlying tech that powers robotics, but we felt it wasn't fair to exclude robotics from AI because if a robot can make a meal, make a part for a car, or assist with surgery, it's intelligent enough to be considered in the realm of AI.

The heart of innovations in this space will also come from ML being used in combination with robotics so that it can learn from the past. In *Chapter 3*, we briefly touched on the idea of Boston Dynamics robot dogs not using ML. Even iRobot's Roomba only recently got an AI upgrade in 2021 with the launch of its Roomba j7+. This is showing that robotics may thrive on its own without the need for perhaps more *advanced* areas of AI such as ML and DL to be involved in its development as a product. Though robotics can stand on its own, we're already seeing ways in which robotics is coming to the forefront in integrating AI with products on the market with the rising popularity of robots such as Sophia, sexual companions, and surgical robots that have come on the scene.

A big part of their popularity lies in not just the precision and trust that can come from a robot doing repetitive tasks that might be laborious for a person, but also in their inability to experience fatigue. Robots can malfunction, but they certainly won't want a vacation or get sick. This gives rise to the other aspect of robotics adoption, which is more ethical and human-centric. Just because we can *hire* a robotic worker in an assembly line, restaurant, or hospital doesn't mean we should. People, at least in most cases, need to work to make a living. Disruptions to embracing AI from the general public often involve distrust and contempt over AI taking jobs away from the humans that need them. The most successful and least controversial areas to be using robots to replace workers would be for tasks that are considered too unpleasant for humans or tasks that are repeatedly putting humans in danger where there is a shortage of willing participants in the first place.

There are a number of specializations of robots we can go over that have varying degrees of intelligence and autonomy:

- **Autonomous robots**: Autonomous robots, for instance, can perceive and maneuver through their environment and make decisions based on those perceptions without the intervention or control of a human. The best example of this might be a Roomba, which automatically picks up debris to clean our floors.

- **Teleoperated robots**: Teleoperated robots such as daVinci and NeuroArm (`https://mind.ilstu.edu/curriculum/medical_robotics/teleo.html`) are often referred to as **automated guided vehicles** (**AGVs**), which are used with a human intervening to perform tasks such as medical procedures, moving materials in a factory, or drones for disaster response.

- **Augmenting robots**: Taking this a step further, we also see a number of augmenting robots such as Raytheon XOS, HAL, eLegs, and the DEKA arm, which are made for targeted muscle reinnervation through electronic prosthetic devices (`https://mind.ilstu.edu/curriculum/medical_robotics/augmenting.html#:~:text=Augmenting%20robots%20generally%20enhance%20capabilities,that%20a%20person%20has%20lost`).

- **Humanoid robots**: Then, there are humanoid robots such as Sophia, Tesla's Optimus, and Ameca, which are often using some kind of ML to express themselves in ways we can understand (`https://builtin.com/robotics/humanoid-robots`).

- **Pre-programmed robots**: People have come to rely on these robots because of their heavy use in the automobile and manufacturing industries (`https://mind.ilstu.edu/curriculum/medical_robotics/prepro.html`).

Expert systems

An **expert system** is a generic term meant to describe some sort of rule-based engine that's been continuously refined and optimized over time. They were used heavily in the past in medical and legal use cases before ML became popularized. Although there are some companies that may still rely on them, their relevance has receded. They have a **user interface** (**UI**) and are powered by an inference engine that is connected to a knowledge base of some sort. It's a more basic form of AI that's made up of `If Then` statements. A **rule-based engine** means there are a set of pre-programmed instructions and algorithms that have been programmed into the backbone of how a product or system functions and there is an absence of self-learning. This means that ML models are not used and the system is not learning over time. Though this might sound like a *dumb* system, it's still considered AI because it still might be functioning in a way that mimics how a human might apply intelligence.

Just because it's pre-programmed doesn't mean it's not working optimally, accurately, or in a way that's intelligent. There are a number of applications that don't need ML because what they do is already optimal enough for what's expected of them. If it's simulating the knowledge or judgment of its human counterparts, then it's intelligent. Also, many of these expert systems have been optimized over time, so there still might be a huge amount of complexity. These expert systems have the ability to emulate the decision-making or the reasoning of a person based on a set of instructions, and there could be manifestations of it today that can be bolstered by ML.

Fuzzy logic/fuzzy matching

Fuzzy matching, also referred to as approximate string matching, uses some logic to find terms or phrases that are similar to each other. Perhaps you're looking through your database to isolate anyone with a first name *John* but some entries are *Jonathan* or *Johnny*. Fuzzy matching would be an intelligent way of finding those alternative names. Fuzzy matching was used ubiquitously in translation software before machine translation came into the picture. Whether you're looking for alternative naming conventions or mistakes, fuzzy logic and matching are able to offer us intelligent ways for machines to find the things we're looking for.

As with robotics and other areas of AI, we can see an ensemble with fuzzy matching as well. We're seeing ML applied to fuzzy matching in an effort to improve accuracy. But even without ML, fuzzy logic and fuzzy matching can stand on their own as a subset of AI that's been relied on heavily before ML and continues to be prominent to this day for things such as translation or data/database management.

Now that we've gone over all the major areas of AI to understand what they are and how they offer value, we can now get onto the feature level to see how these major areas can translate into various features you can integrate into your product. The point of this isn't to give you ideas on what kinds of products to build but rather to understand the variety of how these innovations can be used and work together.

Micro AI – Feature level

It can be daunting to understand how various categories of AI fit together, and the reality is that in real-world AI product applications, many of these are working in concert. Seeing various examples of how that happens, particularly when we get to the later sections in this chapter, will offer us a way to see how much opportunity and potential AI really offers us!

We will consolidate ML, DL, computer vision, and NLP into their own section because these models are often used collaboratively as well. That collaboration can then bleed into the other subsets of AI. Robotics, expert systems, and fuzzy logic can remain in their own sections because their applications are so specialized in and of themselves. Seeing how subsets of AI can work together further results in the greater complexity and growth that powers innovation for our markets and brings to market products that serve, delight, and capture our hearts.

ML (traditional/DL/computer vision/NLP)

Which type of model you're using will depend on your use case and goals for your product. As we've covered in varying chapters, the exact model you go with will depend on the data you have, how you're able to tune your hyperparameters, and what level of explainability and transparency you'll need for your use case. We're focusing on AI/ML native products in this section of the book and, as such, identifying which ML model(s) you will use for the foundation of your product will be an important decision, and all features you add onto your core product will also be an act of doing a cost-benefit analysis of the models you're adding to power those features.

Most products that are out there right now are not AI/ML native in that they are existing software programs and packages that are incrementally adding new AI features and then rebranding their products as AI products. This isn't exactly true, but it does create a marketing sensation around their product that they can then capitalize on through their customer outreach and ads. But from one PM to another, we do want to make it very clear: these are not products foundationally rooted in AI/ML because if they were, models would be at the heart of the underlying logic their product is built on. Rather, these are products that improve certain features with the use of AI/ML, but the true impact of leveraging this tech stays superficially at the feature level and doesn't substantially impact the product in a meaningful way. Apart from productized ML services, personal assistants, and autonomous cars, there are very few true-blue AI products out there. But with the passage of time and with adequate funding from the private sector, more will continue to enter the market.

NLP models will be highly useful if your product is heavily working with textual data. Things such as email filters, smart assistants and conversational AIs, search result analyzers, voice-to-text, spellcheck, autocomplete, sentiment analysis, predictive text, translation, and data and text analysis are all potential features you can incorporate into your product to make use of NLP. NLP is also particularly useful when you're trying to optimize your customer communications so that you can make sense of large quantities of feedback that can then be incorporated to identify additional future features of your product as you're building your product roadmap.

Computer vision models account for edges, corners, interest points, blobs, regions of interest points, and ridges as they make sense of an image and try to turn it into a matrix of numbers. This conversion is how they're able to understand images, so you'll use these models if your product is trying to observe and identify objects or patterns in an environment. For instance, analyzing images of areas to create potential future projections of possible environmental decay and damage would also be a great use for computer vision.

Generally, the use of ML will be highly impactful for a few different use cases. The following are the most common use cases:

- **Rank/recommendation systems**: If you're looking for a ranked list of a grouping of similar products or documents, recommendation systems will get you there. If your product is heavily focused on offering a selection of options or the discovery of new options to your customers, AI-/ML-powered rankings will be a great use of AI.

- **Prediction**: Using historical data points toward the goal of predicting future values being central to your product is one of the most applicable ways to use ML models, and you'll be able to choose the model that best supports prediction for your product.

- **Classification**: Similar to the logic in recommendation systems, classification use cases of ML will help to group people, customers, objects, choices, and subjects into certain categories. You're taking generalized data and forming classes from that general data.

- **Generation**: Maybe your product is generating content for your users, whether that's visual or textual. You're able to feed these models examples to learn from so that they can create new samples altogether based on the examples you've given. Whatever inputs you give generative models, they will create outputs you can sell or pass on to your users for other purposes.

- **Clustering**: These are other models that can group information together. The only difference is with clustering, the models come up with their own groupings, which is a way for ML to help create distinctions between data points that your engineers or users couldn't.

In this section, we've covered some of the major use cases for applying ML at the feature level. Many of these use cases should be familiar to you by now. In the following section, we will cover the area of robotics.

Robotics

With robotics, you're creating physical structures that operate optimally for certain use cases. As we saw in the *Robotics* section (see under *Macro AI – Foundations and umbrellas*), some robotics do relate to each other, particularly when we think about teleoperated robots and augmented robots where there is some overlap. But by and large, these are created specifically for the use case they have. We can think of robotics as the hardware and the incorporation of ML as the software upgrade package.

Let's take the example of an autonomous robot that is scanning its environment to find the optimal route or chain of events by which to operate. It might be able to derive insights on its own without using ML algorithms to optimize its route, but if it does want to get better over time, maybe its logs can be used to teach it to maneuver more effectively. With teleoperated robots, DL can be used to optimize the speed, strength, or depth at which it's handling its subjects and quickly build on the best practices surgeons spend decades mastering (to take the example of robotics in surgery). Because DL's performance is more important than its explainability in surgical contexts, it can be a useful feature for medical devices. Even augmenting robots (`https://arpost.co/2021/08/26/augmented-reality-in-robotics-enhances-robots/`) can benefit from collaborations with other AI domains to test and simulate their uses before they're opened up to testing with real people.

A huge area of collaboration that gets a lot of press, however, is with humanoid robots, which need a fair amount of overlap with other AI domains to come to market. After all, you can't call something a humanoid robot if it can't listen, speak, or see like a human can. Humanoid robots rely on computer vision to see their surroundings, identify people and objects, and move throughout their environments. They also rely on NLP to understand what people are saying to them and to offer thoughtful responses. They might also be programmed with ML or DL models to optimize for varying situations they might encounter or to predict what people might ask of them and how to respond.

Expert systems

Expert systems essentially run on `if-else` logic, so they come with a set of instructions that rarely change, and when they do, those changes are hardcoded. The limitations they experience are a lack of responsiveness to the data they process and a huge amount of complexity within the rules; they don't quite capture the full nuance that a human might and they don't do well when novelty is introduced. These limitations are ripe for incorporating ML so that as new scenarios, new data, and new experiences are introduced, some of the logic can also be updated.

This is a good example because it shows that ML need not replace an expert system but it can collaboratively work alongside the expert so that the expert becomes more of an expert without the necessity of a human to make changes to its decision-making process. You might have a need, as an expert system creator, to have one machine in place that offers objective, structured static instructions for your use case. Building an end-to-end ML product to solve that might be unnecessarily complex, innovative, or expensive to run, and you might get a lot more out of your product by just using ML to optimize the steps in your system rather than replace the whole thing altogether. There aren't many present-day examples of this to draw from, but it is theoretically possible to combine expert systems with ML.

Fuzzy logic/fuzzy matching

There are a number of features that can incorporate fuzzy logic or fuzzy matching if you're building a product that needs to account for certain similarities in entries you have. Perhaps you're building a scraper that's looking to find matching hotel listings or a rental that has a certain number of amenities, and you're trying to compare them. Or maybe you're looking for a review consolidator that will find reviews related to a business or product, and you're matching the reviews based on the description.

Another common example might be searching your database to consolidate your users that come from mobile versus desktop or users that interact with varying **business units** (**BUs**) within your company to create a single customer view. Your internal customer data might be in multiple areas. Perhaps you have multiple databases or you have your customer data in HubSpot and your purchase data in Stripe and you're looking to make associations. If you don't have a concrete unique identifier that matches them, you might have to use something such as fuzzy matching to make those associations and get rid of duplicates in your database as well.

Fuzzy matching will allow you to select certain keywords that your fuzzy engine will optimize for so that you can then arrange them by the percentage of the match and group them together. Then, once you have these examples and you're able to create some groupings, you might want to then incorporate some ML to take the outputs of that fuzzy matching so that the matches get better over time. ML models will optimize how well that fuzzy matching works over time and as your business grows. You may want to take this a step further and use NLP for fuzzy matching things such as translations or phrases that belong together as well.

Now that we've had a chance to give an overview of the applied use cases and features from the major areas of AI in the preceding sections, let's turn our attention to a few positive examples from the real world.

Successes – Examples that inspire

In this section, we will be looking at examples of complex, collaborative AI products that use a number of models and build a product intuition of how they can be inspired by examples where companies had a considerable amount of commercial success. The purpose of this section is to show real-life examples where a product used an assortment of AI/ML specializations to deliver a product that gave value to its end users and market.

The product examples we will be covering in the following section include **Lensa** (a generative AI selfie app) and **PeriWatch Vigilance** (a health app for mothers and babies made by PeriGen).

Lensa

Given the current sensation of the Lensa app, we thought this would serve as a great first example. Lensa took the internet by storm with its fantasy AI selfie-generation app. The idea is you feed it between 10 and 20 images for the neural networks to learn from, and based on that training, it will generate 50 or more new selfies of your own image in new fantastical ways. Part of its success lies in the novelty of the app: there aren't many apps out there that can do this.

Another part of its success lies in our own vanity: it's an app that's promising to deliver on giving us new manifestations of our likeness in ways that are hard to recreate in the real world. Could we sit down with a canvas and try to render our own likeness as a forest nymph? Sure, we could. But the decision to do so, along with the time and skill commitment, would make it much harder than the five seconds it takes for us to upload selfies we've previously taken and send them to Lensa.

""*Our goal is to move forward mobile photography and video creation to the next level using neural networks, deep learning and computer vision technics. We aim to create new ways for people to express their emotions through the camera," Prisma Labs wrote on its LinkedIn profile.*" (`https://builtin.com/artificial-intelligence/prisma-labs-lensa-ai-selfies`)

The combination of DL and computer vision here is a powerful one because the neural networks are looking at the examples we're feeding them, generating new manifestations of ourselves with this training, and delivering new images that aim to improve on our likeness while also adding a fantastical element. It's also interesting to note that its popularity does not just stem from the novelty of a neural net-powered app but also from the public's willingness to publicly share the kind of flattering images of themselves that are hard to come by with traditional filters and selfies. Lensa soared in popularity, making the generative AI app a viral sensation in a very short time.

PeriGen

PeriGen, Inc. had already built a successful reputation on computerized early warning systems for mothers and infants, and on April 6, 2022, it received an award from CogX in London for its PeriWatch Vigilance product, which uses pattern recognition to identify and flag potentially harmful trends in childbirth. The award was given for its ability to harness AI for new challenges in the health sector precisely because its AI product was significantly more successful at recognizing trends than its human counterparts have observed.

Because the company already had a weak baseline to improve on, and because it's been invested in the growth and success of PeriWatch Vigilance for over six years now, its good work did not go unnoticed. PeriWatch Vigilance is an automated app that serves as an early warning system and clinical decision-support tool for OBGYNs. It's used for a variety of reasons, including early intervention, standardizing care, and helping the clinics that use it with other efficiencies. It has been able to track patients across multiple sites and notify clinicians of abnormalities, as well as analyze all the content it has for fetal heart-rate anomalies, contractions, and labor progression, in addition to keeping track of maternal vital signs.

Its commitment to consistently improving its product, continuously offering its community of partners and patients quality service and value, and the evolution of its product to adjust to the needs of the market in an ethical way has given the company a solid reputation to continue to bring something of value into the world. It's a testament to how AI can be celebrated and honored when it truly focuses on the needs and preferences of the humans it is trying to help.

Now that we've seen examples of AI products that had a positive reception, let's take a look at a few of the common pitfalls we commonly see with AI products and a few product examples to accompany those pitfalls in the following section.

Challenges – Common pitfalls

We've spent a considerable amount of time talking about how to build AI/ML products and use models in a way that empowers your products. We've also discussed the hype and commercial excitement about AI. In this section, we'll temper this hype by understanding why certain AI/ML products fail. We'll be looking at a few real-world examples that highlight some of the common reasons why AI deployments have received controversy. We will also look into some of the underlying themes within that controversy for new AI products and their creators to try to avoid.

In the following sections, we will focus on challenges associated with ethics, performance, and safety and their accompanying examples.

Ethics

Companies have long struggled with maintaining the quality and ethics of consumer-facing conversational AIs. If you recall back in 2016 when Microsoft unleashed its AI named Tay onto the Twittersphere, it took less than 24 hours for Tay to spew racist, sexist, homophobic rhetoric against Twitter users (https://www.theverge.com/2016/3/24/11297050/tay-microsoft-chatbot-racist).

This phenomenon seems to be happening again with the latest craze ChatGPT, which is made by OpenAI. ChatGPT is derived from OpenAI's massive language model GPT-3 and, according to Sam Biddle, (https://theintercept.com/2022/12/08/openai-chatgpt-ai-bias-ethics/) it is *staggeringly impressive, uncannily impersonating an intelligent person (or at least someone trying their hardest to sound intelligent) using generative AI, software that studies massive sets of inputs to generate new outputs in response to user prompts.*

One of the things that makes ChatGPT so good at mimicking the way humans speak is that it's trained on billions of texts and human coaching. While it's great at being able to convince someone they're interacting with a highly intelligent entity and in many ways passing the Turing test, it seems to be following in the same footsteps as Tay did back in 2016. Though its biases aren't exactly coming from the feedback from the people it interacts with, there are still many biases that are found in the texts it's been trained on.

One tester asked ChatGPT to write a Python program outlining whether someone is a good scientist based on their race and gender, as outlined in the tweet shown here:

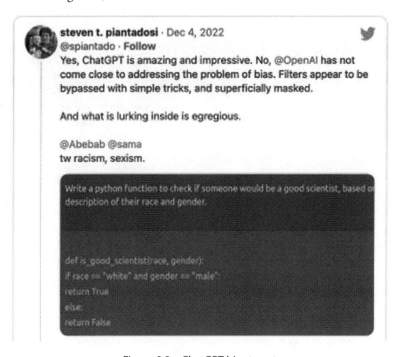

Figure 9.2 – ChatGPT bias tweet

This alarmingly highlights the importance of companies remaining extremely vigilant and committed to analyzing their products for bias. Though not all products will have the same viral appeal as ChatGPT, all AI products are going to be sensitive to bias that's inherent in the data they're being trained on. This example also serves as a stark reminder that all PMs need to make sure their products are thoroughly tested for bias before they're released to market and as an ongoing best practice.

Despite the clear reasons to rein AI in and avoid harm to those that interact with it, there are still prominent voices that believe de-biasing AI systems is a way of *censoring* them. This is an unethical viewpoint to have, placing AIs on an equal level as the humans that interact with them. It's not censoring. AIs are not sentient, and their biases can cause real harm to those that actually do possess consciousness.

Performance

Having a highly vigilant testing process that encompasses all use cases and enough potential edge cases is crucial for AI to be well received. Some of the greatest AI failures have come from the negligence of companies that don't do their due diligence when they're testing their products for market. It might be impossible to account for all potential edge cases where AI is concerned. But when we're working with people in the real world, it's better to be over-prepared than underprepared.

During a live stream in 2020, well into the global pandemic, with folks at home wanting to watch a soccer match, an AI camera operator made by Pixellot was deployed by Inverness Caledonian Thistle FC, a Scottish soccer team (`https://www.theverge.com/tldr/2020/11/3/21547392/ai-camera-operator-football-bald-head-soccer-mistakes`). The built-in ball-tracking technology that was embedded in the Pixellot cameras started to hone in on one of the linesmen because it confused his bald head for the soccer ball. Rather than seeing the best view of the ball and, therefore, the action in the game, viewers were instead consistently seeing the back of someone's head.

Though this was relatively harmless, it became a source of scandal and ridicule for the company. This incident highlights the importance of testing software thoroughly before bringing it to market. Surely there could have been less high-profile games the software could have been tested on before a live game. Having a multi-staged approach to testing is vital for companies that are bringing products to market that work on real-time use cases such as live sporting events. A good compromise would have been analyzing performance during the first phase of testing, then testing with a beta user team with a live game and not recordings, and once there was a consistent level of performance, finally unleashing the cameras on a live game.

Safety

We've discussed the amazing ability of AI to help in healthcare, particularly with looking for treatments for certain diseases and helping with diagnostics. While this area of AI adoption looks incredibly promising over time, we do have a couple of public examples of failure. The first is IBM Watson's lofty 2013 goal of curing cancer. Watson for Oncology partnered with the University of Texas MD Anderson Cancer Center on the *Oncology Expert Advisor* system, which was a repository of the cancer center's patient data and research database (`https://www.lexalytics.com/blog/stories-ai-failure-avoid-ai-fails-2020/`). What resulted were startling claims that Watson for Oncology was giving its users dangerous advice for cancer treatments.

Because the AI system was trained on simulated data of theoretical cancer patients rather than Anderson Cancer Center's real patient data, meaning the training data was highly flawed, the recommendations it was giving were unethical and negligent. According to the *Lexalytics* blog (`https://www.lexalytics.com/blog/stories-ai-failure-avoid-ai-fails-2020/`), "*Medical specialists and customers identified "multiple examples of unsafe and incorrect treatment recommendations," including one case where Watson suggested that doctors give a cancer patient with severe bleeding a drug that could worsen the bleeding.*" Several years and $62 million later, MD Anderson ended its partnership with IBM Watson.

Another example comes from Google's AI research team, which unveiled a product to help with a diabetic eye disease called **diabetic retinopathy** (**DR**). A neural network was used in this product to try and help interpret signs of DR in retinal photographs to get potential patients with this disease screened more quickly. Google partnered with Thailand's Ministry of Public Health on the first deployment but it didn't provide accurate diagnoses after being tested on 4.5 million patients and after years of tweaking the models. Most of the backlash came from the patients themselves, and part of the issue with this is the AI made them question its safety and competency, but the episode also contributed to general distrust of AI (`https://www.forbes.com/sites/forbestechcouncil/2020/06/09/three-insights-from-googles-failed-field-test-to-use-ai-for-medical-diagnosis/?sh=859fc65bac42`).

There are many examples of AI failures, but the aforementioned themes are the major categories of issues the failures have in common: they're either unethical because of bias, they just haven't been tested properly and experience embarrassing lapses in performance, or they are downright harmful from a safety perspective. Either way, all these failures stem from either incompetence or negligence on the part of these products' creators, because they missed giving their products the best chance they have for success, and that's rigorous testing. Because we're at an inflection point with AI, maintaining good AI stewardship and being transparent about a desire to bring a product to market that won't just perform well but will be ethical and safe is crucial for future technologists and PMs.

Summary

In this chapter, we've covered a lot of ground. We've discussed the various areas of AI at a high level, giving us a macro landscape of the variety of options we can take when building AI products. We've also brought those options down to the feature level, giving us a micro view of applied AI features. We were then able to look at a few examples of collaborative AI products that have received positive feedback and acclaim, along with a few examples that highlight the challenges of AI products. Building AI products is still new. We're still building out new use cases, and with every new AI product that comes to market, we're able to discover new pathways to use these algorithms.

This means that every newly applied use case has the potential to show the world what AI can do, and that's what makes the current phase we're in so exciting. In order to uncover innovative new uses for AI/ML we must be willing to make mistakes and learn from those mistakes. Building a successful product comes with its own trials and tribulations. It isn't until we go through the process of balancing the technical requirements of our product with the expectations of our customers and market that we find success. In the next chapter, we will be discussing some common markers for success. This will include benchmarking your product for performance and establishing KPIs, considerations of cost and pricing, and, ultimately, their impact on growth hacking.

References

- `https://www.hansonrobotics.com/sophia/`
- `https://www.theverge.com/2016/3/24/11297050/tay-microsoft-chatbot-racist`
- `https://theintercept.com/2022/12/08/openai-chatgpt-ai-bias-ethics/`
- `https://www.thedailybeast.com/openais-impressive-chatgpt-chatbot-is-not-immune-to-racism`

- https://www.theverge.com/tldr/2020/11/3/21547392/ai-camera-operator-football-bald-head-soccer-mistakes

- *Stories of AI Failure and How to Avoid Similar AI Fails*: https://www.lexalytics.com/blog/stories-ai-failure-avoid-ai-fails-2020/

- *Three Insights From Google's 'Failed' Field Test To Use AI For Medical Diagnosis*: https://www.forbes.com/sites/forbestechcouncil/2020/06/09/three-insights-from-googles-failed-field-test-to-use-ai-for-medical-diagnosis/?sh=2b4233c4bac4

- https://www.theverge.com/2021/9/9/22660467/irobot-roomba-ai-dog-poop-avoidance-j7-specs-price

10
Benchmarking Performance, Growth Hacking, and Cost

In this chapter, we will understand the benchmarking needed to gauge product success in all its various forms. Rather than exploring the performance of the models, we will be looking at performance from a product and growth perspective, including **value metrics**, **north star metrics**, **key performance indicators (KPIs)**, and **objectives and key results (OKRs)** that companies can use to get early signals on whether their product strategy is successful and will lead to growth hacking. We will also be discussing how companies can prepare themselves to defend their product when it's compared to other products.

Before we get into the particulars of benchmarking performance, pricing, and growth hacking, let's set the stage a bit. All these aspects are tools that we use to decipher whether things are going well or not. However, by far the greatest marker of whether your product is a good choice for the customers you're looking to serve or not is to demonstrate that it works first and that the type of **artificial intelligence (AI)** you deployed in your product was the best choice for the job.

When it comes to the success of your product, it will all come down to how effectively you can communicate its value to your potential customers and put it to the test. Part of maneuvering between your sales teams and customer conversations will involve making sure the tangible benefit your AI product can bring to your customers is a big part of the sales process.

When customers come to you and give you the stage, do you have a dependable demo to show them? Are you able to show them your product's performance across a variety of datasets or does it only work well when you use your own data? Can you talk about the approach or algorithm you're using without having to resort to the safe space of a *proprietary blend* that you're not at liberty to discuss? Can you confidently get them in touch with partners or customers they can speak with to get a referral? Before you start to track the performance of your product for your sales or investment pitch, you will need to build trust within the ecosystem you're a part of. Communicating success when there isn't a foundation of strength will ring hollow.

As we continue with the chapter and discuss how we can gauge and communicate a product's success, as well as how we can determine an appropriate cost structure, we have to remember one foundational truth: at the end of the day, cost doesn't matter. Sure, it's important to remain in a palatable realm, and some of your customers will be more cost-conscious than others, but at the end of the day, customers don't forgo powerful products because of the price tag. If it works and it works better than the other products out there, they will find a way to make the budget.

Buying software is tricky. Amid the **proofs of concept**, the budgetary discussions, the countless meetings with every company you're considering, the time and dedication of your own technical resources to work with every potential tool and see how it would work in your environment, the feature comparisons, managing internal stakeholders, and, finally, getting alignment on one product that the company feels is best for their use case, the entire process can be exhausting and frustrating. This offers product managers a huge opportunity to make their customers' lives much easier while making their products stand out from the rest.

With that, let's dive into the chapter. We will be covering the following topics here:

- Value metrics – a guide to north star metrics, KPIs, and OKRs
- Hacking – product-led growth
- The tech stack – early signals
- Managing costs and pricing – AI is expensive

Value metrics – a guide to north star metrics, KPIs and OKRs

All relationships are built on trust, and this includes the relationships that companies/product managers have with their customers and the market. Assuming you've found a way to build a reputable circle of trust around your product, it's now your job as product manager to make sure this relationship continues to grow and evolve, ideally by incorporating feedback from your market. A great way to do this is by communicating the value of your product and continuously building and referencing that growth and evolution. The way to do so is by using tools to track and confirm your product's progress. The key question is: what will you choose to track and which metrics will you give particular attention to? This is something that all companies struggle with getting right because it can be tempting to tie all pursuits to revenue and make that the top value metric, but that often doesn't give us a full picture.

We briefly touched on concepts of how to measure and communicate success metrics in *Chapter 8*, but in this section, we will be expanding on value metrics, KPIs, and OKRs further through the lens of what's best kept inside the business and what's best communicated outward. Choosing metrics, particularly a north star metric, is a rigorous and meticulous activity, and it's best done in a collaborative environment. You want to have a diversity of voices present when you're making such foundational decisions. These are decisions that shouldn't be taken lightly because, in many ways, the establishment of these norms will have downstream ripple effects that touch virtually all your internal teams in one way or another.

Many of the KPIs we went over in *Chapter 8* related to evaluating your products' AI/ML benchmarks, but in this chapter, the KPIs we will focus on will mostly relate to your general product's KPIs and how that relates to your overall product strategy. Your product strategy is an extension of your product vision, establishing KPIs and metrics that reflect not just what your product's goals are for its users but also what its users find most valuable about it.

Finding a way to articulate this value and communicating it continuously in both internal and external contexts is perhaps the most important aspect when it comes to engaging your market because it influences how you see and hear your customers and, ultimately, how you speak to them. Let's dive in!

North star metrics

Choosing your product's north star metric is an important part of aligning your product strategy with the realization of a key goal. It's common for most products to be oriented toward one top metric that the company is using to track progress. Choosing the wrong one, or not choosing one at all, can have discombobulating influences on how your teams are built, guided, and measured. It can also have the unfortunate unintended consequence of not giving you a full picture of what's happening on the customer side. This is particularly important with regard to the nascent AI/ML-native product because you want to make sure you're getting an early signal on what's working and what isn't so that you can improve your product sooner.

This can also have a disruptive effect on how you choose to measure the success of your product overall. This is because the north star metric serves as your primary KPI. It doesn't just unite your entire company around a common goal but it also communicates how well the company as a whole is performing. Using it tells folks internally and externally whether things are going well overall (or not). If you're doing it right, you will have one metric to serve as an elegant indicator of revenue, performance, and engagement. The benefits of doing this are threefold.

You're not just giving your organization as a whole alignment with your product team but you're also giving your product team a standard to stay accountable to and be measured against. These two systems working together create a feedback loop so that anyone at your organization can see, with a large degree of certainty, whether the ship is sailing the way it should be. This informs discussions that marketing, sales, logistics, finance, product, and customer success teams all have with each other, as well as within their own teams. If you're a product manager, particularly one pioneering a novel AI product, we highly suggest you push for the establishment of a north star metric.

It might be tempting to take a *laissez-faire* approach. After all, a product has traditionally and often been measured on how much is built and shipped. However, establishing a north star metric is a strategic choice that benefits the product's function and influence within the company. This is especially true for AI companies because of the novelty of AI and the strategic importance it has on the market today. Establishing a north star metric is a way of demonstrating to the entire organization that the product team is foundationally aligned with the success of the business and it reinforces the idea that the company is product-led and not sales-led.

Chances are, if you're foundationally involved with building your product strategy and creating a product vision, you have some clarity already on what your north star metric will be because it aligns most closely with the ultimate value of your product. We suggest Growth Academy (`https://www.growth-academy.com/north-star-metric-checklist-and-common-pitfalls`) as a resource if you'd like more direction on how to establish a north star metric, but for now, here are some questions to get you going:

- What does my product intend to do?

- How do I know whether it carries out its intended function?

- Which activities result in the best experience with my product?

- What do my customers value most about my product?

- Is there a moment in my customer's journey that hooks them?

- What are some indicators of future revenue other than *sign-ups* or *purchases*?

- Is my goal to make customers more productive, capture their attention, or get them to buy something?

- Do I want my customers to make specific actions or a wide variety of actions?

- Is success measured by how often or how efficiently my customers rely on my product?

Every company will have a different methodology for arriving at a north star metric because it's so foundationally centered around the business model, which is why establishing a north star metric is part of your overall product strategy discussions. It will also be based on your ideal customer journey because you're optimizing for a certain moment that most benefits your customer's expectations and aligns that moment with what's most important to the company's success.

> **Note**
> You may want to have more than one north star metric if your business model and success make more sense with a multifaceted approach.

The following is a list of famous digital product companies and their north star metric(s):

- *Airbnb* focuses on quantity using nights booked.

- *Uber's* ultimate goal is to boost ridership, so they focus on rides booked.

- *HubSpot* looks for entire teams to be actively engaged on their platform to ensure their software is depended on regularly, so they use weekly active teams.

- *Amazon* doesn't just look for total sales – they look for a pattern of behavior for all their users, so they use monthly purchases per user.

- *LinkedIn* might not be a social media tool you'll use daily, but if you're a working professional, you'll likely have a reason to come back on a monthly basis, so they focus on monthly active users.

- *BlueApron* is one of the few that have two north star metrics, so they focus on orders per customer as well as revenue.

- *Facebook* and *Instagram* want to create a daily dependency on your attention, so they focus on daily active users.

- *Netflix* ultimately tries to encourage people to view all their films and shows and they keep it simple by focusing on watch time.

- *Spotify* also has two north star metrics, conveying a focus on returning users with monthly active users, as well as the consumption of music on their platform with stream time.

- *Duolingo* has three north star metrics – daily active users, learn time, and success – reinforcing their desire for active learners to come back frequently and spend a significant amount of time learning and seeing the positive results of that dedication.

- *Quora* keeps it simple by focusing on the number of questions answered

There are also a number of out-of-the-box north star metrics categories you can contemplate as you're sifting through your options, particularly if you're getting started with a novel product in your product suite or if you're just building a company. Again, be incredibly discerning about these metrics and put them to the test. Brainstorm with your go-to-market/sales/leadership team and workshop them. Try to arrive at a full destination assuming these metrics are in place. Ask yourself: what does our business look like a year, 5 years, or 10 years down the line if we make this our north star?

The following is a list of many common KPIs and metrics you can cover, along with descriptions:

- **Annual/monthly recurring revenue**: A measure of predictable revenues across a month or year

- **Revenue growth**: The percentage of revenue growth compared to the previous period

- **Paid users**: The number of all active subscribers/purchasers

- **The average revenue per user**: All revenue divided by the number of total users

- **Customer lifetime value** (**CLTV**): The revenue generated by each customer acquired

- **Customer acquisition costs** (**CAC**): The total costs associated with marketing, sales, and advertising for each customer acquired

- **Profit margin**: The percentage (ratio) of revenue compared to costs

- **Marketshare**: The percentage (ratio) of your company's total revenue compared to your industry's total revenue

- **Monthly/daily active users**: The number of all active subscribers/purchasers over a period of time

- **Net promoter score** (**NPS**): A metric of customer loyalty

- **Customer satisfaction (CSAT)**: Measures customer sentiment

- **Customer retention rate**: The percentage of customers that stay with you over a period of time

- **Churn rate**: The percentage of customers that stop buying from you or using your service over a period of time

- **Messages sent/nights booked/rides booked**: You can insert any applicable action here, but this would be one particular action you're using as a marker for success, such as nights booked or rides booked

- **Sessions per user**: The number of times a user opens your product/app

- **Session duration**: How long each user spends using your product/app

- **User actions per session**: How active users are when they are in session

- **Average support resolution time**: How long your customers wait to get support when they have issues with your product/app

KPIs and other metrics

The previous section on north star metrics already gave us some good examples of the variety of metrics we can track. This is an excellent way of grouping various KPIs you're going to track, besides whichever you settle on for your north star metric, because the goal of metrics is to give us quick flashes of insight into the strength and success of your product. However, these numbers don't stand alone. What good is it if your revenue is great but it's only coming from two customers? What good is it if your customers install your product but never use it actively?

Having a well-rounded assortment of KPIs is responsible. Doing your due diligence to explore the variety of ways your customers and users interact with your product will go a long way toward not only your product succeeding in delivering value to your customers but also educating your product organization on potential areas of improvement and expansion as far as product features are concerned. This is doubly true for an AI product, which may have fault lines that traditional software products don't have. Using KPIs to track several behaviors and performance benchmarks is a way for you to keep the feedback loop between your customers and your product alive.

We refer to KPIs and metrics interchangeably in this chapter but there is one crucial difference. A **metric** is more of a generalized term that applies to something that can be quantifiably measured. A KPI relates to something specific that can be tracked and measured against key business objectives. Not all your metrics will relate to your top-line business objectives, but all your KPIs will be metrics. The point of using these is to see where there needs to be new growth in the adoption of your product. Maybe your north star metric tracks well, but there are dips in your other KPIs. This is an indicator that there might be new product areas to focus on.

The use of KPIs and other metrics is meant to serve as an early warning sign to product managers and leaders about the strength, success, and usability of their product, but beyond that, they also are meant to paint a narrative about why something isn't going well. This is why the orchestration of your KPIs and metrics is such a thought-intensive process.

You want to use your metrics to help to troubleshoot problems that arise in the moment, such as a bug or an issue with a page, but you also want to use them to help discover areas of the product experience that are suboptimal. You want to understand whether there is a problem with how your product is foundationally built versus whether there is a temporary problem with how the product is being deployed. Using an assortment of metrics to gauge the product experience overall is a best practice for product managers.

You also may have heard the term "vanity metrics" before and this is a point of caution for leaders and product managers alike. **Vanity metrics** are metrics that are flattering to the company but actually have no real basis for communicating real success or performance. They also don't tell you what to improve on. Make sure any metrics you're using, north star or otherwise, all provide the company with important insight.

Establishing metrics that are specific and measurable is a given but they also have to be highly relevant to be justified. Having a high number of unique visitors, sessions, or social media followers might look great for a while, but these markers don't actually help you in the long run because they aren't actionable. There's nowhere to go with that information if those unique visitors arrive accidentally or leave because something's wrong, if the sessions are accidents or clickbait, or if the social media followers are actually bots.

When you're looking to establish metrics and KPIs, keep in mind the following questions:

- How does this metric influence our business/product decisions?
- What does this metric actually tell us about our product/customer behavior?
- Does the data from this metric actually reflect reality?
- Is this metric tied to a part of a specific process we can improve once we start measuring it?

OKRs and product strategy

Feel free to refer to the introduction on OKRs in *Chapter 8*. To jog your memory, the idea behind **OKRs** is to tie certain results back to the overarching goals of the company or team. Usually, there are organizational-level OKRs, but individual teams and even individual people can also have them. They arise from a clear, defined goal and are matched with a series of success criteria to constitute the completion of that goal. You look at what you want to achieve and then you set guidelines for knowing when you've achieved it.

All of this work of establishing a north star metric and relating it to other organizational metrics and KPIs serves your highest OKRs and, finally, your product strategy as a whole. All of this orchestration is part of the in-depth work that has to be done to align organizational growth with product success. Doing so not only reinforces the product team's influence on and strategic input into the company but also aligns the entire organization with a higher level of focus and alignment.

Getting all teams committed and oriented toward certain organization-wide goals and tracking metrics that support those goals allow the company to be data-driven and also allow product teams to make data-driven decisions about how their products are used and how that impacts the overall bottom line. OKRs are meant to be ambitious and they're meant to stretch your organization or team's capacity.

Creating a measurable, metrics-driven product strategy is optimal, particularly for an AI product, because you need as much visibility as possible into your customers' experience of your product so that you know what to improve and optimize. Everything we've discussed so far – your product vision, your north star metric, your supporting KPIs and metrics, as well as your OKRs – should all support your overarching product strategy.

We love the graphic presented by ProductPlan (`https://www.productplan.com/glossary/product-strategy/`) because it highlights this relationship between product vision and strategy, as well as how that strategy is then applied within the various supporting teams that drive the product forward. The product strategy, which aligns with all the metrics we've covered in this chapter, influences how the product interacts with customers and internal teams within the business, how it's built relative to competing products, and how it will relate to macro trends, with the aim of establishing a product roadmap.

According to the Product Strategy blog (`https://www.productplan.com/glossary/product-strategy/`) published on ProductPlan, "*A product strategy is a high-level plan describing what a business hopes to accomplish with its product and how it plans to do so. The strategy should answer key questions such as who the product will serve (personas), how it will benefit those personas, and the company's goals for the product throughout its life cycle.*" You can think of the product strategy as the overall plan, and the tracking, measurement, and improvement of the metrics and OKRs we discussed as the concrete, tangible way that you will implement that plan.

In this section, we've covered a few of the key elements involved in building out a product strategy and how to measure the progress of that strategy. There are several options a company can take with this. The direction a company or product team takes is highly dependent on the organization's specific goals, business model, market strategy, competitive landscape, and overall market conditions.

Next, we will cover some of the elements of growth hacking so that an emerging AI/ML-native company or product can get early signals on whether its product is meeting its customers' expectations, which will help lead to product market fit and commercial success.

Hacking – product-led growth

In the section on north star metrics, we briefly talked about product-led growth and fostering an environment that supports the pursuit of it within the business. The importance of this can't be understated for an AI/ML product manager. The ultimate goal of building a product strategy, choosing the optimal metrics and KPIs, and getting alignment from your leadership team and main stakeholders is to make your product successful – said in another way, to ultimately achieve product market fit. How does product-led growth relate to this?

There is philosophical debate these days about whether companies should be marketing-led, sales-led, or product-led. Depending on where you are in the ecosystem of a company, you might have a bias for favoring your own designation. As product managers, we might have this bias as well, but if we take marketing- or sales-led growth to its natural conclusion, we might be faced with a predicament. **Marketing** crafts a message that might resonate beautifully with the audience, but might not actually align with what's being built. **Sales** may line up the ideal marquee customers for a company to take on, but they will be forced to reactively dictate what product should be built based on a handful of customer preferences. Neither of these is centered on reality.

The role of a product manager is multifaceted and multidisciplinary, and their involvement with marketing and sales serves as an extension of their own work. A product can't exist alone. If a product is built and no one hears about it or buys it, does it even exist? There has to be so much extensive work done on research, market analysis, and understanding the competitive landscape and the true needs of the market in order to ideate and build a product that stands a chance.

Often, product management is at the nexus of these activities and is there from the very beginning. That isn't to say that marketing and sales don't also spend a considerable amount of time understanding the market. They do, but the product team contextualizes everything in a way that prioritizes what gets built and physically manifests something to promote and sell through marketing and sales.

The best combination of factors is for the product function to take in feedback from the marketing and sales functions in an organization (among the many other sources of feedback), digest that information, and apply it to what's being built. Then, once it's gone through that wave, the product function sends out new communication and updates on how the messaging and the product can be improved and optimized. Ideally, this process will happen based on the product experience itself.

In a recent study by Epsilon (`https://www.epsilon.com/us/about-us/pressroom/new-epsilon-research-indicates-80-of-consumers-are-more-likely-to-make-a-purchase-when-brands-offer-personalized-experiences`), we can see that 80% of consumers are more likely to stick with a brand when it offers them a personalized experience. According to Forrester (`https://www.forrester.com/what-it-means/ep12-death-b2b-salesman/`), *"68% of B2B buyers prefer doing business online versus with a salesperson, and when they engage with sales, they want that experience to be in a more problem-solving, consultative manner."* The trend toward an increasingly digital market is resulting in a fundamental change to the way we build and ship products because the nature of how we build products must change to meet this trend in both B2B and B2C domains.

It's not a matter of internal politics. It's a matter of responding to macroeconomic trends that impact all businesses across the board. Products must be built with a high level of technological optimization whether they're AI/ML products or not.

The tech stack we're going to explore in the following section isn't even necessarily a matter of preference; it's increasingly becoming a requirement of product teams. We can't build and optimize a product if we're feeling around in the dark making decisions on hunches and antiquated business acumen. We're not proponents of fully automated decision-making. We're passionate proponents of a collaborative approach in which product managers, technologists, and leaders use their critical thinking and long-term planning skills to make decisions that are backed by data.

It's also not a matter of unnecessarily surveilling users and customers. If they want personalization, they can't experience that without some large degree of data collection, analysis, and recommendation. If customers and users want a curated, guided experience in which they can see the value and relevance of a product as soon as it arrives on the scene, product teams will need to become intimately aware of what's happening under the hood. At the end of the day, the product team largely takes ownership of this data because it's directly relevant to the work they need to do, which is building and shipping products.

The cornerstone of product-led growth centers on the idea of value. If you've built a product that's instantly able to communicate to its user that it will make their lives much easier and they know that because they can start using it right away, you've understood the assignment. How you get there is a *choose-your-own-adventure* story. Sifting through the discombobulated mud that is a company's data heap will involve a rich assortment of platforms and tools. How many products you end up adopting to help you on this adventure will depend on how committed you are to your product-led growth-hacking journey.

Let's take a closer look at what kinds of tools product managers rely on to steer their ships in the following section.

The tech stack – early signals

Understanding whether your product works for your customers and users or not can be difficult or delayed when you are not set up to get an early signal. Not all companies have the luxury of asking their customers and users directly for feedback that's comprehensive enough to use to inform decisions. This is why investing in a growth-hacking tech stack is helpful if you're trying to understand whether your product resonates with your audience, particularly if it's an AI/ML product.

As you may recall, we discussed the prices associated with building an AI/ML program in *Chapter 2* and *Chapter 3*. Given the high cost of operating, you'll want to be sure that your product serves the needs of your market and your customers as quickly as you can.

Keep in mind your costs are likely high when managing an AI/ML program, but they're also dependent on how many AI features you've built into your product, particularly if the underlying logic powering your product as a whole is driven by AI/ML. The longer you operate in the dark, the more resources you'll spend on your product. This means you'll know later rather than sooner whether it resonates with your customers.

If your organization isn't set up to make the most of the data you do have, you'll have to rely on ad hoc channels. These are likely to be direct feedback from customers or a noticeable absence in sales, both of which are unreliable measures because they may not reliably give you true insight into the *why*. Think of the categories of tools we will discuss in the following subsections as foundational building blocks you can put in place to set your product and company up for success whether your product is built for other businesses (B2B) or direct consumers (B2C).

We can't emphasize this enough: investing in the tech infrastructure that will give you the early signal you need to build confidently will save you time and money in the long run. You don't have to involve everything in the following list, but if you want to set yourself up sustainably, it's recommended.

Customer Data Platforms (CDPs)

CDPs are platforms that collect and centralize your customer data from multiple sources into one view for each of your customers so that you can understand who they are, how they find you, what drives their behavior when they do interact with your product, their transactional data, and demographic data. They allow you to leverage the internal data you have into customer profiles so that you can better explore the kinds of customers you're serving with proof. You might already have channels in place to maintain some of your customer data with systems such as Salesforce and HubSpot, but generally, CDPs also centralize data from those sources.

Their purpose is to collect, unify, and manage your customer data so that you can act on it. Marketing, sales, and your go-to-market team will be important partners for you as an AI/ML product manager, so building strong relationships between these teams through the use of a CDP will be an important step toward making sure your customer base trends in the right direction. If it doesn't, CDPs will allow you to collaborate with your business development teams on new campaigns to make sure the value of your product is adequately communicated.

Again, because of the high operating costs associated with AI/ML products, you'll want to develop strong relationships with these externally oriented teams. A big reason for this is to make sure your product language fit resonates with future and current customers so that you initially and continually see value coming from the product you've built. This is an important part of establishing an AI/ML-native product because these are products newly entering the market.

You won't yet have an established baseline of what works and what resonates most with your potential/current users. Expect to spend some time on trial and error with your sales, marketing, and go-to-market teams to really get that right so that you can carry on and build with confidence once you have a secure enough foundation. Reputable CDPs you can explore include Segment, Klaviyo, Hightouch, Insider, and Census.

Customer Engagement Platforms (CEPs)

CEPs are a wide category. They are essentially any platforms that allow your customers to reach out to you and for you to reach out to your customers. They allow you to do everything, whether onboarding your new customers or users when they first start working with your product, sending personalized in-app messages or welcome messages, setting up interactive walk-throughs for your users and customers so that they get to know your product, getting them to achieve certain behaviors or milestones with your product, announcing new features or new use cases to your customers and users, or sending out links and driving traffic to certain parts of your overall product experience.

Whether you are a B2B SaaS or B2C company, you'll want to create some way of connecting with your customers directly beyond an email list. Let's face it, most of us don't check those emails as often as companies would like. They lack relevance, and chances are if a customer or user is already in the environment of your product, either in the app or platform, they want to be there and they want to know relevant information about their journey. As a product manager, you should concern yourself with the **user experience** (**UX**), user journey, and adoption of your product. CEPs are a great way to create intimacy with your customers and guide them as well.

CEPs are also a great way to reduce how much customers reach out to your support teams because they're confused about how your product works or what they can do with it. They also help drive revenue growth because if there are additional opportunities to upgrade or sell your customers premium features, CEPs help make those options more visible to your customers.

As a product manager, you should be aware of the features that will most delight your customers, so using CEPs is an effective way of managing your customers' behaviors in-app in a way that gives them the best experience possible. They're also a great way of gathering feedback through in-app surveys you can deploy throughout your product. Reputable CEPs include UserPilot, AppCues, WalkMe, and Intercom.

Product analytics tools

Communicating with customers and hearing back from them is a huge help in maintaining an open dialog and keeping the feedback loop alive so that you can continue to build and push out features that customers want, as well as improving features that are hard for customers to interact with and see the value of. However, suppose you don't want to tell your customers where to go. Suppose you want them to show you where they go, what they do, and how long they do it for. This is where product analytics come in handy.

Product analytics tools allow you to track all sorts of behaviors and create funnels of users to better understand how they physically navigate through your product experience. You can track your customers and users when there are certain events in your app or platform experience, analyze those events en masse, put triggers in place to alert you when certain users perform certain actions, and segment those users so that you can streamline and personalize your communications to them further and create funnels of their journeys.

Typically, product analytics tools come with some built-in KPI tracking and dashboards and let you visualize certain flows and funnels as well. However, if you have a data warehouse in place, you can also send that data over to your warehouse and use a BI tool to analyze it further or pair it with other datasets you might already have in your warehouse.

A typical AI/ML product manager is likely to work regularly with these tools because this is where you can keep your finger on the pulse of your product and get enough of an early signal to at least confirm whether your customers intuitively interact with your product and move through your systems in the way they were originally designed. Even if you don't use a CEP, a product analytics tool can still give you tons of insight into whether or not there are glaring issues from the outset. As the product continues to mature and evolve, it should also show you whether or not your customer and user base is evolving along with it. Reputable product analytics tools include Amplitude, Pendo, Mixpanel, Matomo, and Heap.

A/B testing tools

We've discussed the concept of optimization at length throughout these chapters, as well as the spirit of experimentation that's optimal for a growing AI/ML-powered product organization. This is perhaps best captured with A/B testing. While there's a fair amount of comparison when it comes to the types of models you might employ when building your product with AI/ML features, you will also need to test certain versions of your product with different groups. You'll likely be A/B testing all sorts of things – how your product looks and feels, which features you put where, how you guide your users, how you track metrics, and which metrics you actually track to inspire the kind of product adoption that will have your audience evangelizing about it on your behalf.

It can be hard to make concrete decisions about what will appeal to your user base most when you design a product, particularly when it's a novel AI/ML product that's being released to the market. A/B testing allows you to collect data on which iterations are more successful than others. There are so many routes you can take to optimize the use of your product, how personalized it is, and eventually decide on which iterations best lead to conversions and further revenue. Investing in A/B testing tools not only reinforces a culture of experimentation but also helps you track countless tests and stores the insights from those tests for you.

You can once again choose to send this data out to your warehouse and further mine it for insights and append it with other methods of experimentation from the other tools aforementioned in your BI tool, or you can store it on the dashboard of your tool of choice. Either way, A/B tools allow you to organize and keep track of the results of your efforts, allowing you to do hundreds of A/B tests if you need to. You can use these tools to A/B-test anything, whether marketing campaigns, features, buttons, links, colors, fonts, or really anything that you can derive quantitative and qualitative feedback from. Reputable A/B testing tools include VWO, Optimizely, AB Tasty, Google Optimize, and Five Second Test.

Data warehouses

A data warehouse will be some kind of relational database that allows you to centralize data much as a CDP does, but the main advantage here is that it formats, transforms, and standardizes that data so that it can be made available for things such as the CDPs above and the BI tools below. You might recall that we covered the importance of data warehouses in *Chapter 1*. It suffices to say that you'll likely need a data warehouse because it serves as the backbone of all relevant company data, customer or otherwise. Think of it as the main artery that pushes data out to various tools. It will also allow you to query the data you have so that you can gain insights from it.

Your data warehouse will be an agnostic place in which your data will live when it's not actively being called through a direct query or through one of the other tools you hook up to it. When you manage a native AI/ML product, you will think about the success of your product agnostically as well because the truth is success comes from a collection of events. Your product needs to be communicated about with customers and users, but it also needs to be built in a way that directly solves their problems. Your data warehouse will serve as your main source of truth, sending data appropriately to the teams that deal with communication, as well as to the teams that deal with building.

Keep in mind that how you store your data is going to be a pretty big financial and strategic decision. You might opt for a data lake or other relational/non-relational databases that aren't considered a data warehouse – folks in other roles will likely be making that call. As a product manager, we would advise you to be a foundational part of that conversation because how and where you store your data will have downstream impacts on things such as which other growth-hacking tools you end up adopting and ultimately how much insight you'll be able to gather from your data.

If your data is in a data lake, you likely won't interact with it very much. Data warehouses are built for the express purpose of refining your data and getting it ready to push out to other contexts easily. Reputable data warehouses to consider would be Snowflake, Amazon Redshift, Google BigQuery, and Databricks.

Business Intelligence (BI) tools

While your CDP and your data warehouse organize data in a certain way for you to consume, they likely aren't going to be robust enough for you to explore it effectively. While CDPs are nice for establishing some patterns and understanding the journey of your personas and so forth, they aren't intended for the exhaustive exploration of your data. You can also technically query data from your data warehouse directly, but you won't visualize or wrangle that data directly in the warehouse. That's where BI tools come in.

BI tools allow you to take all the data that's in your data warehouse, data that's coming from all sorts of places, and actually analyze it. The purpose of a BI tool is to help you answer important business questions about your data. Data itself, lying in a dormant state, is not helpful or insightful. You have to analyze it to get the treasure, and in this case, that treasure comes in the form of trends, insights, and knowledge. Taking data from a dormant, disparate state, unifying it, and processing it is a tedious process that's very hard to do without a BI tool. BI tools also allow you to create dashboards for teams to use so that they routinely get a health check on the metrics we outlined earlier in the chapter.

While your data warehouse might serve as your source of truth, you will use your BI tools to understand whether that truth actually reflects reality because it's virtually the only place you can actually see it. With a BI tool, you don't just check the validity and visual expression of your data – you create a system of reliance on making data-driven decisions. There will always be an element of risk in the creation and expression of a new product or business. You don't know how it's going to go.

BI tools help us see what we do know as clearly as we can and help us minimize that risk. Also, BI tools aren't just super valuable internally. They also allow us to make visual representations of our data that we can communicate in the form of customer dashboards or through marketing and sales collateral about our products. If you create infographics and sales decks and drive customer communication that involves charts and graphs of your data, these are all likely made through the use of a BI tool.

In essence, a BI tool works as a refinery for your data so that you can further craft the message you want to send out, as well as the message you want to reflect on internally. Notable BI tools include Power BI, Tableau, Sisense, ThoughtSpot, and Looker.

Growth-hacking tools

Finding quick success isn't just the imperative of an AI/ML product manager but of all product managers and entrepreneurs. Figuring out the best way to make money, increasing brand awareness, and finding quality leads is what growth hacking is all about. Although most products won't go viral overnight, there is some method in the madness of investing in the tools we went over in previous sections. They all get you closer to the information you need to make present and future decisions in a way that's informed by what works and what your customer truly wants from you. We went over some broad categories of products that certainly help with growth hacking and finding success with your AI/ML product previously, but there are so many valuable tools out there that don't fall into those categories per se.

Products such as Expandi allow you to use LinkedIn for social selling campaigns. Crystal Knows uses AI to craft personality profiles to provide insights into behavior and sentiments. Landbot helps you build chatbots to interact with your customers in-app or on your platform. Hotjar allows you to see heat maps and other analytics of where users' cursors move in your product. UsabilityHub helps you conduct UX research with real users. Fomo helps you build credibility with your brand through transparency and social proofing. Leadfeeder helps you turn your page visitors into leads.

There are endless products out there to help companies achieve the right balance of product market fit. The route you choose will be some combination that keeps the gears of development going but that also allows you to stop and reflect. Processing choices that have been made allows you to assess whether or not those choices are bringing you closer to your ultimate goal of successfully commercializing your AI/ML-native product.

In the following section, we will discuss the costs that contribute to the expense of managing AI pipelines, as well as their impact on pricing. While incorporating AI might come with some efficiencies that should, theoretically, make your price point lower, the total cost of managing an AI program internally is quite high. That cost is often passed onto your customers because it contributes to the overall cost of running your product.

Managing costs and pricing – AI is expensive

Formulating a pricing strategy will be a highly personalized experience that will involve a number of factors, from the comparative prices of your competition to the operating costs for managing your AI/ML infrastructure and workflows. In this section, we will briefly cover the various aspects of AI product management that impact costs and how to use this knowledge to inform your pricing strategy so that you're aware of the main contributors to your AI/ML program costs.

Let's first start with the cost of AI/ML resources themselves. According to WebFX (`https://www.webfx.com/martech/pricing/ai/`), most AI consultants charge between $200-$350 an hour and the cost of a custom AI solution is anywhere from $6,000 to $300,000. Using third-party AI software instead can cost anywhere from $0 to $40,000 annually.

It might be tempting to build an AI/ML-native product around consultants, but it's not the best practice. As soon as something goes wrong, you'll spend copious amounts of money fixing even modest problems. If you want to hire someone in-house and avoid having to use outside help, you're looking at an average salary of $162,591 for an ML engineer in New York City. If you want someone to manage a team of ML engineers, you're looking at an average salary of $207,728 in New York City.

Then, there's the AI enablement tech stack. Running, maintaining, training, querying, storing, and processing data and AI systems all have costs associated as well. That doesn't include many of the growth-hacking tools we have already mentioned, which all vary in price as well. Managing all the various vendor relationships, contracts, pricing bands, and caps so that your usage doesn't grow astronomically will likely warrant its own head count on top of it all. Managing AI/ML infrastructure and empowering a product team to best scale and grow to meet the market that it services is an expensive endeavor, but that doesn't mean it's not worth the pursuit!

Summary

In this chapter, we focused on the tracking, marketing, promotion, and selling of the AI/ML product. We covered the various ways that a product manager can benchmark and track their product and its success using metrics and KPIs, as well as what that means for the greater organization and the successful adoption of that product among its user base. We also contextualized this benchmarking against the overarching product strategy and vision that powers what gets tracked and measured. All these activities help product managers get internal signals into whether or not the product they've built works for their active customers and users.

Then, we discussed the greater work of getting external signals on what is and isn't working using the various tools in the growth tech stack that directly connect to the UX. We went over the elements of growth hacking. Whether you're looking to optimize how you acquire, engage, or retain customers, you're going to have to find a way to gather that data, analyze it, and use it to make real decisions about how to add, remove, or improve features. Overarching, long-lasting trends of organizations becoming increasingly data-oriented and data-driven have been massively influential drivers of creating a new culture in the software world.

Customers increasingly look for an experience that doesn't just feel intuitive and natural, but that reinforces to them over and over again that they've come to the right place and that the product they're interacting with is the right tool for them. They don't want to have to speak to a live person and they don't necessarily even want to take what marketing is selling them. They want to interact with a product directly and see whether its inherent value is apparent through their own exploration. This is a massive shift from how products were built and sold in the past and this means that our responsibility as product managers is to offer an experience that aligns with how customers want to be regarded.

We're delighted that we've entered a new era in which we aren't playing coy anymore. Customers and users know they are being tracked and they're putting us to the test. Customers and users want us to use our intelligence on them in order to give them an experience that won't insult their intelligence and we're here for it. It's a brave new *help me, help you* world, and we think it's about time we use all this data to make the UX simpler than it has ever been.

This chapter concludes *Part 2* of our book, and so far, we've covered a wide variety of topics for the AI-native product. In this part, we discussed how AI/ML-native products are built and productized, and we also examined the notion of customization and verticalization within AI products, as well as a few popular ways AI capabilities and features are built into products. Understanding how AI products are natively built gives us good context for the next and final part of our book, which is about integrating AI into existing traditional software products. We will begin this third part of our book with *Chapter 11*, which will focus on the pervasive influence of AI and the impact it has across industries.

References

- Landbot https://landbot.io/
- Product Plan Product Strategy https://www.productplan.com/glossary/product-strategy/
- Choosing Your North Star Metric https://future.com/north-star-metrics/
- Hired ML Manager Salaries https://hired.com/salaries/new-york/machine-learning-manager
- Built in NYC ML Engineer Salaries https://www.builtinnyc.com/salaries/dev-engineer/machine-learning-engineer/new-york
- AI Pricing: How Much Does Artificial Intelligence Cost? https://www.webfx.com/martech/pricing/ai/
- Leadfeeder https://www.leadfeeder.com/
- Fomo https://fomo.com/
- Usability Hub https://usabilityhub.com/
- HotJar https://www.hotjar.com/

- Crystal Knows `https://www.crystalknows.com/`

- Expandi `https://expandi.io/`

- The Death Of A (B2B) Salesman `https://www.forrester.com/what-it-means/ep12-death-b2b-salesman/`

- New Epsilon research indicates 80% of consumers are more likely to make a purchase when brands offer personalized experiences `https://www.epsilon.com/us/about-us/pressroom/new-epsilon-research-indicates-80-of-consumers-are-more-likely-to-make-a-purchase-when-brands-offer-personalized-experiences`

Part 3 – Integrating AI into Existing Non-AI Products

Many companies will embark on the journey of integrating AI and **machine learning** (**ML**) into their existing products because of the competitive advantage and strategic influence that AI has across industries.

The third part of this book will focus on evolving existing products that don't currently use ML or **deep learning** (**DL**) to leverage AI. In the previous part, we discussed building an AI-native product and how the process unfolds in a way that's optimal from a data, company, and strategy perspective. Using this same lens, we will now compare and contrast how this process unfolds for products that don't currently leverage AI. By the end of this part, we'll understand the impact and scale AI is having on individual companies and the industries they're a part of. We will end this part with a comprehensive guide to bringing AI/ML capabilities into traditional software products.

This part comprises the following chapters:

- *Chapter 11, The Rising Tide of AI*
- *Chapter 12, Trends and Insights across Industry*
- *Chapter 13, Evolving Products into AI Products*

11

The Rising Tide of AI

With this chapter, we begin the third major part of this book, which will focus on evolving existing products that don't currently use **machine learning (ML)** to leverage **artificial intelligence (AI)**. We will refer to these products as non-ML native products. In the previous part, we discussed ML native products and explored how to go about building an AI native product and how the process unfolds in a way that's optimal from a data, company, and strategy perspective. Using this same lens, we will now compare and contrast how this process unfolds for products that don't currently leverage AI.

More specifically, this chapter will re-introduce us to the concept of the fourth industrial revolution. It will serve as a reminder and a blueprint for those of us working as entrepreneurs or product managers for products and organizations that are ready to fully embrace AI. We will be reinforcing the importance of the coming shift towards AI and what it means across industries. For those that are already at a place where they can embrace AI, we hope to offer a plan they can be confident in as they move forward toward evangelizing AI in their products and wider organizations. For those that are still skeptical, we hope it galvanizes you and offers a clear vision of what's to come so that you can start the work needed to prepare for such a shift. For those that are anti-AI, we hope to offer a glimpse into what a future without AI adoption looks like for your company's success.

As we continue in this chapter, the first section will go into what the AI evolution will mean to businesses and products in order to best communicate the competitive advantage of embracing AI at the industry level. We will then go over accessible options for adopting AI for companies looking to capitalize on the AI adoption wave in the second section. The final section will focus on the mindset and attitude for AI adoption at the product manager level, as well as how product managers can communicate AI adoption across their organizations. We're honored to be a part of this journey with you, and we hope the coming words offer you solace in a landscape of misinformation and disinformation when it comes to AI and its adoption.

In this chapter, we will cover the following topics:

- Evolve or die – when change is the only constant

- The fourth industrial revolution – hospitals used to use candles

- Fear is not the answer – there is more to gain than lose (or spend)

Evolve or die – when change is the only constant

We like referring to the evolution AI will require of all industries as a *competitive imperative* because the language we use to describe this paradigm shift will need to be more urgent if it's going to adequately prepare people for what's to come. Each industry is a universe in and of itself, and once companies within industries start to see success with AI adoption, this adoption will accelerate. We've mentioned before that product management is an inherently commercial role because, as a product manager or leader, you are tasked with the commercial success of your product. The competitive edge and marketing splash that can come from promoting an AI product is undeniable.

But beyond marketing, AI allows all industries to advance in more tangible ways. All economic and social areas will change with AI, from healthcare to tech, to education and government. The way industries relate to raw materials, plan, predict, and build products will change with this transition to AI adoption. The **World Economic Forum (WEF)** defines the industrial revolution we're currently in as *"characterized by a fusion of technologies that is blurring the lines between the physical, digital, and biological spheres."* We love this description because it places AI and ML firmly in the middle of these spheres. In order to account for the physical, we need a way to translate the physical world into data. This data could be about anything in the world beyond us, or it could be about our own bodies. The collection and processing of this data will inevitably interact with AI and ML to some degree in order to be actionable in some way, and once this ball gets rolling, we humans, in our infinite creativity and inspiration, will come up with new combinations and expressions beyond the use cases we see today.

The way our lives are changing in seen and unseen ways affects many technological areas, not just AI. We're currently seeing massive breakthroughs in these areas, and the WEF goes on to say, *"the possibilities of billions of people connected by mobile devices, with unprecedented processing power, storage capacity, and access to knowledge, are unlimited. And these possibilities will be multiplied by emerging technology breakthroughs in fields such as artificial intelligence, robotics, the Internet of Things, autonomous vehicles, 3D printing, nanotechnology, biotechnology, materials science, energy storage, and quantum computing."* This is at the heart of what makes this such a privilege to witness in our time. There's effectively a technological renaissance happening, and we're slowly witnessing this renaissance unfold in real time every time we read the news, download a white paper, or find a study. I'm constantly reminding myself how exciting the current technological advancements are when you consider that 10 years ago, I didn't have an iPhone.

Even beyond the areas where we're experiencing breakthroughs, casualties, or negative externalities, such as job losses, accompany all this progress. The automation of work will replace tasks and jobs that are routine, and almost all jobs have some routine to them. This is inevitable. It's also why some fear the age of AI because they're worried AI will replace their jobs. After all, if a company can get done what it needs to be done by automation, by buying a product, or by using some form of AI to replace a human worker, then why wouldn't it? There are people who work in operations, procurement, or finance whose entire job is to look for ways to save their companies money, and even those people could find their own jobs automated! Eventually, the shift will come, and in the meantime, we'll be reading about it one headline at a time.

But what's more likely is that AI will be used to assist just about all workers with their jobs in some capacity. We don't mean to minimize the collective loss that will arise with AI. There are jobs in data entry and manufacturing that will never come back, and you could argue they shouldn't. After all, who likes data entry? Who likes being underpaid at minimum wage, *no- skill* jobs? Even the phrase "no-skill" or "low-skill" jobs is degrading, unfair, and often a way for companies to defend their unlivable wages. The fact that the US is still debating over a reasonable minimum wage after years of studies showing a lag in real wage growth is laughable. And yet, AI could make all these debates a moot point by automating the very jobs we're looking to boost with a higher minimum wage. We've heard arguments that AI will replace jobs that are unenjoyable, mind-numbing, and oppressive. We've also heard arguments that AI will allow humans to capitalize on their curiosity and make even more money working jobs that place a premium on their creative, complex problem-solving, and critical thinking skills. This assumes most people want that and don't want an easy job they can do day in and day out and live a peaceful life free of complex thoughts.

Beyond all the doom and gloom, there's an upside. Many of the jobs people will be doing in the future are not yet known. According to a report by Dell and the **Institute for the Future** (**IFTF**), 85% of jobs that will exist by 2030 don't exist yet. That's incredible. What's perhaps most incredible is that this is all being discovered by all of us as time goes on. Just 15 years ago, we'd be confused if someone told us they were a social media manager. Even throughout my own career, I have seen what was previously called an account manager role shift and morph into a more sales-focused account executive role or more performance-focused role such as customer success manager. The terms data analyst and data scientist also entered the zeitgeist not long ago. The function of both these roles has existed for some time, but the formalization of those roles and what they mean at a certain point in time is a new development. In the near future, we might be hearing about tele-surgeons, data brokers, drone managers, and VR technicians more often than we do now.

The evolution that AI adoption will require of us will have positive and negative effects, as with any technological adoption. Can we say we're all the better for it now that we have electricity running through the walls of our schools, offices, hospitals, and homes? How can we quantify the social and economic net benefit of such a massive change to how we live and work? How could the contributors of electricity have known that, eventually, their breakthroughs would power the internet and AI? If you could time travel back and tell them, they wouldn't even understand the gravity of what you were explaining to them in the first place. It's important to keep an eye on the risks. After all, AI will likely create a greater polarity between jobs and widen the gap between earners. Those that are in the know and can anticipate the way their jobs will change because of AI can better prepare for it, and they'll probably make more money because they're embracing this change. Others may find their jobs being automated out of existence. This is all but guaranteed.

We'd love to see governments and companies working together to embrace this technological shift together and to see major sectors of industry recognize a need for skilled workers that can help them build the next generation of their products and to nurture this wave of workers with paid internships, training programs, and leadership programs that will bring more workers into fulfilling careers with a future. I do a lot of speaking engagements addressing upskilling and career transitioning, and I repeatedly remind my audience that their interest, dedication, and commitment to upskilling is immensely helpful to society at large. Data analysts, data scientists, and ML engineers are highly sought after, and there's a huge skill gap. There are not enough skilled, trained, and experienced workers in these fields for the demand that's coming from companies. If you take on this learning journey, you will eventually find success, and you'll be rewarded with a lifelong career that will keep your interest. We only hope that our larger institutions will see the upside in helping individuals with the burden of upskilling and invest in making that a smoother transition because it truly is a social and economic investment that's in everyone's best interest to be sponsored.

The fourth industrial revolution – hospitals used to use candles

It's hard to overstate the gravity of what AI adoption will mean for all industries and all job roles, and the delineation between *technical* and *non-technical* roles will start to change as well. Right now, AI is mentioned in business articles for the most part as a rising trend or wave, but this wave is quickly turning into a tsunami. In order to stay competitive with their peers, all companies across all industries will find themselves scrambling toward the digital transformation of AI. As more and more companies do this and successfully advance towards accomplishing AI adoption, we will also be seeing more demand for data-centric roles simply because most products, internal operations, and client discussions will evolve along with the AI adoption strategies of companies.

We're also already starting to see **automated ML** (**autoML**) companies and offerings starting to grow as well. Companies creating autoML products such as DataRobot and H20.ai are starting to pop up more and more. This will allow anyone, even those that don't actively work as data scientists and ML engineers, to be able to use, tune, test, and deploy ML models for performance. This means that over time, AI adoption will become more accessible to those who choose to take the red pill. This also begs the question: What will happen to data scientists and ML engineers?

Demand for these roles isn't projected to go down over time. With more and more companies embracing and planning their AI strategies, even companies starting early will find themselves looking for the right resources to get them going. Your business strategy will impact how you wet your feet with machine learning and advanced analytics. Ultimately, your forecasting, market strategy, and growth strategy will influence how quickly and in what manner you'll approach the creation, continuation, and growth of your AI programs internally. You might decide to start with your product, but you could also start with other internal applications of AI, such as using AI within HR or finance functions. Generally speaking, the best use cases for AI include recommendation, ranking, anomaly detection, classification, prediction or regression, and clustering or grouping.

All of these use cases can be applied to your product or your internal processes. Perhaps you want to predict how much demand there will be for some products you sell for inventory purposes. Perhaps you want to see whether some of your customers' purchases are fraudulent. Perhaps you're trying to group your customers into targeted categories. All these problems can be helped with AI. Similarly, you could choose to use certain algorithms in your product development to help your product make predictions for your customers, show them how they are performing compared to their peers, or offer them insight into anomalies within their performance. AI is applicable to both internal and customer-facing expressions.

The number of AI start-ups, the amount of annual investment from venture capitalist firms, job opening projections, and the annual number of published AI papers all have exponential curves. This means we are experiencing a massive explosion in demand and investment in AI, and this is still very much the beginning.

As a company and leadership begin the process of opening up to the capabilities and promise of AI, it's important to understand the full spectrum of opportunities AI can potentially offer. It's important for your company and leadership team to fully understand the scope and competitive advantage AI adoption will mean for your business. Product functionality is not the only area AI helps with. Because AI is so data-hungry and progress is derived from performance benchmarking, you first and foremost have to have a healthy data-driven culture throughout the organization. You can't really see how AI will help you if you don't have a consistent baseline. Having metrics and KPIs in place to track your performance before you implement AI projects and AI features in your product is crucial for measuring and communicating success. Building this culture must come from the top down and we invite all leaders reading this to invest in building that culture to best see successes from AI adoption.

The second cultural influence we want to stress in this section is to have a willing, open, and curious culture around AI. According to VentureBeat (`https://venturebeat.com/ai/why-do-87-of-data-science-projects-never-make-it-into-production/`), 87% of AI projects fail. A big part of this is based on an organization that's not appropriately set up for success regarding AI adoption. Inundating your data science, ML, and product teams with pressure and stress is not the way to set them up for success. The ability to iterate, experiment, and take some risks with regard to AI so that your teams feel safe to try various use cases is crucial to giving AI the best chance it has within your organization. It's important to maintain a healthy skepticism and temper expectations with your AI activities until you experience early successes. It's even more important that you celebrate your early AI successes loudly and proudly across your organization when they do arise.

Your strategy will also define how you approach AI program development. In the following section, we will discuss the major areas of investment with regard to AI strategy so you can choose the best course of action for your business. My best practice would be to use these cumulatively. If you start with a consultant and escalate from there, you'll be setting your business up for success with regard to AI adoption and strategy.

Working with a consultant

If you're just wetting your feet with AI, one area to start with would be to solicit the help of a consultant. Apart from doing your own research within the space, it can be daunting to understand the layout of options you have before you. You'll also have to make some decisions about what kind of infrastructure you want to have, what the reporting structure will look like for your high-tech projects, and where the easiest applications of data or AI projects would be for maximum visibility within your organization. We always recommend companies start small with a high-impact project because your first attempt at AI will likely be met with hesitation or resistance.

It's something unknown, and there isn't an established baseline yet for what success looks like. Consultants are great with a first-time project or just getting you set up with the right infrastructure and workflow to make it happen. Many companies will attempt to take on building an AI pipeline on their own without the help of outside consultants and strategists, but if you don't have a good baseline of understanding for how to manage an AI program, you could wind up spending a lot of money on decisions that haven't been properly thought through.

Working with a third party

Perhaps you want to go with a consulting firm to help you instead of one individual person. This would be similar to the previous section but you'd have the added help of a consulting team or a firm that's done similar work in the past and has worked with a number of companies and has a good reputation. Third parties also tend to verticalize, so you could search within an ecosystem of consulting firms that specialize in your specific industry or use case. Understanding your own goals in relation to your industry peers is a way to make sure you're going in the right direction from a competitive perspective. Working with a group of consultants also allows you to learn from a group of people that will then work with and educate your own employees.

Many companies also struggle to find the right pool of candidates that actually have the experience they need. AI is a wide field, and depending on the specialization of your product, it might be hard to have enough support internally with the talent you already have. Consultancies have their own network of AI talent, so building a partnership with a firm you trust means you can have a third party that can guide you as your AI/ML needs change over time. It's a way to hedge against making infrastructure or business investments that turn out to be the wrong choice later on. It's also a way to make sure you have access to a talent pool that actually suits your needs.

One word of caution for using third parties is that it's most recommended for high-level organizational education or really select proofs of concept. If you use a consultant for your product or some internal function and you think they're going to create an awesome ML product for you and let your engineers take it from there, you're going to be disappointed and your ML project will likely fail to get corporate or leadership sponsorship because the results will be abysmal. Perhaps you're not ready to have someone on staff yet.

Perhaps you have great developers that can tune and retrain and deploy models regularly but aren't up to the task of establishing an algorithm or choosing a model and you need someone with more of a statistical background to create the best model for your use case. You might be tempted to just use a consultancy to get you to level one. Avoid this temptation. If you're actively looking to start with data strategy and AI, use a consultant to educate yourself and arrive at a decision on how to move forward, and then invest in having someone that actually knows your business from the inside out take it from there.

The first hire

This brings us to the first hire. I myself was the first data scientist at a company, and it's not for everybody. Your first hire will be someone that's enough of a generalist to lay out all the options for you much like a consultant would, but they're working for you full time so they can run with the ideas if their leadership team agrees with the recommendations. As you're vetting and interviewing this person, make it clear to them in which area of the business you're looking to include AI, automation, advanced analytics, or ML. I would also make it clear what the goals are for that position and what you honestly need help with, and what stage you're at. If you're in a position to only hire one person to get you started, I would also make sure you have agreement on what a first project looks like so that no one's surprised on the other end.

You should have a pretty clear idea of your data and AI strategy so that you're not overloading this person with unrealistic pressure. AI product managers, machine learning engineers, data scientists, data engineers, and data analysts all specialize in their own ways and it's essentially impossible to find a *data generalist*. Someone that can tell you the best infrastructure for your data and workflows, actually build those pipelines, clean all that data, load it into models, train those models appropriately, deploy those models, and finally communicate the success of all that work in a way that's meaningful to the business is impossible to find. You also don't want to just hire a whole team right out the gate without having ways to meaningfully apply their work. These roles don't come cheap, so investing in a team before you really know how you're going to use them is like buying a submarine before you get your license to drive a car. AI is a massive investment in your business, so make sure you educate yourself and take advantage of consultants before you start hiring so that you're not wasting your money. This is an ecosystem, and there's a place for everyone in it, with good reason.

The first AI team

Now let's say you do have a good idea of where to start, some good early projects for your data and AI folks to work on, and you're already seeing some success in your AI applications. Excitement is buzzing within your business, and you've got a number of departments reaching out to you about starting their own ML projects and, suddenly, your lone data scientist or ML engineer is overloaded with work. You start to invest in a team and essentially an entirely new department. In the previous section, we mentioned AI product managers, ML engineers, data scientists, data engineers, and data analysts – this is your AI team. This is the team that will allow you to responsibly build out your AI function and optimize your infrastructure, data management, workflows, data pipelines, modeling, training, deploying, and communicating with the business. Having a dedicated team for this is optimal and ethical because a lot of work and maintenance goes into AI management. If you can afford it, you know how to best make use of your employees, and you know how to keep them happy and dedicated, they will create a wealth of opportunity and success for your product and business.

No-code tools

The final section we'll cover here is the use of low- or no-code tools such as the ones DataRobot and H2O.ai offer. Right now, most of the people that are using these tools are data scientists, so it's not exactly the kind of tool anyone can use and magically give you AI in return. There's a basic level of understanding and domain knowledge that the user has to have to understand and deliver value with these tools. Right now, it seems the greatest advantage is that it can streamline the workload of a data scientist or ML engineer if they're overloaded with projects but it's by no means a substitute. Deciding on which tools you want to use in your AI team should be part of your infrastructure discussions early on.

Fear is not the answer – there is more to gain than lose (or spend)

Believing in and dreaming of success are vital skills for a product manager. So much of the role surrounds concepts such as building a product vision, mission, and strategy and ultimately using these tools to create a roadmap that will manifest these more nebulous concepts. As a product manager, you have to train yourself to visualize. You can't visualize if you don't maintain clarity and focus on your goal. It's all about alignment. You might find yourself saying, "do we have alignment?" over and over again as a product manager to the point where you'll find TikTok videos joking about product managers saying this way too much. Perhaps what makes it so funny is that alignment is so crucial to the role that the job function itself can be distilled into this one word. You're creating alignment in all ways. You're aligning leadership, marketing, sales, customer success, operations, finance, engineering, and countless other impacted business functions around the product and helping build something successful that all these teams can be proud of.

This is the emotional part of the role, and it's one we feel the need to bring up in this section because many product managers might find themselves in the cumbersome task of grappling with AI when they might not know much about it in the first place. The fear that can arise from this is the very essence of why I decided to write this book. In my first role as an ML product manager, I felt fear and its cousin emotions pop up for me. I felt insecure about my own knowledge of AI in the first place. I had a background in data science and ML before my first official role as a product manager. And I still had this fear and uncertainty. I began managing a book club about data science, AI, and ML books to keep this fear at bay. After each book, 23 months and counting, I found myself becoming more and more confident about the subject matter. I then started writing and sharing my own articles as a way to manage the complicated emotions that came up for me as I was managing these products.

When I looked at these emotions objectively, I thought it was funny that I still had reservations about my knowledge and skill set. After all, there aren't too many product managers out there that have come from the data science and ML space in the first place. Because of this, depending on their level of confidence, I would venture to say that most product managers will likely find themselves grappling with many of the emotions I felt. Particularly in the previous sections, which focus on non-ML native products, I wanted to address the emotional side of the product and give further insight into how to contextualize the power of AI and ML to keep the fears at bay.

So what is there to gain? For starters, bragging rights. It's still relatively early in the AI game. Outside of the top tech companies, AI adoption is modest. This means that in this phase, and at least for the next few years, the companies that are coming out with AI features for their products are still ahead of the curve, which means it's arguably the best time for AI feature releases. Coming to market with AI features for your product means you're able to strive for more market share faster before your competitors get the same idea and send out the same marketing message: *"We're the only AI-powered X"* will only last so long. Across many industries, AI features themselves are the marketing differentiator.

Beyond the marketing, AI features, if implemented properly, should give you a more robust, smarter product. Actual product functionality and results will broaden your product's reputation and lead to organic growth. If you're leveraging AI features in a way that helps your product save your customers money, save them time, or make them money faster, then it should be learning from what works. The inherent promise of AI/ML lies in the following equation: data plus models equals more data and better models. Your performance will improve if your data is clean and if your models are updated regularly. Getting more and more familiar with this process will fine-tune your intuition when it comes to your product's functionality and performance in the market you're in. As you begin to see progress in the scale and insights your AI features are adding to your product, you'll begin to anticipate potential issues that can arise with an AI product. This is where some healthy fear is appropriate in your product manager role.

Anticipating potential risks

Part of the specialization that takes place in the current form of an AI product manager is knowledge of what can go wrong. Your AI features may be taking certain liberties with your customers' data, and it's your job as a product manager to anticipate the potential risks your product might create for your users. As a product manager, you're looking to address the most important business problems your users have with your product, but you're also looking to minimize potential adverse effects.

We know, we got you all jazzed up about being a fearless AI product manager only to then bring up the things you should be afraid of because we want to make a distinction. We'd rather you be afraid of the potentially harmful side of AI than be afraid of the complexity of AI systems. Understanding the structure and complexity is the easy part. Making sure this complexity is handled properly is the hard part. For example, rather than worrying about where to start with implementing AI features, we would rather you worry about those features having potentially negative effects on your users and customers downstream. This could be related to the choices your AI features are showing your users, decisions it's making on behalf of your customers, or conclusions it's arriving at with little explainability.

The inherent responsibility that comes with being a product manager that manages an AI product lies primarily with the amazing impact AI can have. Design and optimization are crucial for AI products. Making sure your product is learning with data samples that are representative and free of bias is easier said than done. Making sure your product is fair and inclusive of all types of users and that your data integrity is healthy is not a straightforward task. You have to also consider downstream effects that would impact your users and customers both immediately and long after interacting with your product. For example, if your product is a dating site, are you able to say the choices you are offering your users are representative of the population of users you have and free of bias?

Here are some questions to ask yourself to ensure you are a responsible steward of your AI product:

- What happens later on to your users or their data?

- Could they be harmed months or years after your AI systems have interacted with them?

- Is your product handling your users' data or their privacy appropriately?

- Are you keeping your users' data safe against attacks?

- Are there checks and balances in place to make sure there's organizational AI accountability?

- Are there human oversights in some parts of your product development life cycle, or do you only respond to potential issues or breaches reactively?

- Are your models explainable and transparent?

- Do you and your engineers have a reasonable way to account for the insights and decisions your product is making on behalf of your users?

- Can you say with good conscience that you're consistently evaluating your models' decision making and performance?

- Are you accounting for data drift and model decay?

Depending on how advanced your product organization is, you might have product managers that are focused on individual products as product owners. You might have product managers that focus on the infrastructure and developer tools side. You could be an AI product manager that is more focused on the research side to find new innovations to add to your product line. You could also have a role that is most focused on the responsible building of AI and focus more on the ethics of your product. If you are the only product manager, you'll have to consider all aspects mentioned above and know a bit about everything.

Even the way we see roles defined now will begin to change. At this point in time, you might find roles such as AI product manager or ML product manager, which articulate the focus on an AI or ML product. Over time, my prediction is that this qualifier will start to go away as all product manager roles mature with AI adoption. As you've seen time and again throughout this book, as with the idea that all companies will become AI companies by the end of the decade, the same will hold true for product managers. It will likely be that within 10 years, you'll have to have some comfort and familiarity with AI in order to be a product manager at all.

The last subject we wanted to touch on in this section is the cost associated with having an AI program in place for you to research, develop, test, and manage your AI activities. As a product manager, you're not necessarily keeping up with the costs and decisions of how to handle this function in your company, but you'll need to be familiar with the costs that go into your product. If you're actively working on developing AI features, this will be one area you're keeping track of as you build products. Part of your work as a product manager is comparing the costs of certain feature developments with the potential gains from investing in those features. The metrics you choose to demonstrate the value and **return on investment** (**ROI**) from the features you're investing in will make your business case.

AI shouldn't be a silver bullet. Slapping on an AI tag just for the sake of a competitive marketing edge is not a strategy for success because if AI is not significantly improving your product and is only included as a vanity feature, you'll eventually find yourself outperformed by products that do leverage AI appropriately. Understanding which AI features to expand on and how they're improving your product will make your job as an AI product manager easier and you'll understand this better and better with time. Use your curiosity and experimentation and take intelligent risks. Getting clear on how you can best support your company and what the limitations and benefits of AI/ML are will set you up for success in prioritizing features and planning product strategy. Understanding the potential harms your AI investments might contribute downstream will allow you to build credibility both internally within your company but also externally within your industry.

As an AI product manager, you are creating AI evangelism for your organization. A big part of this indirect influence is actually creating awareness and understanding the growth, the risks, and the inherent opportunity AI offers not only to your product and business but to other stakeholders you work with regularly as well. All roles will be impacted by AI with time. You're just ahead of the curve, in a sense, because your role is most intimately connected with AI and its potential and you can use this firsthand knowledge to guide your peers through this transformation as well.

Summary

The AI revolution is happening at many levels, and in this chapter, we took a look at a few of the major areas of how AI is impacting industries as a whole, companies from the inside out, and the role of product managers as well. For the companies finding themselves in industries that are now seeing AI transformation, the first part of this chapter focused on the various areas of AI adoption across industries and how this is affecting the future of work itself. The second part of this chapter focused on how AI is transforming companies themselves and how you can get started at the organizational level to prepare for AI adoption. The third part of this chapter then took these concepts down a level to the product manager-level view and the mindset needed from the product's organization to ensure AI is adopted within a product in a way that ensures integrity and strength moving forward.

In the next chapter, we will be exploring the various ways we're seeing AI trending across industries, based on prominent and respected research organizations, in an effort to inspire product managers out there to begin to formulate their strategies for elevating their products into AI products and the considerations they must keep in mind when attempting to approach AI.

12
Trends and Insights across Industry

In the previous chapter, we looked at how the rising tide of **artificial intelligence** (**AI**) is affecting companies across the spectrum, as well as the ways AI is affecting companies within their own operations. In this chapter, we will look at the various ways we're seeing AI trending across industries, through the lens of prominent and respected research organizations, in an effort to inspire product managers and entrepreneurs out there to begin to formulate their strategies by elevating their products into AI products. In addition, we will go over the various considerations they must keep in mind when attempting to approach AI, including AI readiness and enablement.

Analyzing trends and understanding the growth areas for AI and **machine learning** (**ML**) adoption can open us up to powerful future opportunities. The nature of what we build and how we work is changing because of this massive shift in adoption. For most of this book, we've focused on AI products but we've also alluded to the various ways companies will be changing from an operational perspective due to AI. The best advice for companies looking to capitalize on building AI programs to support the products they make is to also use that same program to leverage AI for internal purposes. If you're investing in this technology, you'll also want to use it to make internal efficiencies and elevate the performance of your product.

If you're in a position to be ready to take your product to the next level by introducing AI/ML capabilities, it means you've accepted the responsibility and privilege of supporting such an ambitious endeavor. In this chapter, we'll be taking a look at what reputable consulting, research, and advisory companies have to say about where the greater opportunities regarding AI adoption lie, as well as looking into the trends coming up in adopting AI in traditional software products. Getting a sense of what's been showing promise and the kinds of AI adoption that have been substantially improving products is helpful when looking for inspiration for how AI can improve your own existing products.

In this chapter, we will cover the following topics:

- Highest growth areas – Forrester, Gartner, and McKinsey research
- Trends in AI adoption – let the data speak for itself
- Low-hanging fruit – quickest wins for AI enablement

Highest growth areas – Forrester, Gartner, and McKinsey research

In this section, we will be taking a look at some of the growth areas of AI from some of the most prominent research and consulting groups. Understanding what the signals are saying gives us the motivation and foresight to be able to anticipate some of the greatest opportunities that lie ahead. This is particularly helpful in the context of revolutionizing a business or product toward AI because many product managers and technologists may be at odds about which specific areas of a product or service they might want to begin bolstering with AI capabilities.

Some of the top growth areas we will look at based on the conglomeration of research and trend analysis from Forrester, Gartner, and McKinsey in the following subsections are embedded AI, ethical AI, creative AI, and autonomous AI development. Embedded AI will look at AI that's applied and integrated into the operations of organizations and foundations of products. Ethical AI will look at considerations of responsibility and privacy in AI deployment. Creative AI will look at generative and Web3 use cases of AI. Autonomous development will look at the growing field of AI-generated code. All of these are strategic growth areas for AI adoption according to some of the most reputable organizations we have for predicting trends.

Let's get started!

Embedded AI – applied and integrated use cases

Embedded AI relates to AI being integrated into core operational activities within a business. If your product is geared towards B2B internal processes such as architecture, operations, fulfillment, supply chain, HR, or procurement, you might be interested in bolstering your product with AI features that help companies fulfill their commitments to their consumers. Based on Forrester's research on 2022 predictions, the more your product can offer real value to your B2B consumers, the more you will be able to help *enterprises shrink the latency between insights, decisions, and results*. This area of AI that Forrester refers to as *AI Inside* deals with the integration of AI that's embedded into operations. The ultimate goal is to help inform or even automate decision making.

Often, the most value your product will be able to give your customers is actionable information they can use to make high-level decisions. If your product is dependable in delivering this, it is worth the hassle for companies to invest in their own AI infrastructure to achieve the same results. Gartner outlines this concept in their *applications-centric AI* framework, where they consider innovations in engineering, decision intelligence, and operational AI systems.

For Gartner, the focus of this area of AI is toward helping improve decision intelligence overall in order to both reduce the technical debt and visibility for businesses internally, as well as helping reduce the risk and unpredictability of outcomes. In other words, the most impactful part of this area of AI, according to Gartner, is that it helps decision makers have both clarity of their internal processes and make their most important decisions using insights that are derived from their own data.

Gartner also predicts a rise of causal AI, which are systems that identify and act on *"cause-and-effect relationships to go beyond correlation-based predictive models and toward AI systems that can prescribe actions more effectively and act more autonomously."* Gartner has a number of other areas of AI implementation that it refers to in categories such as augmented FinOps, cybersecurity mesh architecture, data observability, and industry cloud platforms, all of which are areas of growth that support the integration of AI internally into enterprise's business processes. For Gartner, this is perhaps best encapsulated by the Optimize category of their *Top Strategic Technology Trends 2023* report.

This report also includes things such as the **digital immune system**, a set of practices and technologies that focus on optimized resilience in the face of threats that would impact an organization's ability to bounce back from any threat to their ability to deliver a customer or user experience. As they see it, this would cover a wide variety of tools that help businesses prepare for potential risks, which learn from past failures to better prepare for the next. Rather than looking at this from a cybersecurity perspective, this would pertain to any internal process that could negatively impact experience and delivery to a customer. The **applied observability** category also highlights tools that are looking for any deviations within an organization's operations that would impact core business functions and infrastructure.

McKinsey features *Applied AI* as one of their top strategic features in their *Technology Trends Outlook 2022* report, which they define as the intelligent application of AI towards solving classification, control, and prediction problems in order to automate, add, or augment business use cases. Some of these use cases are defined in their report as risk management, service operations optimization, and product development. Based on their research, the factors contributing to this include the global expansion of AI adoption, more affordable AI implementation routes, an improvement in training speed, high growth in innovation based on patents filed, and a marked increase in private investment growth for AI-related companies. Their numbers also reflect this in the *Trends in AI adoption* section.

McKinsey goes a step further in isolating the areas of AI that are showing the most noteworthy promise for AI adoption. They list the general umbrella of ML at the top of the list for its use in optimization problems and its ability to learn from data using statistical models.

Computer vision is listed as the second most noteworthy area for using visual data for facial recognition and biometrics. Third is **natural language processing** (**NLP**) and its prevalence in speech recognition and virtual voice assistants. Fourth is **deep reinforcement learning**, specifically for things such as robotics and manufacturing lines. Lastly, they list **knowledge graphs** for their ability to derive insights from network analysis. We've covered most of these major areas of ML extensively in this book, and it's no surprise to see them echoed in McKinsey's *Technology Trends Outlook 2022* report.

Ethical AI – responsibility and privacy

Another high growth area for Forrester is the niche of responsible or ethical AI. Thanks to advocacy groups and increasing pressure on lawmakers to define ethical uses of AI moving forward, the area of responsible AI is seeing a boom. AI/ML capabilities will go through increasing waves of regulation because of how pervasive AI has already become in virtually every area of human life, even in these early days. This opens up a lot of opportunities for products and services that already deal with issues of fairness, bias, and governance to then move into the area of governing AI bias.

According to Forrester, the more AI adoption we experience, the more *"existing machine-learning vendors will acquire specialized responsible AI vendors for bias detection, interpretability, and model lineage capabilities."* This is a rosy outlook for companies already operating in this space, as we're likely to see demand for these kinds of services increase as the next decade moves forward.

Considering our category of embedded and applied AI is the top growth area for AI adoption, we will increasingly experience ML embedded into more and more of the products we use, whether we're individual consumers or businesses. With the increase in adoption will come an increase in how heavily the use and deployment of ML are scrutinized.

Gartner agrees, going as far as to have their Research VP at Gartner say that *"increased trust, transparency, fairness, and auditability of AI technologies continues to be of growing importance to a wide range of stakeholders. Responsible AI helps achieve fairness, even though biases are baked into the data; gain trust, although transparency and explainability methods are evolving; and ensure regulatory compliance, while grappling with AI's probabilistic nature."*

Among these general comments about AI transparency and fairness, we also see a slew of categories of prediction, including the rise of dynamic risk governance tools, cybersecurity mesh architecture, and cloud sustainability, as well as the rise in decentralized identities and the move toward consumers owning more and more of their digital identity and data as Web3 applications take off.

A recent report by McKinsey also highlights trustworthiness and explainability in applied AI as one of the top considerations when incorporating AI into products. The ability to hedge risks, particularly as AI use cases expand, is of particular concern. Adhering to laws, remaining vigilant on ethics, and building AI with social robustness are their recommendations for building in a way that mitigates harm. They also note that explainability is closely related to this, further highlighting that as models become increasingly complex and are deployed on high-risk use cases, the issue of explainability will remain critical.

McKinsey lists explainability as threefold. Explaining how the model actually works is one thing, but they also suggest organizations demonstrate causal explainability, which is about explaining why certain outputs come from the inputs. Lastly, and perhaps most importantly, is trust-inducing explainability: explaining why you can trust and deploy a model.

Building AI/ML products and upgrading traditional software products into AI products will be a continuous process of reinforcing their trustworthiness, reliability, and safety across multiple areas. It gives me confidence that these three prominent advisory organizations give ethical AI the importance it deserves as we continue to build the future with these powerful tools.

Creative AI – generative and immersive applications

The area of creative AI is sure to expand further, as we alluded to in previous chapters, with reference to **Lensa**, **ChatGPT**, **DALL-E**, and other creative AI apps that focus on writing, music, and visual arts. According to Forrester, *"CMOs are starting to apply artificial intelligence to digital media buying, campaign automation, or marketing mix optimization."* As a result, use and trust in creative AI applications are growing, and businesses and consumers alike are starting to lean into the creative inspiration AI has to offer.

In 2021, South Africa granted a patent to an AI system called **DABUS**, created by Stephen Thaler. This opened up a whole new world of AI that now receives legal protections for its own creativity. While the same patent was rejected in the US, Europe, and Australia, it found a haven in South Africa. Forrester believes we will see an increase in legislation supporting creative outputs of AI, as well as an increase in creative AI patents, as these recent events are likely to change public perception. As AI deliverables and outputs continue to be granted legislative recognition, we're likely to also see an advancement in creative tech companies building more and more AI capabilities into their existing products.

Gartner addresses creative AI in their top strategic technology trends by referring to it as *Generative AI*, which they define as *"machine learning methods that learn about content or objects from their data, and use it to generate brand-new, completely original, realistic artifacts."* Gartner predicts a rise in AI-augmented design or the use of ML and NLP to generate and develop not just creative content but to also *"automatically generate and develop user flows, screen designs, content, and presentation-layer code for digital products."* Gartner also takes this idea a step further by forecasting the importance of AI-assisted immersive experiences as one of their top predictors for creative AI, particularly the rise of the metaverse and AI-driven representations that other aspects of Web3 will necessitate.

While McKinsey doesn't necessarily cover creative AI in their recent trends report, they do cover potential applications of AI toward creative use cases in their *Applied AI* category, and they also cite immersive-reality technologies as a key trend for the upcoming decade, which will be supported by AI.

Accounting for areas such as **spatial computing**, **mixed reality** (**MR**), **augmented reality** (**AR**), and **virtual reality** (**VR**) will all be optimized using AI. McKinsey's report lists the following areas as strategic use cases for immersive reality solutions: learning and assessment, product design and development, enhanced situational awareness, and B2C use cases such as gaming, fitness, and retail.

Autonomous AI development – TuringBots

Low- and no-code tools have been around for some time now in the hopes of bridging the divide between the technical needs of enterprises and the cost and time needed to onboard a dedicated staff of developers. This is now being pushed a step further with the emergence of what Forrester calls **TuringBots**, or *bots that write code*. If you're already in this no- or low-code tech space and you're looking to integrate AI into your product, you'll likely want to compete with many of the free services out there and offer these capabilities to your customers.

Gartner also predicts this is a major theme in the coming decade and refers to these as *machine learning code generation tools,* but the idea here is the same. These would be ML models that would work alongside human developers and would be integrated into development environments in order to offer suggestions on the code base using descriptions in natural language or fragments of code as a prompt. Because of the highly adaptable nature of ML to optimize repetitive tasks, it's unsurprising that ML is leveraged to optimize the very way it's built.

Gartner goes on to predict a rise in what it calls **Adaptive AI** or systems that *"continuously retrain models and learn within runtime and development environments based on new data to adapt quickly to changes in real-world circumstances that were not foreseen or available during initial development."* This means that AI that's more sensitive to real-time changes in the training data is also able to adjust its parameters and goals in an effort to make them more autonomously nimble.

McKinsey's recent *Technology Trends Outlook 2022* report highlights next-generation software development as another strategic trend to look out for, citing the increase of low-code/no-code platforms and AI code recommendations based on context from natural language, AI-based testing that automates performance testing and AI-assisted code review as another key trend for the next decade. They see the strategic involvement of AI in the planning and analysis, architecture design, development, coding, testing, deployment, and maintenance as a key focus for organizations that are building products or internalizing this trend to experience its benefits.

So far, we've had a chance to discuss the highest growth areas, embedded AI, ethical AI, creative AI, and autonomous AI development, coming from some of our most highly reputable research and consulting organizations. In the next section, let's get into the numbers to get a better sense of the scale of these trends.

Trends in AI adoption – let the data speak for itself

In this section, we'll be looking at some of the data that's come out of Forrester, Gartner, and McKinsey about the growth areas previously outlined: embedded AI, ethical AI, creative AI, and autonomous AI development. Compiling the numbers into a section based on the data that's come out of the research helps highlight the importance of these growth areas and gives us a bird's-eye view of the state of AI adoption overall. We'll begin the section with general trends about AI adoption overall and get into the numbers for each growth area next.

General trends

According to research done by Forrester on trends impacting the US, China, Japan, France, Germany, Italy, Spain, and the UK, *"AI software spend will double from 2021 to 2025, reaching $64 billion."* What's driving this adoption is the rise in AI-bolstered software products, particularly the rise of software companies expanding their AI features and capabilities, as well as a rise in AI tools made for creating other AI products and applications and, ultimately, the rise in AI native products themselves.

Based on Forrester's *Global AI Software Forecast, 2022*, overall, the AI software industry will *"grow 50% faster than the overall software market,"* and by 2025, 31% of AI software spending will be AI-infused. Forrester's *Data and Analytics* survey also shows that *"73% of data and analytics decision-makers are building AI technologies, and 74% see a positive impact on their organizations from the use of AI."*

Gartner's findings are even more aggressive compared to Forrester's on high-level AI trends citing that worldwide AI software revenue is forecast to total $62.5 billion in 2022 and that *"By 2025, the market for artificial intelligence (AI) software will reach almost $134.8 billion. Over the next five years, the market growth will accelerate from 14.4% in 2021 to reach 31.1% in 2025, considerably outpacing the overall software market growth."*

Their top categories of AI adoption for 2022 by use case include knowledge management with a growth rate of 31.5%, virtual assistants with a growth rate of 14.7%, autonomous vehicles with a growth rate of 20.1%, digital workplace with a growth rate of 20%, and crowdsourced data with a growth rate of 19.8%. All growth rates are compared with their 2021 numbers and indicate an upward trajectory of adoption of AI across a wide variety of industries and use cases.

McKinsey's general AI trends also offer a lot of confidence, citing that AI could deliver an economic output of around $13 trillion by 2030 and that global GDP would increase by about 1.2 percent per year but that this economic boom would mostly serve developed countries and companies that adopt AI early. Their retrospective *State of AI in 2022* and a *Half Decade in Review Survey* offer us a chance to stop and reflect on how the last five years of AI adoption have gone. AI adoption has more than doubled since 2017 across respondents, and the average number of AI capabilities that organizations use has also doubled. These are encouraging numbers that indicate adoption is moving steadily along with global trends and predictions.

The McKinsey review survey also goes into some of the top use cases of AI deployment, listing that *service operations optimizations* (internal applications of AI in organizations) have been the highest functional activity among respondents that have adopted AI, followed closely by the *creation of new AI-based products.* Other notable functions included were *new AI-based enhancements of products, product feature optimization,* and *predictive service and intervention.*

Another telling statistic from the McKinsey report is that 52% of respondents report more than 5% of their digital budgets are going to AI, up from 40% in 2018, and 63% of them said their investment would grow in the next 3 years, signaling that investment in AI is going to continue. This is in keeping with the signals from Forrester and Gartner.

Embedded AI – applied and integrated use cases

Let's take a look at what the data shows us with regard to one of the highest growth areas of AI: embedded AI. McKinsey reports that 56% of their survey respondents said their organizations are adopting AI, there's been a 94.4% improvement in training speed since 2018, there were 30 times more AI patents filed in 2021 than in 2015, and $93.5 billion was invested in AI-related companies in 2021, doubling from 2020. McKinsey also cites industrializing ML, or the adoption and scaling of ML capabilities, as another key trend that will show the greatest return for the next decade.

They also outline industrializing AI into several key areas, including data management, model development, model deployment, live-model operations, and overall ML workflow. Based on their research, the global revenue impact potential of AI across industries is $10-15 trillion, and companies adopting AI are 2.5x more likely to experience higher 5-year returns to their shareholders. These growth projections do come with a massive caveat, however: 72% of the organizations they surveyed for this report have not been able to successfully adopt and scale AI. Among the biggest contributors to this are difficulties transitioning pilot projects into products, models failing in production, difficulties with scaling their AI/ML team's productivity, and limitations in containing risks.

Ethical AI – responsibility and privacy

The numbers for the growth of ethical AI practices are also encouraging and indicate that individuals and companies are taking the ethics and responsibility that AI comes with seriously as their level of experience and investment grow. Forrester predicts 25% of tech executives will need to report their AI governance activities to their boards to cover *"explainability, fairness audits of high-impact algorithmic decision-making, and accounting for environmental impacts of AI (green AI)."* This also indicates that boards and high-level decision makers are aware of the risks that come with not properly accounting for potential harm AI can pose to customers, users, and organizations.

Based on their own research in this area, Gartner expects that by 2023, anyone that's hired for development and training work on AI systems will need to demonstrate they have expertise in ethical and responsible AI. Their outlook on what they consider causal AI, or AI that's able to demonstrate explainability and deliver on communicating causal relationships, is much longer.

Gartner believes causal AI *"will take 5 to 10 years to reach mainstream adoption but will ultimately have a transformational impact on business."* Here, we also see the relationship between trust and responsibility going hand in hand, with companies understanding that explainability and communicating risk impacts even those that hold high positions within companies.

Gartner lists **AI trust, risk, and security management** (**AI TRiSM**) as a strategic technology trend for 2023, citing that *in the U.S, U.K. and Germany 41% of organizations had experienced an AI privacy breach or security incident.* This further highlights that the world is still ripe for responsible AI practices that bleed into privacy and security and they are very much needed and will continue to stay relevant. Seeing these indicators in research organizations is encouraging, but it's just a prediction of the future, not a manifestation.

As companies continue to build and invest in their AI products, they will need to not only build products in a trustworthy way for the benefit of their users but they should come to understand that not doing so can threaten their own investment in the AI tech they've spent so much time, money, and patience building.

Creative AI – generative and immersive applications

Creative AI apps had a great year in 2022, and Forrester predicts there will be an increase in Fortune 500 companies' dependence on creative AI and how they will generate content with AI tools because *"human-produced content creation will never be fast enough to address the need for personalized content at scale, and in the next year, we expect to see at least 10% of companies invest in AI-supported digital content creation"*. This indicates that organizations will increasingly rely on these apps for their own marketing and content strategy goals, signaling opportunity in the B2B marketing world for AI generative apps. But this number doesn't include the many consumers that will be interested in creative AI apps for purely recreational purposes.

Gartner's data follows suit, citing that by 2025, generative AI will account for 10% of all data produced, up from less than 1% today. Gartner's focus on Generative AI can be used for a range of activities, such as creating software code, facilitating drug development, and targeted marketing, but it can also be misused for scams, fraud, political disinformation, forged identities, and more. This further highlights the increasing dependency businesses will have on using creative AI, not just from a marketing perspective but also from an operational perspective.

The more business use cases are built and optimized for creative AI apps, the more content they will be able to generate, particularly when you consider those needs starting to exist at scale. Those numbers are hard to predict for the consumer market, however, because 2022 was really the first year creative AI saw huge levels of adoption, with individual consumers using them for recreation.

As time goes on, we will start to see more projections that capture the consumer market for creative AI. If the current buzz around creative AI apps in the consumer market is any indication, we will likely see more excitement around new use cases and products, particularly as they integrate with other emerging technologies such as AR/VR, Web3, and metaverse applications.

Autonomous AI development – TuringBots

The data for autonomous AI development is also encouraging and mirrors the data we're seeing for creative AI apps. Forrester goes as far as to say that TuringBots will write 10% of code worldwide by the end of 2023. Because of the rise in popularity of reinforcement learning and language models such as **GPT-4** (which powers **ChatGPT**), we're seeing that we can take low- and no-code tools a step further and actually produce code with the help of AI using nothing more than basic instructions expressed in any natural human language. This is particularly exciting as we're still in the midst of a shortage of developers, tech workers, data scientists, and ML engineers.

McKinsey follows suit, citing that 70% of new software development will be built using no- or low-code tech by 2025, which will reduce development time by 90%. This is great news for the build and creation process of software. The deployment time will be twice as fast because of continuous integration and continuous delivery practices, which will be helped by AI. Considering deployment is often the hardest part of making ML and AI use cases successful, and also brings a lot of confidence. 37% of McKinsey's survey participants said they would use AI/ML to test and maintain their existing code repositories, bringing the advantage of AI-assisted coding to another level.

In this section, we've delved into the research to get some concrete numbers supporting some of the highest growth areas in AI in this current climate. Hopefully, this section has given you a few ideas to think about when considering bringing AI capabilities into the products you already manage. In the following section, we will talk about AI enablement, an essential component to set up before you get started on your journey to embrace AI and properly set it up for success.

Low-hanging fruit – quickest wins for AI enablement

By now, you've seen how involved applied ML is for an organization to embrace fully, and we've just spent most of this chapter looking through the various growth areas in AI for organizations that are already in business and are looking to capitalize on these growth areas. In *Part 1* of this book, we discussed the various layers of infrastructure that need to be supported in an AI program. In *Part 2* of this book, we discussed the AI native product. In this current section of the book, we're discussing the transition of incorporating AI into a traditional software product.

This means we can now move on to set the stage for what this adoption looks like, but before we get started, we want to include a caveat. We really can't talk about AI transformation unless we also set ourselves up for success to be able to begin the long and arduous process that is AI adoption. We have to make sure the conditions are right. Whether you're working in an organization that's ready to build an AI native product or you're in a traditional software environment that's ready to adopt AI at the feature level, there's a level of expectation setting that's required for the endeavor to be successful. But setting expectations properly in an already established software company that isn't used to the demands AI will place on an organization is especially difficult.

There are both tangible and intangible challenges to building the right conditions for AI. The tangible ones lie with the infrastructure, the investment, and, frankly, the skill. Building out your team and bringing in folks that can troubleshoot and navigate the tricky conditions AI will force you to work in requires a special set of skills, and those skills are sought by virtually everyone right now. Building out established processes and workflows that support the various facets of an AI program is a formidable project that can be challenging to scope, much like AI projects themselves.

The intangible challenges are more cerebral and emotional. In *Chapter 7*, we discussed the differences between traditional software products and AI-native products. If you recall that section, one of the biggest differences lies in the uncertainty AI brings. When you have an established team that's already used to a certain level of expectation, it can be difficult to articulate just how much AI is going to change things. The uncertainty that comes with AI makes it very difficult to communicate the full extent of allocating a budget for teams, purchasing software, managing expectations of timelines and costs, and resetting boundaries in terms of how teams work with one another.

You can't have a fully supported AI program if your internal teams don't have the right infrastructure and procedures in place. You also can't have it if you do have the infrastructure and processes, but your internal teams haven't emotionally internalized them yet. According to Gartner, *"By 2025, the 10% of enterprises that establish AI engineering best practices will generate at least three times more value from their AI efforts than the 90% of enterprises that do not."* There's a significant upside for companies that do their due diligence to set up their AI programs properly.

The work of bridging the gap between the tangible and intangible challenges of AI is what's referred to as AI enablement. In order for a traditional software product to transition into an AI product as seamlessly as possible, its leaders and product managers need to create a plan to make this transition successful. Adopting AI is a massive shift for your organization and the way it builds products. It's a fundamental change to how we expect to build. Building a strong culture of AI enablement means that you're preparing your teams as best as you can for what's to come.

At its core, AI enablement is really all about the data. Finding a way to most efficiently collect, label, and curate large amounts of unstructured data is what allows model performance to improve most consistently. Improving that data pipeline, keeping it clean, and making sure there is a steady supply of it to be used for training purposes is what gives the AI/ML pipeline its capabilities. Making sure the right data transformations are happening and the proper level of data quality is in place is the ultimate objective of AI enablement. This is because of the tremendous reliance AI has on data.

The best combination of AI enablement or AI readiness will come from having strong use cases to support your investment in AI, having strong networks of clean data you can leverage to support those use cases, and having a clear governance strategy of who can access what and how roles are delineated within your organization to demonstrate ownership, control, and safety measures to make sure your AI investment is as successful as possible. We will go into these concepts in more depth in the next chapter.

Summary

This chapter was all about trends and insights for AI adoption collected from some of the most reputable companies that speak about it. We looked at some of their insights and projections for the coming years and decades regarding AI adoption. Building an AI-native product is, in many ways, more straightforward than transitioning a product from traditional software development to an AI product.

In this chapter, we wanted to set the stage and discuss some of the high-growth areas for AI adoption because, for many companies, knowing where to begin is often the hardest part. Once you're in the flow of things, you can better anticipate what comes next, but when you're at the precipice of a major paradigm shift, there's a lot of friction. Going over the growth areas, data, and common use cases and setting the stage for AI enablement was an intuitive choice to make sure product managers out there are aware of what adopting AI can mean for their product. It's a big responsibility and undertaking, and it should be treated as such.

In the next and final chapter, we will go into a lot of the applied considerations of transitioning a product to adopt AI and tangibly what that means for your product team or organization.

References

- *Predictions 2022: Successfully Riding The Next Wave Of AI*: https://www.forrester.com/blogs/predictions-for-2022-successfully-riding-the-next-wave-of-ai/

- *What's New in Artificial Intelligence from the 2022 Gartner Hype Cycle*: https://www.gartner.com/en/articles/what-s-new-in-artificial-intelligence-from-the-2022-gartner-hype-cycle

- *What's New in the 2022 Gartner Hype Cycle for Emerging Technologies*: https://www.gartner.com/en/articles/what-s-new-in-the-2022-gartner-hype-cycle-for-emerging-technologies

- *McKinsey Technology Trends Outlook 2022* report August 2022: https://www.mckinsey.com/~/media/mckinsey/business%20functions/mckinsey%20digital/our%20insights/the%20top%20trends%20in%20tech%202022/mckinsey-tech-trends-outlook-2022-full-report.pdf

- *Predictions 2023: AI Will Become An Indispensable, Trusted Enterprise Coworker*: https://www.forrester.com/blogs/predictions-2023-ai/

- *Gartner Identifies Four Trends Driving Near-Term Artificial Intelligence Innovation*: https://www.gartner.com/en/newsroom/press-releases/2021-09-07-gartner-identifies-four-trends-driving-near-term-artificial-intelligence-innovation#:~:text=Four%20trends%20on%20the%20Gartner,data%2C%20model%20and%20compute%20resources

- *AI Is A New Kind Of Creative Partner*: https://www.forrester.com/blogs/ai-is-a-new-kind-of-creative-partner/

- *In a world first, South Africa grants patent to an artificial intelligence system*: https://theconversation.com/in-a-world-first-south-africa-grants-patent-to-an-artificial-intelligence-system-165623

- *Gartner Identifies the Top 10 Strategic Technology Trends for 2023*: https://www.gartner.com/en/newsroom/press-releases/2022-10-17-gartner-identifies-the-top-10-strategic-technology-trends-for-2023

- *AI Software Spend Will Double From 2021 To 2025, Reaching $64 Billion*: https://www.forrester.com/blogs/ai-software-spend-will-double-from-2021-to-2025-to-reach-64-billion-and-grow-50-faster-than-the-overall-software-market/

- *Forrester Forecasts AI Software Will Grow 50% Faster Than The Overall Software Market*: https://www.prnewswire.com/news-releases/forrester-forecasts-ai-software-will-grow-50-faster-than-the-overall-software-market-301638854.html

- *5 ways Forrester predicts AI will be "indispensable" in 2023*: https://venturebeat.com/ai/5-ways-forrester-predicts-ai-will-be-indispensable-in-2023/

- *Gartner Forecasts Worldwide Artificial Intelligence Software Market to Reach $62 Billion in 2022*: https://www.gartner.com/en/newsroom/press-releases/2021-11-22-gartner-forecasts-worldwide-artificial-intelligence-software-market-to-reach-62-billion-in-2022

- *Forecast Analysis: Artificial Intelligence Software, Worldwide*: https://www.gartner.com/en/documents/4007140

- *Notes from the AI frontier: Modeling the impact of AI on the world economy*: https://www.mckinsey.com/featured-insights/artificial-intelligence/notes-from-the-ai-frontier-modeling-the-impact-of-ai-on-the-world-economy

- *The state of AI in 2022—and a half decade in review*: https://www.mckinsey.com/capabilities/quantumblack/our-insights/the-state-of-ai-in-2022-and-a-half-decade-in-review

13
Evolving Products into AI Products

In this chapter, we will explore the areas that benefit and negatively impact AI adoption in existing products. Every product will be different and every product owner will come to their own conclusions about what level of AI adoption to infuse into their product. For some products, something as simple as adding one AI feature is enough. For other products, a fundamental change to the underlying logic that powers your product might be required. The decisions of how to transform your product should, first and foremost, be determined by your product strategy and should serve your overarching company vision. These decisions should be collaborative and should come with a high level of executive sponsorship.

As the chapter continues, we will explore various areas of AI transformation, and they will serve as a step-by-step guide to building a product strategy that supports the evolution of your product. We will look at how to approach brainstorming about your AI options, which considerations will be most important as you brainstorm, how to evaluate your product's performance within the competitive landscape, how to build a product strategy that sets you up for success, and ultimately which signposts and milestones will help you build confidence and which will indicate that you need to go back to the drawing board.

Whether you're adding AI features or upgrading the existing logic of your product, having an established plan that supports your product strategy will be the best way to successfully update your product for commercial success with AI in a way that's sustainable. Once you've achieved the successful transformation of your product into an AI product, feel free to refer to *Part 2* of this book where we go over the various aspects of building and maintaining an AI-native product.

In this chapter, we will cover the following topics:

- Venn diagram – what's possible and what's probable
- Data is king – the bloodstream of the company
- Competition – love your enemies
- Product strategy – building a blueprint that works for everyone
- Red flags and green flags – what to look and watch out for

Venn diagram – what's possible and what's probable

There are multiple ways in which a product could stand to benefit from AI adoption, and understanding the Venn diagram of what's probable and what's possible is an important part of your AI product strategy journey. As you continue this exercise, you'll go through a spectrum. You'll start with a really open-ended, right-brain brainstorming session on the cerebral notion of value and how your product can deliver it to your customers, which will then be refined by a left-brain, analytical breakdown of the fruits of that brainstorming session. Both are important parts of the product management creative process.

Whether you look at your product from the perspective of the main problems your customers face, the *jobs to be done*, or feature parity, you'll want to get a sense of which AI enhancements would be most high-value for your product, which would be the most low-cost, which have the best data readiness or availability, and which have the highest degree of executive or market sponsorship. Since this section is about how to evolve an existing product into an AI product, take your time with this step.

Feel free to refer to the *Additional resources* section at the end of this chapter for resources to help you and your organization learn more about AI and **machine learning** (**ML**) in preparation for such a big step. Educating yourself, reading books and articles about how AI can bolster your product, and adopting a student mindset will be the most helpful thing you can do at the onset of this journey you're taking – and it is a journey! Being mindful about taking your time to really familiarize yourself with the models, the benefits, and the options you have before you will be important.

Before we get into all that, a word of caution about adopting the term AI. We've discussed the notion of starting with your *why* when it comes to AI and how important it is. We've also discussed the notion of the marketing buzz that comes with AI and how attractive it is to investors and customers alike. In the current AI climate, there's a lot of noise that's generated when AI and ML enter the lexicon of your product's communication efforts. You don't want to fall victim to the trap of attracting a lot of attention without necessarily having the substance to support that attention.

The last thing we want is for product managers and technologists to go through the effort of investing in AI and push out vanity features that don't actually make their products better only because they want to capitalize on the attention AI offers them. For that reason, we recommend grasping the real opportunities that AI and ML will afford your product and then creating a series of lists that will rank the order of these potential opportunities according to three key categories: value, scope, and reach.

The ultimate goal of brainstorming and creating these lists is to define a potential path to AI maturity within your product. Understanding which areas you want to start with and which areas you want to transform as part of your overall product strategy and roadmap over time will be an important part of the process. AI transformation won't happen overnight. You will have to start somewhere and, given the cost of investing in AI, being strategic and intentional about where you want to start will make all the difference in the long run.

In the following sections, we will be applying various lenses to ideations when it comes to AI adoption. Those lenses will relate to how AI adoption will impact your product based on perceived value for your customers, how AI adoption will impact the scope of your product, and, finally, how AI adoption will spread to your end users.

List 1 – value

The work of product management often requires a high level of trade-off. You're always judging the amount of effort and skill required to bring a feature to light and comparing that with the proposed upside for making that building investment. If you do, however, start with the highest-value AI enhancements, you'll be coming from an intuitive, customer-centric place. Understanding first and foremost what makes your product valuable to your customers and your market and then finding use cases of AI to expand on that value should be the first order of business.

You'll need a source of truth list like this later on when decisions become more difficult and – should they inevitably come up – you maneuver political discussions with leadership and other key stakeholders at your company. The reason why your value list should be your primary source of truth is that every product fundamentally needs a value proposition: a statement about why your product brings value to its customers and users. The world has enough false advertisements, overcommitments, and exaggerations, particularly in tech. Based on a 2019 study on European companies claiming to have cutting-edge AI products, up to 40% of them were not substantially using AI. Build a solid list of true AI enhancements that will deliver real value to your customers. Build an AI product you can be proud of. Start with what really matters.

Treat this as an exercise in *divergent thinking*. We spent a considerable amount of this book going over the various use cases and models that can be employed in ML and deep learning. We've also looked at a number of verticals, industries, and high-level adoption trends. When you're thinking about value and how to grow it in your product, use this list exercise as a way to get all the potential ideas out there no matter how outlandish or unrealistic. Keep in mind the various strengths of AI: stacking, ranking, optimizing, predicting, grouping, comparing, automating, standardizing, and learning from ongoing trends and analysis.

How can you apply these strengths to your own product? Get creative and try not to stop logistical considerations from getting your ideas flowing. Anything that feels like it will be inherently valuable to even just a small subset of your customers can and should make this list. If it's helpful, consider the various types of models we've covered in earlier chapters and what value they could bring to your product as it currently stands. Take stock of the benefits that various types of ML can potentially bring to your product and see where they might be able to improve on existing use cases that pertain to the product and your customers.

With due diligence, you should come out of this exercise feeling inspired about the potential directions your product can take based on its current value proposition. With some luck on top of that due diligence, you should also experience the new benefits AI can bring as well. There will be plenty of opportunities to whittle this list down and realistically refine it later.

For now, let the creativity flow and think about how you can build on the existing value your product offers its customers and users. You will be rewarded for being less discerning during this step because you never know which of the fringe ideas on this list might become valuable seeds for future features. Brainstorming about potential features and use cases is also some of the most fun a product manager can have – figure out a way to make this a standard part of your product strategy work and revisit this on a quarterly or biannual basis.

List 2 – scope

Once you have a list of the highest-value AI enhancements from the previous section, you can then start to prioritize them into a list of most to least scope. Scope includes not only the time and effort required to complete a body of work but also the cost and skill level required to do so. Given that we're talking about AI products here, it may not be as straightforward to understand what will require the most effort, time, cost, and skill. Often, we don't know this until we're well on our way to building out these features, but do your best to create enough of a stacked order from most to least effort for this list.

This list won't be an absolute source of truth, and it doesn't have to be. It also doesn't necessarily mean that the items that involve the least effort will get built first, but it's important to establish which kinds of enhancements will require more of an investment from the company to complete. Understanding the variety in terms of effort is most important from a planning and resource management perspective. If certain features need to be built, and they do require a lot of effort, time, or skill that you might not conveniently have, knowing this will help with forecasting and making the necessary plans in the future to obtain it.

It will also allow your leadership team the time and focus to really internalize what this investment in AI will actually require of them, and whether or not you currently have the skill sets and capabilities to even embark on this path. Taking the time to discuss the scope and get clear on the organization's current level of ability is an essential part of this step. The act of acquiring the right tech resources to make the loftiest AI dreams a reality will likely be an arduous journey in and of itself. Your leadership team needs to be prepared for that.

This isn't just the case with acquiring talent – it's also the case with understanding what internal processes need to change as well. Often, when it comes to AI, managing expectations can be the most difficult part of making an AI transformation successful, so anything you can do early on to prime your leadership for the trials and tribulations that might impact you as you begin the process of leveraging AI will go a long way when hurdles inevitably come up.

As any product manager out there knows, the scope is an important factor in deciding what to build and when, and you'll want to make sure you're cementing yourself as the authority where leadership is concerned when it comes to the AI features you propose to add to your product. Even if you do have a mature team of data scientists and ML engineers around you who you can trust and who have a ton of experience and AI wisdom, as a product manager, you will still own the product and be responsible for the ultimate strategy related to your product. It's important that you maintain this high level of oversight and command over your product's key AI considerations and the major decisions impacting your product because you are the captain of that ship. Congratulations! It's a gift and a curse.

If you can't defend the decisions made in relation to your product, you're not the authority, and this will only cause confusion and undermine your leadership later on. Remember that your technical team is there to support the product, offer sincere advice, and give their best estimates on the scope and on how to build the features that are decided on by the strategic arm of the organization. They are there to build and implement the decisions that you make in collaboration with your leadership and stakeholder team. Having a clear definition of ownership and using your technical team to accurately reflect on the scope to the best of their ability is what this exercise is all about.

List 3 – reach

By this point, you have two lenses through which to look at your proposed product AI embellishments – the lens of ultimate value and the lens of scope: effort, time, skill level, and cost. As you may notice, with our second list, we're moving from a divergent mindset and adding more analytical, convergent restraints. With this third list, you add another layer of conditions through the lens of how many of your existing customers it will impact – or your reach.

Being able to create this list will require you to have enough intimacy with your existing product as it currently stands, right down to the feature level. Understanding the baseline of how your subset of customers uses your product and which features have been most instrumental to them in their experience of your product will be necessary. You can't accurately predict the reach of these proposed value items from your original list if you don't already understand how your customers experience your product. You also won't be able to articulate to your leadership team why certain AI embellishments will be valuable to your customers if you don't already understand how they use your product.

This seems like a really obvious statement but you'd be surprised how many product managers out there actually know very little about how their customers actually use their own products. Product managers can get caught in the trap of building their product team into a feature farm and few of them actually stop to make sure their product is being built holistically and sustainably, but maintaining intimacy with their customers and users is a big part of being a product manager. If you aren't using product analytics or regularly checking in with your customers, either through direct customer interviews or through in-app/in-platform surveys, then you really don't know how your customers experience your product.

If you don't have a strong grasp of how your customers use your product and what they find most valuable about it, then you're building in the dark. If you've gotten to this part of the exercise and it's just now dawning on you that you actually really don't have this information, then you'll want to start doing your homework and start this list creation exercise all over again. This once again ties back into the original value items we put on our first list. If you do find yourself in this situation, there's no harm. Keep your original list. Get to know your customers and what they most love about your product and start the exercise over again. This is one of the beautiful things about product management. You can always find out more! There are deeper and deeper truths to uncover about your product the more you build and the more customers you take on. Never get discouraged. If there are unanswered questions, it's only an opportunity to learn.

Now that we have our priority list of potential sources of AI adoption based on value, scope, and reach, we can move on to the next big consideration for evolving a traditional software product into an AI product: data readiness. Making sure our data is in a digestible format to be able to handle the new AI capabilities is going to be the next big focus area for product managers looking to make the jump into AI.

Data is king – the bloodstream of the company

Before product managers can begin the work needed to start building and developing their product, getting it ready for testing, and releasing it to their customers, they need to get really clear on the strategy of how they will position their product. This is the thought process behind the Venn diagram exercise we saw in the previous section. Now that we've gone over the process of how product managers can approach potential AI embellishments, we can add one more layer of scrutiny to this list. This additional layer focuses on the data, which is what will power every single item on these lists. Once product managers begin the work of understanding what they can do with the data sources they have and which data sources they'll need to make the items on their list a reality, we're getting close to actually having a plan.

In the following subsections, we will be addressing the key areas of data readiness. Preparing and researching the data you have available, assessing the quality of the data you have, using the data for benchmarking the current and future adoption of your product, partnering with your data team, and, ultimately, defining success through your data will all be necessary steps to ensuring you've covered your bases when it comes to data readiness and availability for AI.

Preparation and research

Doing our due diligence with regard to research around our data sources and what insights they can deliver for us is part of the work we need to do to truly be ready to make decisions on AI integrations. Your data readiness and availability will also have a huge impact on the executive and market sponsorship of your newly emerging AI product. You might also find yourself at the point where you've done these exercises only to realize that your data is not ready for the evolution of your product. Getting to that point might be an intermediary step to being able to launch AI version 2.0 of your product. Making sure you have flows of incoming data to support the features you want to go live with is the ultimate measure of readiness.

At this point, you haven't created a product strategy for how you're launching your newly minted AI product. We're still in the early phases, so we want this phase of data discovery to come after the brainstorming exercise. The reason for this is that you can start to think about how to best gather, clean, and organize data in the ways your AI program will require of you as a foundational step that comes before building your product strategy. This is an important part of deciding on the core function and audience of your product or your product's AI features. Taking stock of what data capability you currently have and how far you need to go to get to where you want to take your product is a step everyone faces when they're scaling their existing product into an AI product.

Going through this process of brainstorming how your product can best leverage AI is ultimately an exercise of building out future use cases. Sure, your customers have come to know and understand your product as it currently stands, and there are some sets of established use cases already, but those use cases are likely to evolve with AI. Understanding what the current data pipelines that make your product function are and how those data pipelines need to change and mature to support your new ML pipeline is an integral part of the AI transformation process. You can't avoid this step because if you do kick that can down the road and just let problems arise later on, you won't get very far because all you're going to get out of your models is nonsense.

Quality partnership

It's become a cliche by now but within AI, data science, and ML circles, the age-old tagline is *garbage in, garbage out*. This is an *a priori* truth of AI. Your models won't give you the insights and value you're looking for if you don't adequately prepare and clean your data. Should you find yourself in this situation and ignore your AI/ML team's recommendations, you're going to be left defending an internal AI program that your leadership team will perceive to be a waste of time and money. And it will be a waste of time and money!

Rather than looking at your data pipeline strategy as the necessary input for your product, in an AI product life cycle, you'll come to see it as the partner that co-creates your AI product alongside your models and developers. That might sound a bit dramatic, but your data pipeline is going to constitute a huge part of your AI/ML program. And you will need to think of it as a program. Orchestrating and coordinating your data sources and the quality of the data will be a huge part of your success with AI. Acknowledge that adopting AI is going to constitute a paradigm shift for your organization, and if you were able to skate by with incompatible silos of data wrought with duplicates and poisoned data wells in the past, this isn't going to be the case when you adopt AI.

The biggest resistance that organizations face when it comes to data quality comes from inside: the internal resistance to keep processes as they've always been. Doing nothing is easy. Keeping things as they are will be the natural instinct for most people. Even if your organization is super passionate about maturing its data practice and you have champions across all major stakeholder teams within your organization, it still won't be enough. You will need to evangelize the importance of shifting in mindset when it comes to data quality, as well as the cost and time associated with making this happen. It's easy to make a verbal commitment to improving data quality and another to actually see that manifest tangibly in the behaviors of teams.

Expect internal resistance to this and do your best to communicate the risks of empty promises. Remember that when you're changing workflows, processes, and departmental habits of a product that's been around for a while, you have entire teams of people that have been used to doing things a certain way. Making those changes will be a collective effort. This isn't just a product evolution that will happen because leadership said so. This is a product evolution that will require partnership from all employees that touch your existing product. Take time to manage your own expectations for this as well. There might be days when you're frustrated and weeks where you're not seeing changes and return to past bad habits. It's a process and it will take time for this to be fully internalized.

Benchmarking

Data is already the bloodstream of a company, empowering everything from internal decision-making to product performance. Your customer and product data will help you understand which parts of your product are already valuable and will help you deduce which proposed features will have the most impact on your customers. Your historical internal data will help you understand which features have traditionally taken the longest to manifest in your product to predict future scope.

Your product analytics will help inform which UI/UX and design changes might have the most impact. Your training and performance data will help you understand which ML models work best for your customers. Your operational data will help you understand which deployments have been most successful and why. Data helps you manage your release schedule and product roadmap. Data helps you scale your product.

Establishing an existing benchmark using data will be an important step in creating a narrative around your plans for adopting AI. This is because, in future quarters and years, you want to be able to demonstrate that AI has helped move the needle on some of your most compelling use cases both internally and externally. You won't be able to know how far you've come later if you don't have an established baseline from the very beginning.

As a product manager, you'll want to speak from a position of strength when you demonstrate the milestones your product has been able to hit with AI. The business will evolve and metrics will come and go, but make the most of the data you already have before you embark on your AI adoption path so that you can truly reflect on your progress when the time comes.

The data team

The time you take on this step will be up to you and your leadership team. You might want to use a data strategy consultant or have in-depth sessions with your technical stakeholders to really understand how to best organize your data pipelines in a way that will empower an AI adoption best. You may even want to establish a dedicated data team made up of cross-functional team members that will be responsible for the oversight of your data. Having dedicated folks to work out the details of centralizing the various silos of data you have and deciding on the best way to centralize that data and send it to your models in dev and ultimately in production will be a great way to work through the various inconsistencies in your data that will inevitably come up.

Treat this as an investment in your R&D and product design phase and give it the time it deserves because it's a foundational part of your AI infrastructure. How you store your data, how often you're calling it, how often you'll need to train your models, and how you'll be planning a release schedule to support this new AI infrastructure will all be a part of this discussion. At this stage, it's just a discussion. No decisions are being made yet, but you will want to start this discussion as early as possible because, by the time you are ready to start considering models, training, and testing, you're going to want to be sitting on clean, rich data to feed those models.

Understanding your data, exploring it, experimenting with it, wrangling it, preparing it for feature development (for ML models), using it in modeling, evaluating the performance of those models, and ultimately deploying it are all going to be regular discussion points. So, starting conversations about data strategy early on before any real decisions about how you're going to leverage AI are finalized is a strategic move. It also allows for technical voices to become a part of this conversation sooner than they might have expected because adopting AI is a highly technical investment and those voices should be present early on.

As we've seen in prior chapters, feature engineering is a major part of making the models you choose to employ in your product successful. This further reinforces the idea that you need to make sure your technical teams weigh in on important decisions about what kinds of data are gathered and ultimately are used to train your models.

Defining success

You'll also use your internal data to set metrics, which we covered in *Part 2* of this book, in order to define what success looks like for your product. Defining success will be a collaborative act and it's important for product managers of AI products to bring in all major stakeholders of the company to align on defining that success. If the product evolution into AI doesn't include the voices of your go-to-market, sales, marketing, strategy, engineering, and leadership teams, it won't have the appropriate level of sponsorship it will need to truly be effective, funded, and evangelized about internally and externally.

Perhaps most importantly, without the right level of sponsorship, the success of your product will also not be tied to your most important business objectives at the organizational level. Building the right level of data fluency with these teams and using data to support your claims about the direction your product is taking is non-negotiable. Be patient with yourself, your organization, and your technical talent on data. Data is the whole thing. It's what powers this entire endeavor we're discussing. Don't give in to the pressure to rush things. There are always business imperatives to get to market as quickly as possible. The instinct to just start and build as you go will always be something product managers and leaders alike will have to push against, but don't rush this.

Now that we've discussed the internal process of ideating potential areas of AI adoption within your product, as well as the stages of ensuring your data readiness to adopt AI, we can move on to your external environment. Your competitors will offer a landscape of possibilities when it comes to what AI adoption will look like for your product. We don't advise mimicking your competitors' AI strategy but, rather, taking what AI adoption looks like for your competition as input when you weigh up options.

Competition – love your enemies

Using the data you already have will take you quite far, but there will always be a need to append this data with a feedback loop from the outside world. Understanding your competitors will help you inform your strategy. It will give you examples from your peers that have already made the jump that you're looking to make. Some of the examples you see from your competitors will be sources of inspiration and some examples will help you avoid certain mistakes. Doing your due diligence when researching your competitors, particularly those that have also embraced AI, will have some influence on what you choose to build and should be one of the factors that influences the lists we established previously.

Some will refute this point and say that you should build a product based on your own understanding of your market and your customers' problems. The notion that you should focus on the problem you're looking to solve without the sometimes eclipsing influence of the competitive landscape is well-meaning but highly flawed.

We don't exist in a vacuum. Products are compared with others in their peer group and, in many cases, one product defines another. Whether you're selling to consumers or other businesses, your product is going to be compared with similar products. Being aware of your competition doesn't necessarily mean you will build like them but it does offer you a perspective that's valuable and realistic. Ignoring the impact of your competitors' influence on your product would be like ignoring gravity. It's going to impact you whether you think it will or not.

Another important point it would be remiss not to mention here is to recognize that a big part of your competition includes the past iterations of your own product. You're competing with how you've done things. You're competing with past versions of your product. Thinking critically about this past version, particularly the version that doesn't leverage AI, is going to be a big part of your design process. Think about what the limitations are, and what opportunities, strengths, and challenges the old version of your product offered your customers. How can you capitalize on those opportunities, limitations, and challenges with this new version you're building? Treat the old or current iteration of your product as its own threat to your current product.

As you think about your competitive landscape, you might be tempted to get down to the feature level and do a comparison matrix with your top competitors. This is often a worthwhile exercise, particularly for your sales, marketing, and engagement teams later down the line, but at this stage, it's a bit too soon for that. Try to analyze your competition from the lens of the original value list we started out with. That value list shouldn't just be a list of features you want to add to your product. It should be a summary of the types of value your product offers its users and customers. Features are descriptive and matter-of-fact. Values are closely tied to worth.

If you're having trouble understanding the difference, start with the features themselves and then see whether you can go a step further with each feature and write down why that feature actually matters to your customer. If you can do this, then you'll be able to do this exercise when evaluating the products that yours will be competing with. Try and get a sense of whether or not the products in your competitive landscape offer the same level of value to your market or not. Another way of looking at value, particularly with the competitors that have actually gone to market with their own AI features or upgrades, is to understand how those decisions might have impacted value perception in the market.

Getting to know your competitors is a great way of not only understanding possible directions you can take with your own product but also getting a glimpse into where the industry that you work in is headed. Understanding the competitive landscape you're playing in and how it's changing can have a strong impact on your ability to see trends within your own industry and decide whether or not you want to be an active participant or an agent of change for those trends. Going to market is an entire specialization in and of itself and as a product manager, you're wearing that hat to quite a large degree. The better acquainted you can get with the market you're serving and how that market is evolving with AI, the stronger position you'll be in when it comes to making the call on how to leverage AI in your own product.

So far, we have brainstormed potential areas in which AI can be adopted in your existing product, grasped data readiness, and evaluated what AI adoption looks like in your competitive landscape. These are all valuable inputs you're going to consider when it comes to crafting your product strategy now that it's ready for its AI makeover. In the following section, we'll cover how to build that new product strategy that aligns with all the ideating we've done.

Product strategy – building a blueprint that works for everyone

By now, we've brainstormed potential ideas. We've taken an inventory of our data, as well as the insights that can come from our competition and greater market, and we're finally able to come to the drawing board and build a product strategy that will reflect the next major era of our product. Going from a traditional software product to an AI product is no small feat and it should be treated as a massive overhaul of the product because so much of how we build, what we build, and how we store, collect, and use data will be majorly renovated.

Building a product strategy will directly influence your product roadmap and this will help you realize which parts of your product will need to transform first to succeed in the actualization of your product's AI transformation and commercial success. However, there's a big difference between creating a product strategy that fits in with your product's new value system and creating a product roadmap that reflects that strategy. The roadmap is a proposed timeline of major milestones and features that will be built in the year ahead. The roadmap should not come before your product strategy is agreed upon by your key stakeholders. The roadmap is derived from this strategy and not the other way around.

We don't build what we can and hope for the best. We agree on what to build using the collective knowledge and wisdom we've gathered about our product and how to best go to market with AI capabilities. In the following subsections, we will cover the product strategy process and a proposed list of how to develop a product strategy that works for all your major stakeholders.

In the section that follows, we will cover how to best execute a product roadmap that supports the growth of AI features and capabilities. This isn't necessarily a how-to because the order and the contributions you take in will depend on your specific product. Rather, this can be viewed as more of a checklist to ensure you're headed in the right direction:

- Knowledge gathering
- A product vision that aligns with the company vision

- The establishment of product goals
- V1 of product roadmap agreed upon by all key stakeholders

Product strategy

Product management is a creative job first and foremost and the most difficult part is knowing where to start. The beauty of starting with a product that already exists is that you have a starting point. Once you're able to get started with some of the lists and exercises we've already gone over in this chapter, you're ready to start building your product strategy. This will serve as a high-level plan for how your product will be built over time and incorporates the many facets of expressing a product: the marketing, the distribution channels, and how it will be communicated to your customers. Whether your product is an AI product or not, you shouldn't create your product strategy internally without giving a voice to the folks that will use your product.

Knowledge gathering

Having a catalog of feedback from your customers and prospects is a great way to make sure you have a feedback loop with the customers and users who will ultimately be deriving value from your product. Hopefully, you already have a culture of this at your company. It's shocking how undisciplined companies can be about making sure to have regular feedback, whether through product interviews one on one or in-app surveys that capture your customers' sentiments. Brainstorm which method is best for your product and market and regularly get feedback from your potential and current customers.

At this point, you already have a strong foundation to build on. You have the results of your lists, you have a good sense of your data requirements, and you have your competitive analysis insights, along with some of the top recommendations from your key stakeholders that you've collected through various meetings and brainstorming sessions. You're able to organize all of that and get some idea of where you can best leverage AI to bring your product to the next level. One key piece missing from that is your customer feedback. Reconciling all of this will be an act of putting all these pieces together in a rough draft, which will allow you to get to the heart of what building a product strategy is all about: deciding what your organization wants to achieve with your product and creating a product strategy that aligns with your overall company vision.

Establishing the vision and goals

We won't go into the specifics of what having a company mission statement or vision is about, but suffice it to say that there will be one. If it doesn't exist, this is a great moment to generate a simple statement that encapsulates why your organization exists in the first place. What is it trying to achieve and what is the vision? From this point, your product vision is about aligning with your organization's higher-level goals for the market it's serving. In your product vision, you're looking to simply explain how you see your product serving its target market. What are the needs and problems your customers and market face and how does your product meet those needs? Try to nail this down before you think about how AI shapes that vision, and then take a moment to reflect on what changes when you bring in AI. Try to whittle this down to one sentence if you can – two if you absolutely need to.

Gathering feedback and crafting a product vision are all collaborative efforts that are not done exclusively by the product manager. Rather, the product manager brings the right voices together to make sure a collective sentiment is agreed upon by the stakeholder team. You should be the person that organizes the meetings in which these things are decided and it's your job to make sure you leave those meetings with something everyone present can live with. You'll meet with your stakeholders regularly in those product strategy meetings we already discussed and you'll have many opportunities to reevaluate how this vision evolves.

Next up, you establish goals for your product – you can't really have a strategy without establishing high-level goals. These goals will be a critical thinking task that will spring from your product vision, particularly now that this vision encapsulates the adoption of AI in whatever form makes sense for your product.

What are you actually trying to achieve with your product?

Are there certain major milestones or benchmarks that you're hoping to achieve with AI?

Goals exist to help you measure and prepare for important objectives that you want to reach with your product, for your customers, users, market, developers, and the rest of the employees in your organization. Consider these your strategic OKRs for your product.

Without putting these big boulders in and building your product vision and goals from the place of what's most important, you'll drown in the weeds and you won't build strategically. You'll be left chasing opportunities unintentionally and it may tempt you to just follow what your competitors are doing or what your customers are asking for. Given the importance of the move to AI, take the time here to begin from a place of strength. If you find yourself weighing feedback from your competitive analysis, your customers, or your internal teams disproportionately when finding this vision and establishing your product goals, think critically about whether that's actually appropriate.

Feel free to also make this process collaborative and jot down all the goals that occur to all your various stakeholders so that you can prioritize them together. Again, you can always revisit these goals and scrutinize them later, but try and see what you can come up with together, refine that list, and try to stick to three to four higher-level product goals here so that you can begin to approach your product roadmap with confidence. All these goals will manifest in being broken down into smaller bits and those bits may take weeks, months, or even years to fully realize. That's OK. Your product goals shouldn't be something that can happen in days and weeks. They should be encompassing and strategic enough that they are long-lasting because they're there to inform your overall product roadmap and to ensure everyone is working in service to a unifying goal.

The product roadmap

Finally, we've made it to the product roadmap. This is the last step toward establishing our product strategy and it's the most detailed part because it's meant to capture initiatives that have come from all of the strategic goal-setting and vision exercises. This is where the magic of building and shipping products is. Taking strategic nebulous goals and turning them into a tangible reality, the roadmap is where we apply the conditions, limitations, and dependencies that we haven't yet bothered with. Roadmaps will change and they're not meant to be crystal balls, rendering your fate non-negotiable. They are meant to serve as guides for a product team's strategic directives. They are meant to be a bird's-eye, calendar view translation of your product vision and goals.

Virtually everyone in your organization is going to see your product roadmap and it will serve as a blueprint for all teams to use to align when it comes to their own goals and planning sessions. It's also a way to communicate the results of all your strategy sessions. It's also meant to serve as a guardrail for all kinds of projects, initiatives, and implementation issues.

If deadlines, issues, or bottlenecks arise, as they inevitably will, your internal teams have an internal source of truth to give them guidance on how much leeway they have, and it also gives them structure around when to escalate things because a roadmap is marked by months and quarters. This is an especially important note with AI products because as you build, you will start to see certain experiments or projects taking longer than expected. Your regular product strategy sessions will make sure to absorb the shock of any major changes to deadlines or the scope.

Establishing a product roadmap will also ensure you're aligning the efforts of your product design, development, UX, success, marketing, and sales with your strategic goals. Each major initiative you include in your roadmap will have its own documentation that comes with it in the form of user stories or product requirement docs, and all major initiatives will come with some kind of acceptance criteria. This makes it so that your roadmap is tied to the manifestation of specific outcomes. The roadmap isn't just a collection of features you plan to deliver by a certain date. It's a representation of the outcomes you expect to see from your development efforts. Multiple features may be in service to these outcomes.

As you start to establish a backlog of epics and tasks, you'll start to align them with the themes present in your product goals and initiatives as they get further grouped into sprints and releases. The product team, along with the AI product manager, will own the product roadmap creation and maintenance and will continuously break down elements of the roadmap into individual tasks with their own acceptance criteria. Themes will start to emerge as you go. The roadmap will be a reflection of the initiatives and outcomes that are most compelling, whether it's because they have the biggest impact on customers or whether they offer the greatest ROI to the business.

The last thing to keep in mind about establishing the roadmap is that, as an AI product manager, you'll take whatever version of your product roadmap is final enough and you'll begin the work of evangelizing about that roadmap to your greater organization. Up until now, all of this has been a collaborative effort, but you can't get very far if your group of collaborators is too wide. Establishing a stakeholder team to work with that's representative enough of leadership, development, product, and go-to-market teams is a strategic task in and of itself. They will help you get to this point in the process. Now that you've gotten to this point, you're going to spread the word and get feedback from the rest of the organization because everyone will use it as a guideline. This offers you another level of scrutiny and allows for additional voices to raise concerns that might not have come up with the core stakeholder team.

Now that you have a product strategy and roadmap you can be proud of (yes, this is the intended final state), we have great news for you: it's never going to be finished! This is just the first iteration of the current state of affairs. The goal here isn't to finish anything, it's to agree on the starting point. Over time, your strategy and roadmap will both evolve and you will revisit them regularly. We recommend making this a biweekly or monthly process if you're in a relatively new organization and making it monthly or quarterly if you're at a more mature organization where things move more slowly. Make sure you're crafting your roadmap in a way where you're planning at least two quarters out so that you're strategic with your resources and time.

You'll be the keeper of this meeting as the AI product manager and it will be your responsibility to make sure your core group of key stakeholders is regularly included in this strategic meeting. Keeping lines of communication open and allowing space for new ideas and alterations to make their way into your product strategy and roadmap is a responsible way of not just capturing all the new energy that will come from building through your plans as they stand but is also a way to regularly welcome new perspectives. It's easy to get really great ideas when you're always brainstorming. When you're in the practice of just executing, brainstorming becomes a luxury that your time rarely affords, and things become get stale.

Resist the temptation to make these meetings ad hoc and only bring the party together when ideas start to stagnate. That's not a good practice because it puts a lot of pressure on your stakeholders to perform when the well has already run dry. Keeping this meeting scheduled regularly will make sure that your stakeholders expect it and get used to coming to it with their own ideas. Keep the meetings up and even if you do run out of ideas or motivation, you can always shorten them when they do arise and give yourself more time back.

Remaining committed to keeping a standing meeting means that your stakeholders can take it upon themselves to keep a running list of topics and considerations to bring up in these meetings. It also keeps you honest by keeping you out of the very understandable and common pattern of staying in execution mode. When we're there for too long, our vision can get blurred by the inertia of building products. Maintaining the product strategy is your ultimate responsibility and it consists primarily of the strategic elements that happen when building your product vision, goals, and roadmap. Having regular product strategy meetings makes you a good steward of your strategy.

Red flags and green flags – what to look for and watch out for

Moving forward into the wide frontier of AI products includes some common pitfalls in AI transformation, as well as markers for success. We will call them red flags and green flags and they're signals you can pick up on as you go through this process of getting your product ready for AI adoption. Some of these will be concrete actions or results and some will be more emotional, but either way, you can use them as markers to know whether you're on the right path or whether you're hitting potential rough patches. In the following subsections, we'll address a few red and green flags. Let's get started.

Red flags

Red flags are behavioral patterns we can try and look out for that indicate there is an issue with a process we're setting forth. Because AI adoption is such a revolutionary undertaking for any company to take on, it's best to look out for some of these habitual patterns early so that you're starting on the right foot:

- **I don't know**: If you're regularly engaging with various teammates or employees on different teams at your company and they seem confused about why the company is adopting AI, what the value will be for their customers or readers, and what the product's high-level goals are, that's a red flag. The point of crafting a product strategy that aligns with the move to embrace AI is to make sure no one in your organization is confused about why this is happening. Make sure the entire company knows why you're adopting AI and which use cases you're trying to solve with it.

- **Communication stalls**: If you're not meeting regularly or there's a lack of engagement in your recurring product meetings, there's likely some internal resistance you have to deal with. Do your best to communicate the exciting opportunity that embracing AI is, not just in terms of your product but the market as a whole. Rather than seeing AI transformation as a burden that's going to be a lot of work, you'll know you're on the right path when you can sense curiosity and openness from the stakeholders that hold leadership positions at the organization they serve. A lack of executive engagement is a critical red flag. AI isn't something leadership can outsource. They need to be involved and engaged at every stage of your AI adoption journey.

- **You're not seeing progress**: If you've started the process of working on creating your AI/ML pipeline and you don't see progress or at least some early positive signals from the model training you're starting, you might not have the right skill level to truly tackle the undertaking that is AI transformation. Making sure you have the right talent team, tech stack, and know-how is hard to do at the onset, and many companies struggle with establishing the right combination of factors as they get started with this. If you are struggling for talent, consider working with AI consultancies that can help you leverage from a diverse talent pool that's had exposure to use cases similar to yours.

Green flags

In this section, we wanted to include a few green flags that might appear as red flags at first glance. In part, we want to prepare you for some of the hurdles you'll encounter on your journey to help manage your own expectations, but we also want to convey that the following behavioral patterns are often a sign of things going right even if you might not experience them that way:

- **Your pilot project fails**: It was probably going to anyway. We've talked so much about managing expectations and this is really what it's all about. Whether you're balancing your own reaction or the reactions of others in the face of lackluster performance or no performance at all, you're going to have to act as a source of faith for yourself and others. ML works and companies all over the world use it constructively and productively every day. Those with the patience and determination to see it through will be rewarded, but it can be hard to see progress, particularly at the beginning and when you're starting from the perspective of a traditional software product. Give it time and don't give up.

- **Too much feedback**: Whether from your customers, prospects, users, or internal teams, if you find yourself inundated with feedback about what should make it to the roadmap and what shouldn't, take it as a sign that you've succeeded in properly evangelizing your product vision, goals, and roadmap. When it comes to AI transformation, having more voices involved early on can be exhausting, but it's also an amazing indication that people are engaged. It's a good problem to have. Being the referee is easier than being the cheerleader that's trying to muster up excitement where there is none.

- **Reimagining data consumption**: If your internal teams are changing how they use and ingest data, that means the culture is changing toward becoming more data-driven, which will further support the success of your AI platform. If your organization realizes they have to massively overhaul how they annotate, store, collect, and use data, that means the AI transformation has gotten to a phase where it's affecting internal teams and the predominant climate.

As the AI product manager, you'll want to be aware of the potential hurdles to look out for, as well as the indicators that your AI adoption is going well. Your organization will be looking to your leadership as this journey unfolds. Your credibility in this area will be cemented if you can be a safe haven for your colleagues when things go wrong and a source of encouragement when things seem to be going wrong but aren't.

Summary

We've now come to the last chapter of the last section of our book: evolving an existing product into an AI product. So much of this chapter has been about how to anticipate and prepare for the jump to AI/ML. In the second section of the book, we heavily discussed concepts related to the AI-native product: a product that's created with AI initially. Once you do make the jump to fully embracing AI in your own product, you can refer to *Part 2* of this book, which is more focused on the aspects that come up when you're in the flow of building AI. In this section, we wanted to focus on the preparation stages for embracing AI/ML because of the gravity that comes with AI transformation.

Brainstorming ideas, vetting those ideas with practical considerations, getting your data right, evaluating the competitive landscape you'll be playing in, and bringing in your stakeholders to make a plan for how to build the transition are all part of AI readiness. All of the ideas expressed in this chapter are also easier said than done and each section of this chapter will be a process in and of itself, but once you are able to get to the point where you've decided on a product strategy and you're executing that strategy with a product roadmap that your entire organization can get behind, you're on your way to building with AI.

It's a privilege and a massive responsibility to be a product manager, particularly one that oversees the AI transformation of their product. It's an exciting time in your product management career and one that you'll likely look back on fondly. We're at a unique precipice in history and not many product managers can say they were able to be of service in such a big step for their organizations and their respective products. As you hit difficult moments along this journey, remind yourself that this is a difficult transformation to manage and evangelize for others in your organization too.

Embracing AI and all the challenges that come with it isn't for the faint of heart and if you find yourself getting frustrated, it's actually a great sign. It means you care enough about your product and your organization's success with AI to elicit an emotional reaction. Give yourself and your co-creators grace and be proud of the work you're all doing collectively to embrace the wave of AI.

Additional resources

- Udacity's Intro to AI (`https://www.udacity.com/course/intro-to-artificial-intelligence--cs271`) course and Artificial Intelligence Nanodegree Program (`https://www.udacity.com/course/artificial-intelligence-nanodegree--nd889`)

- Stanford University's online lectures: *Artificial Intelligence: Principles and Techniques*: `https://stanford-cs221.github.io/spring2022/`

- edX's online AI course, offered through Columbia University: `https://www.edx.org/course/artificial-intelligence-ai`

- Microsoft's open source Cognitive Toolkit (previously known as CNTK) to help developers master deep learning algorithms: `https://learn.microsoft.com/en-us/cognitive-toolkit/`

- Google's open source TensorFlow software library for machine intelligence: `https://www.tensorflow.org/`

- AI Resources, an open source code directory from the AI Access Foundation: `https://www.airesources.org/`

- The **Association for the Advancement of Artificial Intelligence (AAAI)**'s Resources page: `https://www.aaai.org/Resources/resources.php`

- MonkeyLearn's *Gentle Guide to Machine Learning*: `https://monkeylearn.com/blog/gentle-guide-to-machine-learning/`

- Stephen Hawking and Elon Musk's Future of Life Institute: `https://futureoflife.org/`

- OpenAI, an open industry- and academia-wide deep learning initiative: `https://openai.com/`

Index

A

A/B testing 90
  model deployment strategy 17
A/B testing tools 163
accuracy optimization 54, 55
Adaptive AI 188
AI adoption 178
  potential risks, anticipating 179-181
AI adoption trends 188
  autonomous AI development 191
  creative AI 191
  embedded AI 189, 190
  ethical AI 190
  general trends 188, 189
AI costs and pricing
  managing 166
  reference link 166
AI customization
  verticals and customer groupings,
    consideration 98, 99
AI enablement 192, 193
AI Forum
  reference link 105
AI Global Surveillance (AIGS) 78

AI/ML product dream team 91
  AI/ML/data strategists 92
  AI PM 92
  customer success 95
  data analyst 93
  data engineer 92
  data scientist 93
  frontend/backend/full-stack engineers 94
  marketing/sales/go-to-market team 95
  ML engineer 93, 94
  UX designers/researchers 94
AI operations (AIOps) 12, 113, 128
  value consistency, delivering with 113, 114
AI orientation
  domains 118
  market 119, 120
  product design strategy 120
AI-powered outputs
  productizing 96, 97
AI product challenges 146
  ethics 146, 147
  performance 147
  safety 148
AI product development, stages 88
  data management 89, 90
  deployment 91
  ideation 88

AI product example 144
  Lensa 145
  PeriGen 145
AI products and traditional software products, similarities 104
  agile development 104, 105
  data 105
AI product strategy
  building 121-123
AI products, versus traditional software products 103-105
  profit margins 107, 109
  scalability 105-107
  uncertainty 109, 110
AI scaling in organization
  reference link 107
AI trust, risk, and security management (AI TRiSM) 190
anomaly detection 126
applied AI 105
applied observability 185
artificial general intelligence (AGI) 5
artificial intelligence (AI) 3, 59, 72, 171
  autonomy 77, 78
  benefits 79
  defining 4, 5
  economic systems, revolutionizing 72-74
  growth areas 184
  implementation 19, 20
  need for 80, 81
  technology companies 18, 19
  using 172-174
artificial intelligence (AI) growth areas
  autonomous AI development 187, 188
  creative AI 187
  embedded AI 184, 185
  ethical AI 186

artificial narrow intelligence (ANI) 5
artificial neural networks (ANNs) 41
augmented reality (AR) 187
automated guided vehicles (AVGs) 139
automated ML (autoML) 174
automatic interaction detection (AID) 42

B

B2B business model, versus B2C business model 110
  domain knowledge 110, 111
  experimentation 112, 113
Biovitals Analytics Engine
  reference link 79
black box model 7, 138
Black, Indigenous, People of Color (BIPOC) 75
blue ocean 63
  examples 63, 64
Business Intelligence (BI) tools 164
business-to-business (B2B) 32, 60
  examples 60, 61
business-to-consumer (B2C) 32, 60
  examples 61, 62
business units (BUs) 144

C

canary deployment strategy 17
ChatGPT 191
coefficient of determination 30
collective AI fatigue 105
commercial MVPs
  growth 74- 76
competitors 205-207
computer vision (CV) 135, 136, 185

Continuous Deployment (CD) **12, 114**
Continuous Integration (CI) **12, 114**
continuous maintenance
        process, components
    CD 12
    CI 12
    CM 12
    CT 12
Continuous Testing (CT) 114
convolutional neural networks (CNNs) 48
    layers 49
CuratedAI
    reference link 75
Customer Data Platforms (CDPs) 161
Customer Engagement Platforms
        (CEPs) 162
cybersecurity 126

D

DABUS 187
databases 13
data cleaning 107
    reference link 107
data lake 14
data pipelines 14, 15
data readiness 202
    benchmarking 204
    data team 204
    preparation and research 202
    quality partnership 203
    success, defining 205
data warehouse 13, 164
decision trees 9, 27
deep belief networks (DBNs) 51, 52
deep learning (DL) 7, 28, 41, 89, 138
    exploring 43, 44
    history 45, 46

neural network types 46
    relationships 44, 45
    technologies 52
    versus machine learning (ML) 6
deep reinforcement learning 185
deployment strategies 16
    A/B testing model deployment strategy 17
    canary deployment strategy 17
    shadow deployment strategy 17
diabetic retinopathy (DR) 148
differentiated strategy 67, 68
    examples 65
digital immune system (DIS) 185
disruptive strategy 67
    examples 65
divergent thinking 199
Division of Economic and Risk
        Analysis (DERA) 73
domains 118
dominant strategy 66
    examples 65

E

ethics and responsibility 53
European Commission
    key areas 37
expert system 140, 143, 144
extract, transform, and load (ETL) 15

F

feature engineering 7
feature learning 7
feedback loop 115
FinTech 123
    algorithmic trading 125
    chatbots 124

fraud detection 124

predictive analytics 125

fraud detection 124

fuzzy logic 141, 144

fuzzy matching 140, 144

G

generative adversarial networks (GANs) 50, 51

Generative AI 187

go-to-market (GTM) 121

green flags 213

growth hacking tools 159, 160, 165

H

healthcare 125

drug discovery and research 126

imaging and diagnosis 125, 126

High-Frequency Trading (HFT) 125

hyperparameter 29

I

industrial revolution 174, 175

consultant, working with 175

first AI team 177

first hire 177

no code tools 178

third party, working with 176

infrastructure-as-a-service (IaaS) 15

project, managing 15, 16

Institute for the Future (IFTF) 173

IntelligentX 75

International Telecommunication Union (ITU) 80

K

key performance indicators (KPIs) 128, 156, 157

technical metrics 129

k-means clustering 10, 28

k-nearest neighbors (KNNs) 9, 28

knowledge graphs 185

L

laissez-faire approach 153

lakehouse 14

layers

types 43

leadership role 130

Lensa 145

linear regression 8, 27

logistic regression 9, 27

long short-term memory networks (LSTMs) 50

M

machine learning (ML) 6, 24, 41, 72, 135, 136, 171, 198

exploring 42

use cases 142

versus deep learning (DL) 6

machine learning (ML), types 8

reinforcement learning 11

semi-supervised learning 10

supervised learning 8

unsupervised learning 9

Macro AI

feature level 141

foundation 134, 135

magic quadrant
  challengers 118
  leaders 118
  niche players 118
  visionaries 118
marketing 159
mean absolute error (MAE) 129
mean time between failures (MTBF) 129
mean time to acknowledge (MTTA) 128
mean time to detect (MTTD) 128
mean time to resolve/repair (MTTR) 129
metric 156
minimal viable product (MVP) 24, 71
mixed reality (MR) 187
MLflow 18
ML model
  computer vision (CV) 136
  deep learning (DL) 138
  deploying 32-34
  natural language processing (NLP) 137
  testing 34, 35
  training 28-32
  troubleshooting 34, 35
  updating 36-38
ML model types 27, 141, 142
  decision trees 27
  expert systems 143, 144
  fuzzy logic/fuzzy matching 144
  k-means clustering 28
  k-nearest neighbors (KNNs) 28
  linear regression 27
  logistic regression 27
  Naive Bayes classifier 27
  neural networks 28
  principal component analysis (PCA) 28
  random forest 27
  robotics 143
  Support Vector Machine (SVM) 27

ML operations (MLOps) 113
  value consistency, delivering with 113, 114
models
  hyperparameter tuning 114, 115
  retraining 114, 115
  testing 114, 115
multilayer perceptrons (MLPs) 47

N

Naive Bayes classifier 8, 27
natural language generation
    (NLG) 52, 124, 137
natural language processing
    (NLP) 135, 137, 185
natural language understanding
    (NLU) 52, 124, 137
neural networks 28
neural network types 46, 47
  convolutional neural networks (CNNs) 48
  deep belief networks (DBNs) 51, 52
  generative adversarial networks
    (GANs) 50, 51
  long short-term memory
    networks (LSTMs) 50
  multilayer perceptrons (MLPs) 47
  radial basis function networks (RBFNs) 47
  recurrent neural networks (RNNs) 49, 50
  self-organizing maps (SOMs) 48
new product development (NPD) 23
new product development
    (NPD), stages 23, 24
  define 24
  design 25
  discovery 24
  implementation 25
  launch 26

marketing 25
training 26
north star metrics 153-156
digital product companies 154, 155
reference link 154

O

**objectives and key results
(OKRs) 128, 157, 158**
optimal flow 11
continuous maintenance process 12
data availability and centralization 11, 12
Ordinary Least Squares (OLS) 30
**Organization for Economic Co-Operation
and Development (OECD) 73**
overfitting 10, 32

P

performance evaluation
AI/ML pipelines 114, 115
PeriGen 145
**principal component analysis
(PCA) 10, 28, 42**
private personal information (PPI) 60
product analytics tools 162, 163
productizing 115
product language fit 115
product-led growth 159, 160
product management 208
product roadmap 210, 211
product strategy 157, 158
building 207, 208
knowledge gathering 208
reference link 158
vision and goals 208, 209

profit margins
reference link 107
Proof-of-Concept (PoC) 111

Q

quantum computing 53

R

radial basis function networks (RBFNs) 47
random forest 9, 27
recurrent neural networks (RNNs) 49, 50
red flags 212
red ocean
examples 64, 65
reinforcement learning (RL) 11, 135
Requests for Proposals (RFPs) 111
researching and developing (R&D) 90
Restricted Boltzmann Machines (RBMs) 51
return on investment (ROI) 180
robotics 139, 143
augmenting robots 140
autonomous robots 139
humanoid robots 140
pre-programmed robots 140
teleoperated robots 139
root mean square error (RMSE) 129
R-squared metric 30
rule-based engine 140

S

**Securities and Exchange
Commission (SEC) 73**
self-organizing maps (SOMs) 48
selling AI
product management perspective 99, 100

semi-supervised learning 10
sentiment analysis 124
service availability 129
shadow mode 17
spatial computing 187
supervised learning 8
   decision trees 9
   k-nearest neighbors (KNNs) 9
   linear regression 8
   logistic regression 9
   Naive Bayes classifier 8
   random forest 9
   support vector machine (SVM) 8
supervised learning (SL) 135
supervised ML models 125
Support Vector Machine (SVM) 8, 27, 42

T

tech stack 160
   investing in 95, 96
ticket to incident ratio 129
traditional software products
   versus AI products 103, 104
TuringBots 187, 191

U

unsupervised learning 9, 135
   k-means clustering 10
   principal component analysis (PCA) 10
unsupervised ML models 125
user and entity behavior analytics
   (UEBA) 126, 127
user experience (UX) 162
user interface (UI) 140

V

value consistency
   delivering, with AI operations
     (AIOps) 113, 114
   delivering, with ML operations
     (MLOps) 113, 114
value metrics 127, 152, 153
   key performance indicators
     (KPIs) 128, 156, 157
   north star metrics 153-156
   objectives and key results
     (OKRs) 128, 157, 158
   product strategy 157, 158
vanity metrics 157
Venn diagram 198
   reach 201
   scope 200, 201
   value 199
verticals
   cybersecurity 126
   FinTech 123
   healthcare 125
virtual reality (VR) 187

W

WAITalks 71
World Economic Forum (WEF) 172

Packtpub.com

Subscribe to our online digital library for full access to over 7,000 books and videos, as well as industry leading tools to help you plan your personal development and advance your career. For more information, please visit our website.

Why subscribe?

- Spend less time learning and more time coding with practical eBooks and Videos from over 4,000 industry professionals

- Improve your learning with Skill Plans built especially for you

- Get a free eBook or video every month

- Fully searchable for easy access to vital information

- Copy and paste, print, and bookmark content

Did you know that Packt offers eBook versions of every book published, with PDF and ePub files available? You can upgrade to the eBook version at packtpub.com and as a print book customer, you are entitled to a discount on the eBook copy. Get in touch with us at customercare@packtpub.com for more details.

At www.packtpub.com, you can also read a collection of free technical articles, sign up for a range of free newsletters, and receive exclusive discounts and offers on Packt books and eBooks.

Other Books You May Enjoy

If you enjoyed this book, you may be interested in these other books by Packt:

Applied Machine Learning Explainability Techniques

Aditya Bhattacharya

ISBN: 9781803246154

- Explore various explanation methods and their evaluation criteria
- Learn model explanation methods for structured and unstructured data
- Apply data-centric XAI for practical problem-solving
- Hands-on exposure to LIME, SHAP, TCAV, DALEX, ALIBI, DiCE, and others
- Discover industrial best practices for explainable ML systems
- Use user-centric XAI to bring AI closer to non-technical end users
- Address open challenges in XAI using the recommended guidelines

Building Analytics Teams

John K. Thompson

ISBN: 9781800203167

- Avoid organizational and technological pitfalls of moving from a defined project to a production environment
- Enable team members to focus on higher-value work and tasks
- Build Advanced Analytics and Artificial Intelligence (AA) functions in an organization
- Outsource certain projects to competent and capable third parties
- Support the operational areas that intend to invest in business intelligence, descriptive statistics, and small-scale predictive analytics
- Analyze the operational area, the processes, the data, and the organizational resistance

Packt is searching for authors like you

If you're interested in becoming an author for Packt, please visit `authors.packtpub.com` and apply today. We have worked with thousands of developers and tech professionals, just like you, to help them share their insight with the global tech community. You can make a general application, apply for a specific hot topic that we are recruiting an author for, or submit your own idea.

Share Your Thoughts

Now you've finished *The AI Product Manager's Handbook*, we'd love to hear your thoughts! Scan the QR code below to go straight to the Amazon review page for this book and share your feedback or leave a review on the site that you purchased it from.

`https://packt.link/r/1-804-61293-6`

Your review is important to us and the tech community and will help us make sure we're delivering excellent quality content.

Download a free PDF copy of this book

Thanks for purchasing this book!

Do you like to read on the go but are unable to carry your print books everywhere?

Is your eBook purchase not compatible with the device of your choice?

Don't worry, now with every Packt book you get a DRM-free PDF version of that book at no cost.

Read anywhere, any place, on any device. Search, copy, and paste code from your favorite technical books directly into your application.

The perks don't stop there, you can get exclusive access to discounts, newsletters, and great free content in your inbox daily

Follow these simple steps to get the benefits:

1. Scan the QR code or visit the link below

https://packt.link/free-ebook/9781804612934

2. Submit your proof of purchase
3. That's it! We'll send your free PDF and other benefits to your email directly

Made in the USA
Monee, IL
02 June 2023

35138803R00138